BAD WORDS

PHILIP GOODEN

(GOOD struck through)

BAD
WORDS
AND WHAT
THEY
TELL US

ROBINSON

ROBINSON

First published in Great Britain in 2019 by Robinson

1 3 5 7 9 10 8 6 4 2

A CIP catalogue record for this book
is available from the British Library.

ISBN: 978-1-47214-157-6

Typeset in Adobe Garamond Pro by Hewer Text UK Ltd, Edinburgh
Printed and bound in Great Britain by Clays Ltd, Elcograf S.p.A.

Papers used by Robinson are from well-managed
forests and other responsible sources.

MIX
Paper from
responsible sources
FSC® C104740

Robinson
An imprint of
Little, Brown Book Group
Carmelite House
50 Victoria Embankment
London EC4Y 0DZ

An Hachette UK Company
www.hachette.co.uk

For Richard and Cath

Contents

Introduction: Red Rags

IN NOVEMBER 1965 the drama critic and provocateur Kenneth Tynan deliberately uttered a bad word in the course of a discussion on a late-night BBC television chat show, and the nation went ape. Apparently. Banner headlines in the newspapers, motions in Parliament, demands that Tynan be sacked from his post at the newly created National Theatre, and the suggestion from Mary Whitehouse of the National Viewers' and Listeners' Association that the distinguished if wayward critic should have 'his bottom smacked' for using 'little boys' language', a notion that would probably have pleased Tynan for reasons unknown at the time. The bad word uttered by Ken Tynan exhibited contradictory qualities: on the one hand, its use displayed a juvenile, even infantile mindset; on the other, it was so shocking that even hardened adults seemingly couldn't hear it without either blanching or going red-faced with outrage. The word, of course, was 'fuck'.

As times change, so too do some words, not in their form or spelling but in the weight and significance attached to them.

Prime Minister Tony Blair was not pleased as he watched the unfolding results of the elections to the Welsh National Assembly in May 1999. Welsh Labour had won more votes than any other party but they hadn't done well enough to gain majority control over the Assembly; instead, they were forced to enter into a coalition with the Liberal Democrats. The Prime Minister registered his disappointment at the results as they came in with the repeated and insightful commentary of 'Fucking Welsh'. Or at least those were the words he was alleged to have said by Lance Price, a Downing Street adviser, in the draft version of Price's book *The Spin Doctor's Diaries*. (The published version had the more innocuous 'TB f-ing and blinding about the whole thing'.) Blair's 'F****** Welsh', to adopt the asterisked form used in several newspapers, was enough to prompt a complaint to North Wales Police about anti-Welsh insults. As the *Daily Mail* dead-panned on 28 September 2005: 'North Wales Police has a history of investigating slurs against the Welsh.' An embarrassed Lance Price tried to minimise the damage by suggesting that Blair was angry and frustrated only with the Welsh Labour Party rather than with an entire nation.

Move forward a dozen or so years into a new millennium and a new government in the shape of a Conservative and Liberal Democrat coalition. In September 2012 the police guard on duty at the entrance to Downing Street refused to open the main gate to the government chief whip, the Tory Andrew Mitchell, so he could take his bicycle through. Instead he was instructed to dismount and make his exit through the pedestrian gate. Losing his temper, Mitchell said: 'I thought you guys were supposed to fucking help us.' The police log, as reproduced in several newspapers, had a rather more elaborate tirade, one which Mitchell always denied. According to the *Daily Telegraph*, his alleged words were: 'Best you learn your f------ place . . . you don't run this f----- government . . . You're f------ plebs.' Two years later the affair climaxed in a libel trial, instigated by Andrew Mitchell but also lost by him when the judge declared: 'For the reasons given, I'm satisfied, at least on the balance of probabilities that Mr Mitchell did speak the words attributed to him, or so close to them as to amount to the same, the politically toxic word pleb.'

These two instances of the f-word in the area of Downing Street when put beside Ken Tynan's deliberate, unsweary use in 1965 tell us quite a bit about the way Britain has changed over the last five decades. It's not so much that senior figures in government, from the Prime Minister to a chief whip, routinely employ the word 'fuck' or one of its several derivatives. Perhaps they always have, even if it may be hard to imagine Clement Attlee or Margaret Thatcher unleashing a four-letter tirade. Nor is it the fact that such comments, made in semi-private situations, can now be reported on in the media, though the reports generally require a modest veil of asterisks, dashes or bleeps to cover the word in question. Tony Blair's verbal offence and Andrew Mitchell's too were quite different, and they were different from each other. They involved the breaking of newer kinds of taboo, ones to do with class and ethnicity. The subject of *Bad Words* is, in part, the shift in taboo topics and expressions, and what these shifts tell us about ourselves.

Bad words are expressions which, whether written or spoken, cause responses ranging from silent disapproval (raised eyebrows, pursed lips) to vigilante outrage (anonymous letters, death threats). Some expressions, it seems, have an actual physical effect. Now that taboo terms, whether four-letter swearing or racist insults, have become legitimate subjects for scientific study, research reveals that saying and hearing them may involve enhanced activity in the parts of the brain connected with emotion. The resulting electrical impulses can be measured on the skin. In other words, saying or hearing 'fuck' is more stimulating – in a good or bad way – than saying or hearing 'duck'. The users of the first word and others, which is to say most of us, may well be aware of the effect they are producing, and intend it; alternatively, they may just be ignorant or careless. In a sense, the motivation hardly matters. What is significant are the depths of fury, anxiety and grief that such words seem to both provoke and plumb. A few letters of the alphabet, particularly when they occur in combinations of four, are apparently dangerous enough to shake society, to undermine morality and decency, even to herald the end of civilisation.

A peculiar fact, though, is that what is lethally dangerous in one period may turn almost harmless after a few years have passed. The snakebite is transformed into a pinprick. What would once have caused the user to be roundly condemned is now taken as being edgy, a rejection of convention, a sign of daring or, maybe, mere routine. Meanwhile other terms, which in their day were common verbal currency, suddenly assume new and life-threatening proportions.

George Carlin was an American comedian, noted for his dark humour. Now we'd call him transgressive. His monologue entitled 'Seven Words You Can Never Say On Television' was recorded on disc during a live performance in a civic auditorium in Santa Monica in 1972. He was arrested when he performed the same routine in Milwaukee some months later, but it was only after a New York radio station broadcast a version of it that a complaint to the Federal Communications Commission (FCC) and a legal back-and-forth between the radio station and the FCC eventually clambered its way up to the Supreme Court, and so set the parameters for allowable obscenity for many years afterwards. The seven words in Carlin's schtick were: shit, piss, fuck, cunt, cocksucker, motherfucker and tits.

Things were never quite the same in Britain as they were in the US, in ways that are explored and explained in this book. But at the time Carlin delivered his comic rant there would have been some shared territory between his list and an equivalent British one. (Specifically, fuck, cunt, cocksucker and motherfucker were largely taboo, while shit, piss and tits were merely dubious.) Nearly half a century later things have advanced, if you call the ability of the media to use certain hitherto forbidden words an advance – which I do.

Take this, for example, from the *Guardian* in February 2018 reporting on a revelatory interview given to the *New York Magazine* by the veteran US composer and arranger Quincy Jones, who had plenty of sacred cows in his sights, including the Beatles, whom he described as 'the worst musicians in the world' and 'no-playing motherfuckers'. Jones also remembered time spent hanging out with Marlon Brando, and talked about his charm and his sexuality: 'He'd fuck anything. Anything! He'd fuck a mailbox. James Baldwin. Richard Pryor. Marvin Gaye.' Richard Pryor's fourth and seventh wife (they married twice), Jennifer Lee Pryor, confirmed her husband's bisexuality, again as reported in the *Guardian*, ' "It was the seventies," she told the celebrity news site TMZ. "Drugs were still good, especially quaaludes. If you did enough cocaine, you'd fuck a radiator and send it flowers in the morning."'

This was gossip as news and was duly covered in the other papers. *The Times* asterisked out the offending words almost in their entirety (f***, m************s) while the *Daily Mail* lifted the veil a little further (f*ck, motherf****rs). You could object that the papers didn't have the nerve to print out fuck or motherfucker in full, though it is the policy of *The Times* and the majority of British papers to treat these contentious words by using asterisks. If you've got a long memory you might also conclude that *The Times* and the 'quality' press of forty or more years ago wouldn't have been interested in this kind of scabrous, gossipy comment. You might even conclude that the world is going to hell in a handcart, again. What you could not deny, though, is that when it comes to taboo terminology, things have changed. A report like this, even in the asterisked version, would not have appeared in a British newspaper forty years ago.

Yet as one hitherto shut door opens – or is at least pushed ajar – another one will be closing. Racist terminology is much more shocking to contemporary opinion than the traditional four-letter expressions. Even a glimpse of potential racism can be as alarming and scandalising as a glimpse of ankle apparently was to the Victorians. When he was editor of the *Sun* during the 1980s Kelvin MacKenzie seemed to relish sticking his head above the paper parapet, and earned the enduring hatred of an entire city through his newspaper's false assertions about the behaviour of Liverpool fans during the Hillsborough disaster. Years later, MacKenzie had a slot as a columnist on the *Sun* when the twin themes of football and Liverpool came together once again to derail him, this time for good. Part of MacKenzie's offence was that he made some disobliging remarks about Liverpool and drug dealers, but the core reason for his departure from the paper in 2017 was what he wrote about Ross Barkley after the Everton footballer had been involved in a bar fracas: 'Perhaps unfairly, I have always judged Ross Barkley as one of our dimmest footballers. There is something about the lack of reflection in his eyes which makes me certain not only are the lights not on, there is definitely nobody at home. I get a similar feeling when seeing a gorilla at the zoo. The physique is magnificent but it's the eyes that tell the story.'

If MacKenzie was unaware that Barkley is of mixed race descent – one of his grandfathers was born in Nigeria – he certainly found out about it after the appearance of the article which, online, was complemented by adjoining pictures of the footballer and a gorilla captioned 'Could Everton's Ross Barkley represent the missing link between man and beast?' The mayor of Liverpool described the original comments as a racial slur, the footballer's lawyers made a formal complaint, Merseyside Police launched an investigation, and Everton banned *Sun* reporters from attending their matches and training sessions. Perhaps unfairly – to borrow the meaningless rhetorical flourish used by MacKenzie to introduce his comments on Barkley – the paper's parent company, News UK, cut its ties with their old editor. MacKenzie himself said he had no idea of Barkley's family past and that 'to describe the article as racist is beyond parody.'

So much can hinge on a single word, if that word is a taboo one or hints at a taboo area. A transatlantic version of the gorilla to-do took place also in 2017 when the cable network ESPN sacked a tennis commentator, Doug Adler. His offence was to describe the hard-hitting play of black tennis star Venus Williams as an example of the 'guerrilla effect'. ('And you'll see Venus move in and put the guerrilla effect on, charging,' were his actual words.) Perhaps Adler was thinking of a Nike advertisement from the mid-1990s in which Andre Agassi and Pete Sampras play an impromptu, scrappy game in a New York street, an encounter which was dubbed 'guerrilla tennis'. The word is a diminutive of the Spanish *guerra* (war) and means 'small war', usually with the implication of pinprick attacks and the strategy of grinding down one's opponent. But guerrilla sounds very like gorilla, which is what some ESPN viewers thought that Adler was saying. In other words, some viewers thought he was using 'gorilla' as a racist slur. There was an eruption on Twitter and within days the Disney-owned company had removed the commentator for 'making an inappropriate comment that was viewed negatively by everyone but Adler'. At the time of writing Adler was suing his one-time employer for wrongful dismissal. A less severe penalty was meted out to an Oklahoma commentator who, in April 2018, described a black basketball player as being 'out of his cotton-picking mind' following a complicated pass during a broadcast match. Brian Davis, taken to task for his 'inappropriate and offensive' language, was suspended from commentary for a single match. 'Cotton-picking', originating in the South, is a direct reference to the work on slave plantations. The *Oxford English Dictionary* equates it with 'damned'.

Only a few years ago, 'gorilla', 'guerrilla' and 'cotton-picking' would have passed without remark, whatever the context. The shift in taboo terms, in bad words, isn't confined to the cultural change surrounding traditional four-letter ones, some of them very old indeed, or more recent expressions relating to race and nationality. It extends, for example, to mental illness and the ways in which it is talked about. In the late 1960s and early 1970s there was a vogue for cheap-and-uncheerful exploitation films which employed mental disturbance not just as a key plot driver but as a come-on to the audience. *Twisted Nerve* (1968) used Down's syndrome as an element in the murderous behaviour of the lead character, prompting a hastily added voice-over before the film started: 'Ladies and gentlemen, because of the controversy already aroused, the producers of this film wish to re-emphasise what is already stated in the film, that there is no established scientific connection between Mongolism and psychotic or criminal behaviour.' The 1976 *Schizo* didn't bother with any psychological niceties but went straight for the jugular on the poster tag-line: 'When the left hand doesn't know who the right hand is killing!!' It's safe to say that a mainstream film today would not be issued with the title of *Psycho* or *Schizo* or use Down's syndrome as a plot driver. Political correctness, some would claim. Possibly. But I think political correctness is in general a good thing, and in the section titled 'PC Snowflake' I explain why.

In fact, the bad-word business occupies a wide spectrum, whether we're talking about body size and shape; about health and sickness, both physical and psychological; about political allegiances; about gender, sexuality and parenting; about religion; about culture; about history. Far from contracting in a supposedly permissive era, the reach of taboo words is actually expanding. It may seem that we've reached a desirable position in deciding what is and isn't taboo, a position in which it is possible to be frank about sex and bodily functions, but proper to be more circumspect in matters of race or ethnicity or disability. Yet I'm not sure that this is how most people perceive it. Although the old days – for the purpose of this argument, let's say the period from the end of the Second

World War until the early 1960s – are depicted as repressive and buttoned-up, the truth is that there were fewer things it was taboo to say, aside from what comedian George Carlin called the 'Seven Words You Can Never Say On Television', than there are now in the early twenty-first century.

But *Bad Words* doesn't only deal in taboo terms. I also examine a number of words that have lived quiet lives, in some cases for centuries, but which now find themselves damned to hell. Examples from the last half century or so include 'establishment', 'elite', 'expert' and 'liberal'. An example which seems as recent as a week or two ago is that harmless natural object, the 'snowflake'. A mid-range example is 'paedophile' or, in tabloidese, 'paedo'. The word remained buried away in the lexicon of sexual deviance for most of the twentieth century, describing an adult sexually attracted to children (the *Oxford English Dictionary* cites the first use in this sense in 1912). It remained an acceptable enough term to be used as part of the title of the Paedophile Information Exchange (PIE), an activist group that lasted from 1974 to 1984 and campaigned for the abolition of the age of consent. The emergence of the group, and the toleration for it in some quarters, is generally seen as an offshoot of the sexually liberalising 1960s. Yet the 'paedophile' and the 'paedo' are now the stuff of horror stories, tabloid headlines, government enquiries and special commissions.

Of course, terms such as 'elite' or 'paedophile' don't carry the visceral charge of the standard four-letter terms, especially the sexual or excremental ones. Yet they have a clout that they didn't possess a few years ago, and it's a negative one. 'Elite' was until recently an expression, generally, of approval even if there might be some resentment at its connotation of exclusivity; now the term is thrown around to condemn whole groups who are supposedly 'out of touch' or who might dare to defy the 'will of the people'. The metaphorical 'snowflake' stood for purity and innocence; now it stands – or rather melts – as a symbol of feeble, self-indulgent sensitivity. And 'paedophile' has shifted from an expression of sexual pathology to a red rag.

It's some of these red-rag words and their history I look at in *Bad Words*. A few of them have got a bit faded, and a handful have lost their colour almost completely, but others have been dipped in fresh dye, and have the most astonishing power to shock, distress and enrage.

***

Bad Words is arranged in a rough chronology, dealing briefly with long obsolete terms that invoke God or parts of his body, then with the standard obscenities, some of which by a quirk of history could be uttered openly in only two historical periods: the later Middle Ages and the late twentieth century. In the same period, and intensifying in the beginning of the new millennium, comes the rise in the taboo-rating of expressions to do with race and ethnicity. Finally, I look at terms which have just, as it were, popped into public consciousness, 'elite', 'snowflake' and the like.

This book focuses almost entirely on English as the language was and is used in Britain and America and, to an extent, in Australia. Looking at obscenities and profanity in other languages would reflect things about those cultures, for example the still widespread use of religious cursing in some Catholic countries. But it's a very big subject and another book altogether.

The Old Ones

QUEEN ELIZABETH I was a great swearer. She used the phrase 'God's death!' so frequently that it caught the attention of foreign ambassadors at her court. During a dispute with a favourite, the Earl of Leicester, she declaimed, 'God's death, my lord, I will have here one mistress but no master.' In asserting her power and superiority over the men in court, even those who believed themselves close to her, she used what was traditionally regarded as a man's weapon: strong language. In a famous speech at Tilbury in 1588, the year of the Spanish Armada, Elizabeth conceded that 'I have the body of a weak and feeble woman' but immediately laid claim to 'the heart and stomach of a king'. Clad in a silver breastplate, she invoked her father, Henry VIII, a ruler well-known for his temper and profanity. But Elizabeth's strong language wasn't carving out a new path for queens or for women in general. Rather, it was something of a last gasp for old-style profanity invoking God or Christ. Soon it would be banned altogether. And then when such terms came back many years later, such swearing had lost its force.

In 1606 a play called *The Isle of Gulls* by John Day was staged at the Blackfriars Theatre by one of the children's companies that were fashionable in the London theatre of the early seventeenth century. It caused a major scandal. The play is long forgotten, as is the playwright, but at the time it was thought dangerous enough for those involved – including the boy players – to be committed to Bridewell prison and for the stage company, the Children of the Queen's Revels, to lose its royal patronage. A wider result was a parliamentary Act 'to Restrain Abuses of Players' which threatened 'that if at any time or times after the End of this present Session of Parliament, any Person or Persons do or shall in any Stage-play, Enterlude, Show, May-game or Pageant, jestingly or profanely speak or use the holy Name of God, or of Christ Jesus, or the Holy Ghost, or of the Trinity, which are not to be spoken but with Fear and Reverence, shall forfeit for every such Offence by him or them committed Ten Pounds.'

Snitching was encouraged: half of the ten-pound fine went to the king's treasury but the other half was to be pocketed by the individual who alerted the authorities to the offence. In view of this it may be surprising that there is no trace of any fine at all being levied on an acting company. Yet it seems that this was not because potential tell-tales were asleep on the job but because the players' companies, faced with these severe penalties, straightaway cleaned up their act – and kept it clean.

Ironically, the immediate cause of the trouble in John Day's *The Isle of Gulls* wasn't the language, profane or otherwise. The play provided a satirical if disguised look at the court of King James I. The arrival of James from Scotland after the death of Elizabeth I in 1603 had not been greeted with universal acclaim. Plenty of important people, and Londoners in particular, saw him as an interloper, a cuckoo in the nest. The new king came down south with his own retinue of nobles; he cultivated favourites, closely; he wasn't English. *The Isle of Gulls* was not the only drama to have looked satirically at the alien court in Westminster, even if the satire in this instance didn't lie in the language and might only have consisted in the boy actors guying Scottish accents or sending up particular members of the court. But the authorities had to respond and so they seized on an aspect of drama in performance that might have been troubling them for some time. It was the frequent swearing on stage, those occasions when, in the words of the parliamentary Act, the 'Name of God, or of Christ Jesus, or the Holy Ghost, or of the Trinity' was uttered 'jestingly or profanely'. It wasn't so much throwaway utterances such as 'for God's sake!', though that would be disallowed. Rather it was a peculiarity of this historical period of swearing that not simply the names of the Trinity were evoked in a casual spirit but, in the case of Christ, bodily parts too: By God's arms! By his foot! By his (eye)lid! By his blood! By his wounds! The opening 'by' was often dropped and the rest elided so the oath emerged sibilantly as 'sfoot or 'slid or 'swounds. The greatest playwright of the age frequently put such imprecations into the mouths of his characters. ''Swounds' or ''sblood' exclaims Shakespeare's Hamlet at moments of anger or frustration. ''Sblood' is a favourite exclamation of Falstaff's, one he uses half a dozen times in *Henry IV, Part 1*. And it is the first, angry word uttered by the villainous Iago in *Othello*.

Well, all of that would have to go, by order of Parliament. No more invoking of Christ and his body parts. It wasn't merely the new plays that had to avoid profane language, but the old ones too, which, if revived, required going through and cleaning up before being restaged. This vindictive measure imposed real constraints on companies and their writers. One wonders how often an experienced player dealing with a familiar text had to check himself momentarily on stage in the run-up to a familiar line. When Hamlet is next to Ophelia's open grave he angrily challenges her brother Laertes to a kind of duel of public grief: ''Swounds, show me what thou'lt do:/Woo't weep? woo't fight? woo't fast? woo't tear thyself?' That's how the lines appear in an early published version of the play, which was first staged around 1601. But in the First Folio, containing all of Shakespeare's surviving plays and published in 1623 after his death, Hamlet's graveside challenge has been watered down to 'Come show me what thou'lt do./Woo't weep? Woo't fight? Woo't tear thy self?' Every character in every play, tragic or comic, has to watch his mouth from now on. All Falstaff's 'sbloods – as in ''Sblood, I am as melancholy as a gib cat or a lugged bear' – simply disappear.

These little cuts and amendments might seem small but cumulatively they affected the punch and drama of what was happening on stage, and were a small foretaste of the growing influence of Puritanism which would lead to the closing down of the theatres in the middle of the sixteenth century. The new law may even have affected settings and subjects for playwrights such as Shakespeare. As James Shapiro writes in *1606: William Shakespeare and the Year of Lear* (2015), because of 'the new constraints on how characters could express themselves, it was much easier to locate plays in classical or pagan lands than in Christian ones, and this is likely to have influenced the choice of the plays that followed, most immediately *Antony and Cleopatra* and soon *Coriolanus* and *Pericles* as well.'

Swearing that invoked Christ and parts of his body was nothing new. In 'The Pardoner's Tale', written in the late fourteenth century and one of best-known of the sequence of narrative poems that make up Geoffrey Chaucer's *The Canterbury Tales*, we're told of the debauched lives of the three yobs at the centre of the tale. Along with drinking, whoring and gambling, their profanity is vehemently condemned by the Pardoner with an anti-Semitic note that was routine in the medieval period and long afterward.

> Hir othes been so grete and so dampnable
> That it is grisly for to heere hem swere.
> Oure blissed lordes body they totere –
> Hem thoughte that Jewes rente hym noght ynough.

(Their oaths are so great and damnable, that it is grisly to hear them swear. Our blessed lord's body they tore to pieces – they thought the Jews did not tear him enough.)

In the course of the story, the Pardoner gives examples of the offensive things the young men routinely say: 'Goddes precious herte [heart]', 'by his nayles', 'By the blood of Crist', 'Goddes armes', 'Goddes digne [worthy] bones'. The Pardoner stresses the sinfulness of 'ydel swering' and says that God placed the injunction against it – 'Thou shalt not take the name of the Lord thy God in vain' – high up in the Ten Commandments, well before what might seem more significant offences such as murder. The three young men in the story get their comeuppance when they go in search of Death during a time of plague and discover instead Death lying in wait for them. They are punished for their greed and by implication for their other vices, including the casual way they tear to pieces in words 'oure blissed lordes body'. Whatever the view of the authorities and the church, this kind of 'bad language' was a well-established habit that was to last several hundred more years, as the fuss in Shakespeare's time indicates.

What to our ears sounds like a peculiar but relatively harmless use of language would have sounded very different to medieval ones. In part this is no more than a reflection of the gap between a modern secular society, at least in the West, and a historic community permeated with Christianity, with its beliefs and its terminology, its signs, symbols and relics. Of the thirty or so characters described by Chaucer in the 'Prologue' to *The Canterbury Tales* as they embark on their pilgrimage to the shrine of Thomas Becket, a third are directly connected with organised religion. It is their life and their living, even if several of them, such as the well-fed monk with his taste for hunting, fall short of the ideal while others, such as the Pardoner selling papal pardons to the ignorant and passing off sheep's bones as saint's relics, are actively corrupt. Ironically some of the characters who are not dependent on the church, such as the knight or the ploughman, lead better Christian lives than those who supposedly have vocations. Chaucer's pilgrims are a moving frieze of medieval life. Men and women, young, middle-aged and old, professionals and artisans, chivalrous and crooked, they represent all the social strata except the aristocratic and the down-and-out. And almost every single rider on the way to Canterbury is either genuinely devout or pretending to be devout or paying lip service to religion, if only by virtue of taking part in a pilgrimage.

It may be hard for us to imagine the emotional, intellectual and psychological landscape of a culture so steeped in religion, but less hard perhaps to see why oaths and imprecations that invoked God and Christ, as well as his body parts, should have been taken so seriously and literally. In her instructive and entertaining account, *Holy Sh*t: A Brief History of Swearing* (2013), author Melissa Mohr describes how 'certain vain oaths were believed to actually tear apart the ascended body of Christ, as he sat next to his Father in heaven. Phrases that incorporated body parts, like swearing "by God's bones" or "by God's nails," were looked upon as a kind of opposite to the Catholic eucharist – the ceremony in which a priest is said to conjure Christ's physical body in a wafer and his blood in wine.' For the medieval believer – that is, almost everyone – this sundering of Christ's body wasn't a mere metaphor but actuality. A wall painting in St Lawrence's church in Broughton, Buckinghamshire, depicts a scene generally believed to be a warning to swearers. In it a group of men surround a central image of Christ and Mary, in the style of a Pietà, each clutching a body part, such as a foot or even the heart. This, the picture tells the congregation more in sorrow than anger, is what you do when you swear falsely or in vain.

In addition, this was an era very familiar with body parts in a religious context. Saints' relics were venerated and credited with magical powers. Chaucer's Pardoner exploits this when he shows ignorant country folk 'crystal stones' containing bits of rag and bone which, when dipped in a well, give the water curative powers for livestock as well as bringing prosperity to the farmer who drinks a draught once a week before cockcrow. People were used to sanctified body parts and other religious remnants. In the royal chapel of Charles V, a king of France in the late fourteenth century, could be seen jewel-encrusted reliquaries cradling a piece of Moses' rod and the top of John the Baptist's head, a flask containing the Virgin Mary's milk, and Christ's swaddling clothes as well as a fragment from the True Cross. There must have been enough pieces of the True Cross scattered throughout Europe to construct another Noah's Ark, relics of which were also eagerly sought. In contrast to these A-list remains, the odd saint's fingernail or foreskin housed in your local church or abbey must have seemed less remarkable though still worthy of attention. All this is to say that, to the medieval mind, the linguistic anatomising of Christ's body – by his nails! by his wounds! – wouldn't have been so strange. If the low-life characters in Chaucer's stories are anything to go by, these expressions were in regular use, despite the strictures of the church, and their very familiarity suggests they had been in circulation for a long time. They were still around more than two hundred years later.

But by the time we get to the Jacobean age, and that 1606 Act of Parliament which banned the use of 'sbloods, 'slids and 'swounds, profane language has become a weapon not in the hand of the user but in that of the authorities. If they don't like your tone, your attitude, your message, then one of the things they can pick on – and perhaps punish you for with fines or imprisonment – is your (bad) language. The bad language may not even be the real or main reason for a prosecution but it is the obvious one. Bad language, in all its lurid look-at-me-ness, sticks out like a sore thumb to those inclined to go looking for sore thumbs. It was observed at the time of the *Lady Chatterley* trial in 1960 that some people on the prosecuting team were bothered less by the 'fucks' and 'cunts' which D. H. Lawrence had seeded through the book than by the way the novel dramatised an adulterous affair between a man and a woman from different social classes. Bad language and sexual explicitness were the ostensible targets of the prosecution but the real aim was to tamp down a subversive threat to social order and hierarchy.

What happened to all the 'sbloods, 'slids and 'swounds after the stage ban? They didn't disappear altogether but they slowly fizzled – 'sfizzled – away, sounding more and more quaint until by the nineteenth century, if they're used at all, it is usually in the context of a historical novel by the likes of Walter Scott. Here's another aspect of bad language and the shift in taboo terms: the process reflects larger historical and cultural changes. In an era when religion was woven into daily life, expressions such as 'sblood or 'snails, which to us sound comic or peculiar, had some charge, and could lead to moralising condemnation and even legal penalties.

In *Holy Sh*t*, Melissa Mohr focuses on the great shift from religious swearing to what one might call secular swearing, or in her terms the shift from the 'holy' to the 'shit'. She identifies several reasons related to major social, cultural and religious changes – none of them occurring overnight, but all having the effect of slow earthquakes. The decline of feudalism, which was based on a system of oaths, explicit or implicit, made to God and then spreading downwards through society from the monarch to the nobility to the clergy and then the lower classes meant that everyone was tied together by a web of obligation. The rise of a capitalist system not only produced an element of levelling to this hierarchical, pyramid-like structure, but made the swearing and oath-giving less necessary. Under the old arrangement, the oath-breaker might wait for God to strike him down (or not) if he broke his word. Under a new proto-capitalist dispensation, the oath-breaker – i.e. the producer or merchant who didn't keep his side of the bargain – would soon find himself going out of business. Honesty was the best policy, not so much from a moral viewpoint, but as a matter of trade.

Casual religious cursing relating to Christ still causes offence to some, but their number is fairly small and that reflects the diminished role Christianity plays now.

That said, as an exclamation of surprise or frustration, 'Jesus!' still has a bit of voltage, acting as relief for the speaker and perhaps jolting the listener. Popular variants include 'Jesus wept!', the shortest sentence in the Bible, 'Jesus Christ!', 'Jesus fucking Christ!' and 'Jesus H. Christ!' The origin of that curious H in a phrase that first appears towards the end of the nineteenth century is a mystery. Michael Quinion speculates on his 'World Wide Words' blog that it may have come from the monogram representing the first three letters in Jesus's name in Greek, ΙΗΣΟΥΣ, rendered IHS (sometimes IHC), where the H is the capitalised version of the Greek letter eta (e). Quinion notes that an especially strong and satisfying emphasis can be placed on the central H. The monogram might have been familiar, even if not completely understood, because it figures on clerical vestments. Then there are the euphemistic shortenings of 'gee' and 'jeez' and a rhyming extension in 'jeepers creepers'. As an exclamation 'God!' seems less versatile and popular than the Jesus permutations, although OMG/omg (Oh my God!) is a strong contender among the most popular abbreviations in messaging.

The offensiveness of some of these expressions is going to vary from speaker to speaker – or perhaps more accurately listener to listener – but in general they rate very low. Some idea of the social attitude can be gauged from the British Board of Film Classification's rating system whereby 'God', if used infrequently, counts as 'very mild bad language' and earns an everyone-welcome U certificate, while 'Jesus' and 'Christ' get PG or Parental Guidance ('General viewing, but some scenes may be unsuitable for young children'). Similarly Ofcom, the body that regulates TV and radio, regards the invocation of God or Christ as 'generally of little concern' although there is 'some recognition that this may offend religious people'. An exception would be 'Jesus fucking Christ!' but this is more on account of the central word and not the two framing it.

Bloody hell!

One of the most famous and lavish scenes in the stage and film musical *My Fair Lady* does not appear in George Bernard Shaw's play *Pygmalion*, the source of the story of the cockney flower-seller Eliza Doolittle and the attempt by Henry Higgins, a professor of phonetics, to pass her off as a member of the upper class. The new musical scene is set at the Ascot races and, in the 1964 film version directed by George Cukor, shows the disintegration of Audrey

Hepburn's facade of gentility as she instinctively reverts back to cockney and screams at a horse: 'Come on, Dover, move yer bloomin' arse!' Rex Harrison, playing Henry Higgins, claps his hand to his mouth in horrified amusement. The racegoers, hitherto so stilted as to be almost motionless, now begin to shift, gasp and mutter. One lady is badly affected and swoons into the arms of her husband. The point of the Ascot scene is to show Eliza's introduction to society, and whether all her training in gentility by Professor Higgins will hold up under the glamour and colour of one of society's great occasions. And amid the cut-glass accents and the finery of the costumes, designed for the film by Cecil Beaton, the point of Hepburn's arse is to shock.

This moment, hinging on a particular word, was lyricist Alan Jay Lerner's way of echoing and commemorating another particular word, more taboo than 'arse' and uttered on stage during the first night of George Bernard Shaw's *Pygmalion* in April 1914. As with the Ascot racegoers in the film and their response to 'move yer bloomin' arse!', Shaw's word provoked near-hysteria in the audience at His Majesty's Theatre in London's Haymarket. Their laughter lasted seventy-six seconds, as timed by the stage-manager's stopwatch. It was so wild and uncontrolled, wrote Shaw afterwards to a friend, 'that it was really doubtful for some time whether they could recover themselves and let the play go on'. Outrage wasn't confined to His Majesty's Theatre but rattled round the upper echelons of society. Bishops called for the play to be banned. There were letters to *The Times*, debates at Eton and the Oxford Union, and petitions to the Prime Minister.

The cause of the uproar occurs during a scene set in the flat of Henry Higgins's mother on the Chelsea embankment. It is the old lady's afternoon to receive visitors, and Higgins plans to use the occasion as a test for how far he has succeeded with Eliza. The problem is that, as he explains to his mother before the guests arrive, 'I've got her pronunciation all right, but you have to consider not only how a girl pronounces, but what she pronounces.' Eliza is the last to arrive and makes awkward conversation until finally, when asked by a young man if she's walking back across the park, she replies: 'Walk! Not bloody likely. [Sensation] I am going in a taxi. [She goes out]' Shaw, who paid almost as much attention to his stage directions as he did to his dialogue, inserted [Sensation] to show the effect of Eliza's 'bloody' on Mrs Higgins and her guests.

Sensation would be an understatement for the impact of the word on Edwardian England or the risk that Shaw was running on his own behalf and others, even though he knew that it was a word in widespread use. Indeed, a dialogue between Professor Higgins and his housekeeper indicates that he uses the word himself, and that she doesn't like it ('Only this morning, sir, you applied it to your boots, to the butter, and to the brown bread'). Yet the fact that the stage-manager at His Majesty's Theatre was waiting with a stopwatch to time the laughter, or other reaction, from the audience indicates that there was a big difference between saying it in private and uttering it before hundreds of people. The actor-impresario Herbert Beerbohm Tree, who staged the play and who also took the part of Higgins, had begged the dramatist to substitute a more acceptable term such as 'blooming' or 'ruddy' for 'bloody'. The actress playing Eliza was thought to have endangered her career by saying those three words on stage. Straightaway, and for years afterwards, the word 'Pygmalion' became a humorous substitute for 'bloody', as in 'not Pygmalion likely!' As late as 1960 *The Times* could refer to a town councillor causing trouble by using 'a pygmalion word' and know that readers would understand.

It took centuries for 'bloody' (coming from a Germanic word and initially appearing in Old English as *blodig*) to turn into an outrageous term that Shaw knew would jolt his audience into hysterical laughter. Originally the word applied literally to someone smeared in blood, as with the question early on in Shakespeare's *Macbeth* 'What bloody man is that?', a line always good for a schoolboy snigger in more innocent days. Metaphorically, it was used about someone with a taste for shedding blood or about an especially violent battle or era. Bloody doesn't definitively become the bloody with which we are familiar until the mid-eighteenth century in references such as 'bloody bad news' and a 'bloody good song'. The word is an intensifier, like 'absolutely', 'extremely', and most often appears in a negative context. Hearing a piece of bloody bad news is more likely, linguistically speaking, than hearing a bloody good song.

But why did this blood-related word make the leap from describing something matter-of-fact, if potentially unpleasant, to a term which was for many years a very bad word? No one knows, and this makes 'bloody' unusual among taboo terms in which their sexual, excremental and other associations at once provide a reason for their risky appeal. It seems astonishing that for plenty of English speakers it was once the strongest expletive available – yet it was. 'Bloody' is not obscene and not profane either, despite attempts to make it so. Theories as to its origin that don't hold water include a contraction of 'byrlady' or 'by our Lady', an old oath or interjection, and even a Protestant suspicion of the Catholic doctrine of transubstantiation (the conversion of the red wine of communion into Christ's blood). Apart from anything else, the shock value of such 'religious' swearing and allusion was fading by the late Middle Ages yet 'bloody' retained some of its power well into the secularised twentieth century. The most likely reason for its taboo status seems to be class-based. 'Bloody' was seen as the kind of language typical of the lower classes, and not the hard-working sort; rather it was the preserve of 'dirty drunkards' and 'shrewish women' in the words of one Victorian commentator.

Incidentally it's worth noting that Alan Jay Lerner, the New York librettist of *My Fair Lady*, opted for the euphemistic 'bloomin'', and in doing so he followed exactly what Beerbohm Tree had begged George Bernard Shaw to do. Perhaps 'bloody arse' would have been a bit too vulgar, a double linguistic whammy; more likely Lerner avoided 'bloody' because Americans aren't familiar with the word when used as a taboo intensifier. Indeed those Americans who do use it may be regarded as affected, trying to ape British manners. Also worth noting is that part of the comic and slightly shocking value of the *My Fair Lady* Ascot scene for the cinema audience, as opposed to the racegoers, is that the words were uttered by Audrey Hepburn, famous for the grace and charm of her performances.

Like other contentious expressions, 'bloody' has spawned a handful of related terms that indicate its shadow presence but mean that the user doesn't actually have to say those dangerous syllables. It might be stripped right back to 'bee', as in 'bee nuisance', or even appear simply as 'B/b', as in bf/BF, short for bloody fool but more likely now to stand for 'boyfriend'. Other alternatives include 'bleeding' and the contorted 'sanguinary'. None of these carries much force any longer. Like a dying battery, 'bloody' can at best administer a slight tingle if used in an inappropriate context such as a wedding or funeral speech. A child might once have been ticked off, or worse, for saying it, but now there are other, more taboo terms for a child to use. 'Bloody' has started down that route to defunct taboo-dom once taken by expressions such as 'slid and 'swounds.

Body Parts

If the poet and journalist Henry Reed (1914–86) is remembered at all now it is for his much anthologised poem, 'Naming of Parts'. Published in 1942 and one of a sequence of three collectively called 'Lessons of the War', 'Naming of Parts' parodies the way an army instructor inducts his recruits into the mysteries and functions of the various components of a rifle, parts such as the bolt, the safety-catch and the lower and upper sling swivels 'whose use you will see/When you are given your slings.' Through the mind of one of the half-attentive recruits there floats an alternative commentary, half mocking, half wistful, combining the back-and-forward motion of the rifle bolt that opens the breech – a movement known as 'easing the spring' – with the back-and-forward motion of the bees in the nearby gardens 'assaulting and fumbling the flowers'; that process too might be called 'easing the Spring'. The poem's title punningly links reproductive and rifle parts.

The other two poems in the sequence are not so well known but they are more emphatic about the gap between army life and the ordinary world, especially the world of love and sex, now denied to the recruits. In 'Judging Distances' the squaddies are informed that in the army they have to use terminology such as 'at five o'clock in the central sector' when referring to a landscape. On this basis the reluctant listener concludes that the gap between him and the 'apparent lovers' he can see in the distance is 'about one year and a half'. The final poem, 'Movement of Bodies', is the slyest. Around a table-top 'brown clay model' of a potential battle terrain the recruits stand attentively to be instructed in tactics. Although the instructor is completely unaware of it, the model has incongruously human attributes: at the top is a 'wooded headland', lower down a 'variety of gorges and knolls and plateaus and basins and saddles'. The instructor can't understand why, as he lumberingly talks about the target they must capture, one which is secluded and protected by 'a typical formation of what appear to be bushes', some of the privates seem overcome with emotion. One is crying. Two of them are snivelling. Yesterday one soldier was so badly affected that he was sick. The instructor tells five of them to fall out and sit at the back of the room until they've recovered themselves. Then he returns to the clay model, starting again further north towards the head-like area. The last line of the poem is 'Here are two hills.'

The reaction of the army privates to the instructor, the sniggering and the tears in their eyes as he waves his hands over the nudgingly feminine terrain and talks about 'our point of attack' and whether what is hidden may be 'friend or foe', is the reaction of the schoolkids they were until recently.

Schoolkids find bodies funny, as well as frightening and embarrassing, interesting and exciting. Just like adults, in fact. Children have plenty of slang words to describe bodies and their parts. Adults have plenty as well, many of them of them carried over from childhood. This may explain why there's a bouncy, childish quality to many of the slang terms for human bodies and their parts. Just consider the bonce, block and nut with its kisser, gob, trap, cakehole, choppers, beak, conk, snout and lugholes, and elsewhere the tits, boobs, bristols, breadbasket and bum, all supported by pins and plates of meat.

Most of these terms aren't polite and probably wouldn't, or shouldn't, be used in the most formal situations. But they are far from being bad words, in the sense which I am using in this book, even if it is arguable that the many slang synonyms for breasts come close to the taboo. It is only when we get closer to the centre, as it were, that things get more heated. When parts of the body intersect with two of the principal taboo areas – the sexual and the excremental – the topic suddenly becomes linguistically dangerous and problematic as well as more fascinating.

Almost all of the slangy terms relating to the genitals and their functions and quite a few of the expressions to do with the human backside provoke reactions such as those of the squaddies round the instructor's table in Henry Reed's poem: suppressed giggles, embarrassment, and perhaps a touch of excitement and fear too.

It is significant but not surprising that these two areas, the sexual and the excremental, are among the most productive and inventive fields for slang. In his historical survey *Slang Down the Ages* (1994), Jonathon Green says, 'Other than terms for drinking, which run substantially over 2,000 according to one recent compiler, and those for sexual intercourse the slang terms for the vagina outstrip any rivals, and certainly those for the penis.' Proving his point, Green devotes fifteen pages of the book to the body, twenty to the vagina, sixteen to the penis, four to the posterior and a further ten to defecation and the lavatory. A small handful of these terms are still regarded as obscene or taboo, and need more extended consideration. But we will do things back to front, so to speak, and start at the more innocuous bottom. Specifically, bum and arse.

Elephant & Castle

Bum is quite an old word, even if not as antique as arse, which predates the Norman Conquest. Bum has a cheeky, comic innocence to it, fitting with linguistic speculation

about the word's origins in 'bump', in the sense of a protu-
berance, a bodily swelling. 'Bump' started off as an
onomatopoeic word, signifying a blow and its sound, and
like most onomatopoeic words it has a bit of comedy lurk-
ing in its makeup. Then bump got transferred to the swelling that might be the result of a blow, and from bump to
bum, a ready-made bodily swelling, is but a short step.
The word was included in the most important and author-
itative of the early English dictionaries, Samuel Johnson's
Dictionary of the English Language (1755), where he
defined it as 'The buttocks; the part on which we sit'.
Incidentally, Johnson also included a number of other
terms* that later and more priggish centuries would desig-
nate as 'not in polite use', among which are: piss ('Urine;
animal water'/'To make water'), fart ('Wind from behind'),
turd ('Excrement') and arse ('The buttocks').

---

* One of the many hundreds of anecdotes featuring Dr Johnson
tells us of a 'literary lady expressing to Dr. J. her approbation of
his Dictionary and, in particular, her satisfaction at his not having
admitted into it any improper words; "No, Madam," replied he,
"I hope I have not daubed my fingers. I find, however that you
have been looking for them."' There are several differing versions
of the story, a couple of which have the lady not complimenting
Johnson but complaining because he had included improper
words. His reply, though the wording varies slightly, is always to
the effect that she could only know this if she had been searching
for them.

The 'tramp' definition of bum, originating in the US in the middle of the nineteenth century, comes not from the human posterior but more probably from a bummer or idler, someone who bums around (the German word *Bummler* means a stroller, dawdler). The American equivalent for bum as a body-part is 'butt', a return to the source-word for 'buttock', which probably developed as a diminutive of 'butt'. There's some evidence, however, that 'bum' in the bottom sense is gaining traction in the US. As with other British linguistic imports, there may even be a certain cachet to the bum over the butt. According to Jim Boyd from Des Moines: 'I have seen an increasing use of "bum" for a person's backside here, both from local friends and from Americans on the web. While I am still perfectly fine with sitting on my butt, everyone else is getting all fancy talking about their bums' (quoted on the *BBC News Magazine* website, 17 October 2012).

Linguistically speaking, the arse came before the bum. The *Oxford English Dictionary* gives its first citation around the year 1000, though in a different spelling. Arse is more of a borderline word than bum, slightly further from respectability and a little more of an insult when applied to someone, although arguably a man who is a bum is engaged on a lifetime's (non-)work while he may only be an arse on occasion. When not used as an insult but as a 'compliment', arse also carries a stronger sexual charge than the low-voltage bum. Geoffrey Chaucer was happy enough to use the 'ers' in his *Canterbury Tales*, but he made sure the word was attached to the comic or villainous characters. In his story the Summoner, who's engaged in a feud with the Friar on the Canterbury pilgrimage, discovers what the devil has up his backside in hell when:

> Right so as bees out swarmen from an hyve,
> Out of the develes ers ther gonne dryve
> Twenty thousand freres [friars] on a route,
> And thurghout helle swarmed al aboute.

And in 'The Miller's Tale' the unwary would-be lover Absalon pleads for a night-time kiss from the beautiful Alison through an open window. Fed up with his badgering and already occupied with another lover called Nicholas, Alison offers not her face. Instead:

> And at the wyndow out she putte hir hole,
> And Absolon, hym fil no bet ne wers [it happened to
>   him no better no worse],
> But with his mouth he kiste hir naked ers
> Ful savourly, er he were war of this.

Humiliated, Absalon goes to a friendly smithy, gets a hot metal plough blade and goes back to the window demanding another kiss in exchange for a ring. It's a different kind of ring he receives when it's Nicholas who now sticks his bottom out of the window and farts in Absolon's face. The luckless suitor, though, is 'redy with his iren hoot,/And Nicholas amydde the ers he smoot.' This is far from the end of the tale. It's easy to see why in more buttoned-up days some of Chaucer's raunchier and dirtier stories did not figure on the English Literature syllabuses of secondary schools. Now they do appear, probably because the sex and bad language are sugar coating the pill of poetry written in Middle English.

After all this medieval exuberance, 'arse' seems to take a back seat, not appearing much in print before the twentieth century. Ass is a slightly different matter. In this spelling it describes 'a long-eared animal of the horse kind', as dictionaries put it, and is respectable company anywhere. It's also synonymous with a slow, stupid person and has been employed in this sense in English since at least the early Middle Ages, even if there's occasionally a note of exasperated affection when it's coupled with 'silly'. The arse (bottom) and the ass (donkey) have no etymological connection: the first comes from an old Germanic word – *Arsch* is still modern German slang – and the second from Latin. But there is an overlap between the 'bottom' meaning and the 'donkey/slow-witted' one. Shakespeare, always alert to puns, uses 'ass' dozens of times in his plays. Usually Shakespeare's ass simply equates to the donkey, the idiot. But occasionally it hints at the other 'arse'. He even transforms one character – Bottom, naturally enough, in *A Midsummer Night's Dream* – into an ass, an absurd creature with whom the Queen of Fairies is besotted. When Puck describes how 'Titania waked and straightway loved an ass' the double entendre can't have been far from his or the audience's minds, especially as 'ass' rhymes with 'pass' in the previous line, though both words could be pronounced with a short 'a'.

Meanwhile in the US the double-s version has always been the preferred spelling for what the British term 'arse'. It can mean a fool, a slow person, but much more often it is slang for the bottom, the posterior. As in Britain the term frequently occurs in an aggressive context: Kiss my ass! Get your ass outa here! The rather prim US President Jimmy Carter surprised listeners when he said that if Senator Ted Kennedy ran against him in 1980, he would 'whip his ass', a remark that caused problems for news outlets unwilling to reproduce the word in those more sensitive days. The under-appreciated Florida noir crime writer Charles Willeford wrote a book called *Kiss Your Ass Good-Bye* (1987), and it's not about saying farewell to your pet donkey.

The US spelling and pronunciation are becoming more familiar in the UK. As far back as 2003 the Renault Mégane brand got into trouble with a campaign on British TV featuring the soundtrack song 'I See You Baby (Shakin' That Ass)' to visuals of gyrating bottoms, mostly young and female, intercut with occasional glimpses of the rear view of the car. Ruling only that the commercial should not be shown during programmes specifically made for children, the advertising regulator said it believed the words would be regarded by viewers as 'relatively mild American slang' and that the dancing was 'humorous and energetic rather than sexual'. The duo that produced the song, Groove Armada, is English but it's interesting to speculate whether they would ever have produced a number with a one-letter difference, a number titled and pronounced 'I See You Baby (Shakin' That Arse)'. Rather than hip, such an anglicised version sounds faintly sleazy or, worse, comic. Ironically but unsurprisingly, when the ad was aired in America the line was changed to 'shakin' that thang'.

As demonstrated by the Renault Mégane campaign, 'ass' can easily carry a sexual note whichever side of the Atlantic it occurs, though it's more usual in this sense in the US. Not just the backside, 'ass' long ago expanded to become a generic term for a woman viewed exclusively in sexual terms, 'a piece of ass'. This is objectionable enough but the reason why it should be has changed over the years. The phrase 'piece of ass' is recorded from the first half the twentieth century but then the offence would have lain in the coarse, vulgar employment of the term 'ass', rather than the reductive view of women it entails. By contrast, a man commenting on 'a nice piece of skirt' would probably have got away with it. Now all such expressions are out of court because they are demeaning in general rather than on account of any particular word. Of course, to claim that such things are 'out of court' is not to say that they aren't said.

Of the several expressions or compound words featuring arse/ass, a handful are innocuous enough such as going arse over tip, not knowing your arse from your elbow, half-arsed (= carelessly). The word is a shadowy presence in 'bottle' phrases such as 'bottling out', 'losing your bottle', which signify loss of nerve and derive from the rhyming slang of 'bottle and glass' for 'arse'. But other related terms suggest aggression or disgust or a combination of both. As part of the catalogue of bodily slang, arsehole – Elephant & Castle in rhyming slang – dates from the fourteenth century (in the spelling 'ers hole') but its metaphorical application either to an unattractive place, as in the 'arsehole of the universe', or to a person doesn't come until the twentieth century. Surprisingly, the *Oxford English Dictionary*'s first citation for the word to mean a stupid or irritating person is as recent as 1981 even though the US asshole had made its debut in this sense in the 1940s. D. H. Lawrence, obviously no fan of fan letters, scrawled 'arse-licking' on a flattering letter he received in 1912, so the expression is likely to have been in circulation well before then. Henry Miller described himself as not being an 'ass-licker', in the sense of toady, in *Tropic of Capricorn* (1939). The satirical magazine *Private Eye* invented Arslikhan to cover the practice, as in 'a graduate of the Arslikhan school of biography', as well as a regular feature titled 'O.B.N.' or 'Order of the Brown Nose' and covering egregious examples of servile flattery. (Brown-nose and brown-nosing originate in the US.) 'Arse bandit' for a homosexual man has been in slang circulation for well over half a century and earns the dictionary accolade of 'derogatory and offensive'. The related 'botty burglar' was apparently one of Kelvin MacKenzie's favourite taunts during his editorship of the *Sun* newspaper.

Botty itself appears in British English in the early nineteenth century, a childish diminutive of bottom as suggested by 'botty-wotty', the form in which the word is first recorded. This piece of kidspeak has never had much currency in the US although the rappers' favourite 'booty' may derive from it; the word may also be connected to booty in the sense of plunder. Incidentally, 'twerk' – a portmanteau combination of twitch and work/jerk – which sounds so very new was first noted in British English around the time Queen Victoria ascended to the throne, even if the 'shakin' yer booty' sense didn't come in until the 1990s.

In the US fanny has been a slang term for the buttocks since the early twentieth century. Although it is sometimes used in British English for the backside – Noël Coward has the line in *Private Lives*: 'You'd fallen on your fanny a few moments before' – the word has more generally been slang for the vagina. The travel item which in the UK is referred to as the 'bumbag' is known as a 'fanny pack' in the US, a possible source of confusion – and delight – to British visitors. The source of the term, whether it applies to the back or front, is not known. There is no truth to the notion that it comes from the abbreviated form of First Aid Nursing Yeomanry (FANY), the women's military/nursing organisation, founded in 1907, if only because the genital sense of fanny dates from the mid-Victorian period. Nor is there any connection with the well-known phrase Sweet Fanny Adams* or Sweet FA (sometimes appearing as sweet fuck all). One suggestion is that the British version comes from John Cleland's erotic classic *Fanny Hill, Memoirs of a Woman of Pleasure*, although this seems unlikely as the novel was prosecuted and suppressed for most of its existence after publication in 1748. Possibly Cleland was making a punning genital reference in the full name of his heroine, Fanny Hill, and

* Fanny Adams was an eight-year-old murdered by a solicitor's clerk in Alton, Hampshire, in 1867. His hanging outside Winchester Gaol before a crowd of five thousand was one of the last public executions in Britain. Soon afterwards the Royal Navy started to issue ships' crews with meat that was tinned, not preserved by salting. The mutton in the tins was not to the sailors' taste and, with grim humour, they were said to contain the remains of 'Sweet Fanny Adams'. At some point the story of the unfortunate Fanny got tangled with the abbreviation for 'fuck all'.

if so then the British fanny has been around a lot longer than the American one. The verb form meaning to 'mess about', 'waste time', as in 'Don't fanny around', is dated as late as 1971 in the *OED*. This is merely the first time the usage has been spotted in print; it was likely in spoken use some time before the 1970s.

Altogether it is not surprising, considering its centrality in human (and animal) life, that the bottom can be referred to in so many ways, several of them slang. Perhaps the very variety and the inventiveness of the expressions tell us that people don't quite know what to make of this basic part of our anatomy, and that curiosity, discomfort, excitement, even indifference, are all legitimate responses. Is the human bottom to be treated coldly, clinically, functionally? Is it to be giggled at and sniggered over at the back of the class? Is it to be appreciated aesthetically, in the style of a classical sculptor or painter? Is it to be eroticised and ogled? All of these things and probably more, at different times and occasions. Accordingly there are plenty of linguistic possibilities. Among them are functional, positional descriptions such as 'backside', 'behind', 'rear (end)', 'seat', 'posterior', 'bottom' and 'fundament' together with perhaps less enticing ones containing faintly animal overtones: 'hindquarters', 'rump', 'haunches'. The half-humorous 'cheeks', 'buns' and 'derrière' convey a tabloid sexiness. American English has plenty of slang terms, including 'booty', 'tail', 'can' (also slang for lavatory), 'duff' (dough?), 'fanny' (as above), 'heinie' (diminutive of 'behind') and 'tush/tushy' (from Yiddish *tochus* = buttocks).

Bristol City

Causing less angst than the buttocks and so less problematic in slang/taboo terms are the breasts. And also unlike the buttocks, breast slang is not an equal-opportunity employer. As Jonathon Green observes in *Slang Down the Ages*: 'For the purposes of slang, men have no breasts. Men boast of their pecs . . . but beyond such jargon the concept is essentially meaningless.' Simply to list a few of the many colloquial terms for breasts is to be overwhelmed by linguistic plenitude and a faint sense of silliness: baps, bazookas, bazooms, boobs, boobies, bristols, bubs, charlies, globes, headlights, hooters, jugs, knockers, lungs, melons, norks, puppies, rack, tits, titties . . . Aside from these, there are the nudging euphemisms such as assets,* cleavage, décolletage and embonpoint, or rather elaborate formulations such as 'pleasure pillows', as Helen Mirren said when she described her decision to no longer reveal hers by appearing nude in

---

* The *Daily Mail* in particular is fond of 'assets' often coupled with 'perky'. Rather like the tiles for a game of fridge scrabble, the *Mail* has a restricted arsenal of words that it deploys to describe the models, slebs and TV stars in its online 'sidebar of shame'. They include: pert, perky, toned, svelte, scooping/plunging (neckline), buxom, stunning, slender, busty, cheeky, racy, skintight.

films. Of these the most commonly used – and probably the most acceptable – is boobs, a shortening of booby which is, in turn, a variant of bubby. Some of the slang expressions such as tit and rack – from the US and probably a reference to a frame dependent on a larger structure rather than a rack of meat – carry a note of aggression. In fact, tits was one of the items on comedian George Carlin's (in)famous list of 'Seven Words You Can Never Say On Television', the routine he performed in the early 1970s. Yet even then it seemed out of place among much stronger terms, as Carlin's riff shows: 'And "tits" doesn't even belong on the list, y'know? Man! That's such a friendly sounding word. It sounds like a nickname, right? "Hey, Tits, come here, man. Hey! Hey Tits, meet Toots. Toots, Tits. Tits, Toots." It sounds like a snack, doesn't it? Yes, I know, it is a snack. But I don't mean your sexist snack! I mean New Nabisco Tits! and new Cheese Tits, Corn Tits, Pizza Tits, Sesame Tits, Onion Tits, Tater Tits.'

'Tits' has moved from this taboo area but is not altogether acceptable, as the Ofcom guidelines indicate by the description of 'medium language, potentially unacceptable pre-watershed. Vulgar or sexual use heightens the impact.' Nevertheless, breast slang isn't an area that generally causes much offence or presents linguistic puzzles since practically every word on the list testifies to its own obviousness. Is there anyone who doesn't know that bristols is rhyming slang (Bristol City = titty)? By contrast only a few people are aware that the Australian term 'norks' may come from a butter manufacturer in New South Wales, the Norco Co-operative Ltd, and a large-uddered cow that featured on their product labels, although an alternative explanation holds that it derives from the initials of New Orleans Rhythm Kings, a band on the Melbourne jazz scene in the 1950s, and that the word was used by band members to alert each other to the presence of a big-breasted dancer. Both explanations sound plausible enough, and illustrate the difficulties in pinning down the origins of some slang terms.

Yet breasts haven't always been relatively uncontentious. The word itself was evaded in polite society in the nineteenth century and even into the twentieth. Decorative breast-knots and breast-pins became bosom-knots and -pins. In the novel *Peter Simple* (1834), by Frederick Marryat, the naval hero is in Barbados and a guest at the governor's ball:

Supper was now announced, and having danced the last country dance with Miss Minerva, I of course had the pleasure of handing her into the supper-room. It was my fate to sit opposite to a fine turkey, and I asked my partner if I should have the pleasure of helping her to a piece of the breast. She looked at me very indignantly, and said, 'Curse your impudence, sar, I wonder where you larn manners. Sar, I take a lilly turkey bosom, if you please. Talk of breast to a lady, sar; – really quite horrid.'

The very faint taboo still attached to saying 'breast' out loud emerges in the turkey-and-chicken question, 'White meat or dark?' as an alternative to 'Breast or thigh?' Indeed, there is a Winston Churchill story – when isn't there a Churchill story? – in which, having been rebuked by an American society hostess for asking for breast meat, he was told: 'In this country we ask for white meat or dark meat.' Churchill supposedly sent the offended lady an orchid with a note reading 'I would be delighted if you would pin this on your white meat.' A similar euphemistic twist underlies another chicken query when 'Drumstick?' might be regarded as preferable to the unadorned 'Leg?'*

---

* Victorian prissiness is sometimes overstated. The story about covering up furniture legs seems to have been a British dig at American prudery, which then became a belief about the Victorians in general. It ignores the fact that there are practical, and decorative, reasons for covering furniture legs. There must have been something, however, in the idea of Victorian priggishness. Charles Dickens has this in *Martin Chuzzlewit* (1844), the novel which is partly based on his own US travels: ' "The most short-sighted man could see that at a glance, with his naked eye," said Martin. Mrs Hominy was a philosopher and an authoress, and consequently had a pretty strong digestion; but this coarse, this indecorous phrase, was almost too much for her. For a gentleman sitting alone with a lady – although the door was open – to talk about a naked eye!'

The c-word

There are two-and-a-half c-words in the English language, words which point to realities so daunting or alarming that instead of uttering them out loud some people can refer to them by initial letter only. The half-word is Christmas, not quite at taboo levels but nearly there if we are to believe the propaganda of the anti-PC lobby, and a word explored elsewhere in this book. The second is cancer, which came to be the c-word (or the big C) some-time during the 1980s and originated in the US. The third c-word is cunt, a term which probably has its roots in Old English. In this case age doesn't make for respectability but the reverse. An alternative expression to the c-word – the c-bomb – suggests its shocking, disruptive potential.

Yet the expression that the *Oxford English Dictionary* describes as 'the English word most avoided as taboo' hasn't always enjoyed such dubious status. It was once on the map in a literal sense since, in the thirteenth and four-teenth centuries; it is cited as part of a street name vari-ously spelled Gropecuntlane, Groppecuntelane and Gropecountelane in at least twenty English towns and cities from Bristol to Norwich to York. The earliest exam-ple of Gropecuntlane, from around 1230, occurs in Oxford (the street is now the narrow Magpie Lane running south from the world-famous High Street). It's quite prob-able that such street names marked the sites of brothels or at the least were downmarket lovers' lanes. Keith Briggs of Nottingham University has suggested that the concentration of the name in major ecclesiastical centres such as Norwich, Wells and York, which would be visited by Oxford-educated clerics, could indicate that the name began as an academic joke (*Journal of the English Place-Name Society*, vol. 41, 2009). Later on the names were cleaned up: Oxford's Gropecuntlane had turned into Grope or Grape Lane by 1605.

In confirmation of the fact that when it came to body parts the Middle Ages were less mealy mouthed than later periods, there's evidence in the nicknames or alternative titles that were given not just to streets but to natural places with a suggestive topography. Recorded names of places now lost such as Cuntelowe probably pointed to the presence of wooded gullies, of clefts with streams running through them, or small mounds. This is the kind of humanising – or sexing-up – of landscape that Henry Reed treats in the poem 'Movement of Bodies'. There is even record of the word being assimilated into the surnames of both men and women: John Fillecunt and Robert Clevecunt, Gunoka Cuntles and Bele Wydecynthe.

And above all, as proof of medieval frankness, we have Geoffrey Chaucer – even if he's perhaps not quite as frank as he first seems. Chaucer uses a version of the word several times in *The Canterbury Tales*, putting it into the mouth of those unabashed speakers, the Wife of Bath and the Miller.

It was obviously a topic that cropped up frequently in conversations between the Wife of Bath and her five husbands, one of whom told her 'I hadde the beste queynte that mighte be'. She assures another that he'll get enough sex at the end of the day:

> 'For, certeyn, olde dotard [fool], by youre leve,
> Ye shul have queynte right ynogh at eve'

And since that's the case he really shouldn't be possessive and start grouching:

> 'What eyleth yow to grucche thus and grone?
> Is it for ye wolde have my queynte allone?'

In 'The Miller's Tale', the young student Nicholas – the one who has his bottom or 'ers' branded by a hot iron – gets frisky with Alison, the wife of the carpenter with whom he's lodging.

> As clerkes ben ful subtile and ful queynte,
> And prively he caughte hire by the queynte,
> And seyde, 'Ywis, but if ich have my wille,
> For deerne love of thee, lemman, I spille.'

(Students are very subtle and ingenious, and in private he seized her by the delightful thing and said, 'Unless I get my way, I will spill [perish] for secret love of you, darling.')

Chaucer is playing on the adjective 'queynte' which from the early thirteenth century meant 'crafty', 'ingenious', 'skilfully made'. Like other writers of the time he exploits the word's similarity to 'cunt', for which the curious 'queynte' stands as a punning or euphemistic alternative. Which came first, the similarity of sound or the idea of something skilfully made and pleasing? Who knows? But Chaucer must have been pleased that Nicholas the clerk, being 'queynte', was after Alison's 'queynte', even if his method of getting her attention echoed Donald Trump's boast of grabbing 'them by the pussy'. These lines, as delivered by the Wife or the Miller, show that although Chaucer is often held up as an early and fearless user of 'cunt' this isn't quite accurate. And the fact that the word is uttered by the less respectable or more outspoken of the Canterbury pilgrims suggests that even as a euphemism it was edging towards non-respectability by the later Middle Ages.* So sometime between 1230, when Oxford's

---

* Chaucer had other euphemisms and alternative expressions. Elsewhere the Wife of Bath talks of her 'bele chose' (literally 'pretty thing') and, more obscurely, of what in some versions she calls her 'quoniam' (literally Latin for 'since' or 'whereas' but probably chosen for its alliterative value with 'queynte'). In 'The Miller's Tale', Chaucer also uses 'nether eye' and the no-nonsense 'hole' for the anus.

Gropecuntlane first appears in the records, and the 1390s, when *The Canterbury Tales* was written, 'cunt' was being superseded by 'queynte'. Soon even this substitution would be out for the count. Indeed, counts were out too. In his highly entertaining history of bad language, *Filthy English* (2009), Peter Silverton refers to the claim that 'English counts were renamed earls because of their titles' homophonic closeness to the word'.

Obviously, different kinds of wordplay would be needed. Step forward, that master of wordplay, and especially of sexual punning, William Shakespeare. He plays on cunt, quite extensively. There's the well-known exchange in *Hamlet*, which needs to be quoted in full, partly to prove that, yes, Shakespeare really did mean the cunt pun and partly to show that he could be pretty relentless in his wordplay.

Hamlet: Lady, shall I lie in your lap?
Ophelia: No, my lord.
Hamlet: I mean, my head upon your lap?
Ophelia: Ay, my lord.
Hamlet: Do you think I meant country matters?
Ophelia: I think nothing, my lord.
Hamlet: That's a fair thought to lie between maids'
    legs.
Ophelia: What is, my lord?
Hamlet: Nothing.

This may not be very subtle – and becomes even less so when the actor playing Hamlet places too much emphasis on the first syllable of country – but it gets a laugh from the more knowing in the audience. The same pun occurs when Touchstone in *As You Like It* describes those about to get married as 'country copulatives'.

Then there's the bit in *Twelfth Night* when the pompous and ambitious steward Malvolio reads out a love letter written, as he believes, by Olivia, the mistress of the household. It must be genuine, he says, because he recognises her handwriting: 'By my life, this is my lady's hand, these be her very C's, her U's and her T's and thus makes she her great P's. It is, in contempt of question, her hand.'

The letter is a forgery but the cunt is real enough, spelled out with the 'and' between the U's and T's substituting for the 'n', and the dirty line is continued by the thought that this is how she makes 'her great P's'. Shakespeare's spelling out of a taboo word as an evasive yet teasing way of not actually saying it also appears in the present-day pleasantry 'See you next Tuesday' (i.e. C-U-N-T).

There are other cunt puns in Shakespeare. The passage in *Henry V* when Catherine, the daughter of the French king, is being taught some English not only has fun with the strange way foreigners speak – 'neck' becomes 'nick', 'chin' becomes 'sin' – but has Catherine reacting with comic outrage when her lady-in-waiting tells her that the English for 'le pied et le robe' is 'de foot et de coun' (i.e.

gown). The king's daughter at once links these to the French obscenities *foutre* (= fuck) and *con* (= cunt, but also fool, idiot, etc.), which are not so far from the English equivalents. In *Henry VIII*, Anne Boleyn is asked by an old lady whether she'd contemplate being, if not a queen, then a duchess: 'Have you limbs to bear that load of title?' When Anne denies any ambition, the old lady presses forward even more suggestively: 'Then you are weakly made . . . I would not be a young count in your way/For more than blushing comes to.' The 'young count' is both a would-be husband and the youthful Anne.

Then, like fuck, cunt goes underground. If it appears at all it's in material intended for private circulation as in the Earl of Rochester's poems ('Her Hand, her Foot, her very look's a Cunt.') from the Restoration era, or under-the-counter publications such as Victorian pornography. There doesn't seem to have been a before-and-after moment as there was with the 1960 *Lady Chatterley* case, which more or less licensed the open printing of 'fuck'. Before the 1960s, authors such as Henry Miller in *Tropic of Cancer* (1934) and *Tropic of Capricorn* (1939) employed it liberally but such books could only be smuggled back from Paris, one of the homes of English-language 'obscene' publication. James Joyce used it metaphorically in *Ulysses* ('The grey sunken cunt of the world', though this was altered by Ezra Pound to 'sunken crater' in early versions), while Samuel Beckett used it both metaphorically and literally in

Malone Dies ('His young wife had abandoned all hope of bringing him to heel, by means of her cunt, that trump card of young wives'), published in his own translation from the French in 1956. But Joyce's and Beckett's experimental books were never going to achieve the kind of mass audience aimed at by Penguin when they published *Lady Chatterley's Lover.* The c-word appeared in a couple of dictionaries in the early eighteenth century but was then excised until 1961 in the US (*Webster's Dictionary*) and 1965 in the UK (*Penguin English Dictionary*). Many years before then the word had extended from being an anatomical term to an insult although in this non-genital sense, as with other comparable terms such as 'twat' and 'pussy', it tends to be applied to men rather than to women.

The c-word made its first appearance in the British press in the *Guardian*, predictably enough, in February 1974 during the course of an interview with Marianne Faithfull who commented on bad reviews: 'They're entitled to say it: just as I'm entitled to think they're a cunt for saying it.' It had already been uttered during a late-night ITV show, *The Frost Report*, when one guest described another – both males – as 'the most unreasonable cunt I've ever met'. And, as Peter Silverton points out, it seemed to have a wide appeal for the first generation of transgressive British artists such as Tracey Emin, Gilbert and George, and the Chapman brothers, who use the word as part of a title or incorporate vaginal images in their work.

The media have generally been more uncomfortable with 'cunt' than with any other obscene or offensive term, apart from a handful of racial expressions. It is particularly taboo in the popular press. When Mike Gatting, the captain of England, got into trouble in 1987 while on a winter tour of Pakistan by calling the (Pakistani) umpire a 'fucking, cheating cunt', the *Independent* newspaper printed the three words in full. This so outraged the *Sun* editor Kelvin MacKenzie that he complained to the Press Council, the regulatory body that was generally the object of his contemptuous mockery. What the *Independent* ought to have done, according to MacKenzie, was to use the acceptably asterisked form of c***. Otherwise, the printing of such words in full legitimated them and 'could only have a harmful and deleterious effect upon moral standards'. When the case was heard by the Press Council, the defence offered by the *Independent*'s editor was that his newspaper reported news – unlike others that concentrated on entertainment (by implication, the *Sun*) – and that Gatting's outburst was part of a significant story. The Press Council rejected MacKenzie's complaint. Shortly afterwards, the *Sun* splashed on Gatting's 'sex romps' with 'brazen barmaid Louise', accompanied by a topless picture and the headline I'M 48 NOT OUT – HE'S LEFT ME TWO SHORT OF A HALF CENTURY IN LOVERS. It's easy to point at MacKenzie's double standards, but outlets such as the *Sun* take care to walk the line between respectability and explicitness. Suggestive puns and nudging headlines are fine but naked four-letter expressions, and especially the c-word, are taboo.

What is the public status of 'cunt' now? Has it gone the way of fuck, a word to be read or heard fairly regularly in media outlets and television channels, at least after the watershed? Not quite. There seems to be an extra layer of taboo covering the c-word. Guidance from the regulator Ofcom in 2016 following an audience survey which included coverage of bad language stated that: 'Responses to the word "cunt" were particularly strong. A significant number of participants were uncomfortable with its use even after the watershed. Women were more likely to say it was completely unacceptable, based on its strong vulgar cultural associations. Some women and a few men said they were personally offended and would prefer "cunt" not to be used on TV or radio at all.'

Its use when the audience has not been forewarned is still provoking, even if there is sometimes laughter rather than indignation in the response. In December 2010 the Radio 4 presenter James Naughtie caused some spluttering over the cornflakes when he announced an upcoming interview on the *Today* programme with Jeremy Cunt – in fact, Jeremy Hunt, at the time the Culture Secretary. This wasn't a Freudian slip so much as a verbal inevitability: the collocation of Hunt and Culture pretty well ensured that it was bound to happen to someone, sometime. Naughtie struggled to stifle his own laughter as he went on to read the news headlines before retreating into silence on account of a 'coughing fit'. He later apologised, explaining he'd fallen victim to a verbal tangle 'courtesy of Dr Spooner'.* When Andrew Marr alluded to James Naughtie's slip-up on his own discussion show later that morning he declared firmly that he wouldn't be repeating the mistake, only to refer almost straightaway to Jeremy Cunt. No senior BBC news panjandrum seems to be immune. In January 2011 Jeremy Paxman opined on *Newsnight*: 'Supposing though some of the people who ought to be paying taxes so the cunts – cuts – aren't so bad, aren't actually doing so.'

And the word caused a stir in a court case in Chelmsford in August 2016 when a man who was being sentenced for

---

* The Victorian-era Dr Spooner was an Oxford don famous for his absent-mindedness and verbal confusions, particularly in swapping letters between words at their beginnings. He is supposed to have said to an errant student: 'You have hissed all my mystery lectures . . . Having tasted two worms, you will leave by the next town drain.' The same spooneristic process is at work in the old joke: Question: What's the difference between a circus and a strip club? Answer: The circus has a bunch of cunning stunts . . . Along the same lines, Kenny Everett dragged up in his 1980s BBC series to play a silly starlet called Cupid Stunt. A similar wordplay came in high-camp Kenneth Williams's declaration: 'I'm a cult figure. I'm an enormous cult. I'm one of the biggest cults you'll get round here.'

using racist language towards a black woman and her two children told the judge that she was 'a bit of a cunt'. To which the judge replied: 'You are a bit of a cunt yourself.' When the defendant, who had multiple previous convictions for offences ranging from firearm possession to common assault, screamed back 'Go fuck yourself', the judge returned the ball with: 'You too.' He got eighteen months, she was referred to a judicial conduct body (and subsequently exonerated).

What is significant here is that the c-word still has the power to shock, or at least to draw attention, but only in certain circumstances such as when it accidentally slips out of the mouth of a respected broadcaster or when it is uttered in public by a woman who occupies a position of authority. Otherwise, not so much – at least as far as the majority of people are concerned. Of course, there is quite a difference between hearing the word and being, as it were, on the receiving end of it.

Elsewhere across the English-speaking world there are big differences. In Australia the word has come quite close to general acceptability. In 2015 an activist called Danny Lim was convicted in Sydney for holding up on a busy roadway a placard attacking the then Prime Minister, Tony Abbott. According to the *Sydney Morning Herald*, one side of the placard read: PEACE SMILE PEOPLE CAN CHANGE TONY YOU C---. LIAR, HEARTLESS, CRUEL. PEACE BE WITH YOU. The insult was cleverer than it looked in the newspaper version since Danny Lim had included an apostrophe as if the word was CAN'T and inverted the A to suggest a U. In August 2017 a judge overturned a magistrate's conviction pointing out the play on words and saying that 'c--- was referenced in Shakespeare's *Hamlet*, was used regularly on television, and was less offensive in Australia than in other English-speaking countries'. The judge didn't add, though he might have done, that to term someone a 'good cunt' in Australia means that they're a decent person.

In the US things, by contrast, are very different and the c-word remains the c-word, never to be spelled out in full in mainstream publications. Indeed so unusual is the expression, it seems, that it may occasionally need to be explained: 'The Twitter account for Sid Miller, a conservative Republican who is an adviser to Donald Trump, referred to Hillary Clinton as a "c---" (an obscene term for female genitalia) in a now-deleted tweet Tuesday afternoon' (*Washington Post*, November 2016). When John McCain was running for president against Barack Obama in 2008, a biography revealed that some years previously McCain had called his wife a 'cunt' in the presence of several reporters – a moment that revealed his quick temper. Yet, in a culture where the slightest verbal misstep by a politician will be pored over and dissected, the incident went unreported, not out of loyalty to the Arizona senator but because the media had no way of dealing with such a coarse term.

As discussed elsewhere in this book, things have slackened a bit in the US, and not only because of the Trump presidency. Even so, 'cunt' remains largely off limits. In May 2018 the comic Samantha Bee used the word on her cable TV show referring to Trump's daughter, Ivanka. She was talking about the administration's policy of separating parents and children of illegal immigrants, and contrasting that harsh measure with a soft-focus photo tweeted by Ivanka. 'You know, Ivanka,' said Bee, 'that's a beautiful photo of you and your child, but let me just say, one mother to another: Do something about your dad's immigration policies, you feckless cunt! He listens to you! Put on something tight and low-cut and tell your father to fuckin' stop it.' The Manhattan studio audience erupted in delighted laughter at the c-word, but the comic later apologised for it, while media reaction ranged from right-wing outrage, some of it no doubt genuine, to liberal anxiety that a worthwhile message about an inhumane immigration policy had been lost in the turmoil over a badly chosen word. For the *New York Times* it was 'a vulgar epithet' while the *Chicago Sun-Times* was relatively explicit in referring to the 'c-word'. In Britain, the *Guardian* not only printed the word in full, and got a couple of columnists to speculate on the significance of the event, but provided an unbleeped link to the relevant segment of the TV show. It's hard to believe there would be an equivalent uproar if a British female comic used the c-word about a female member of the government during her act. Needless to say, it would be quite different if a male comic was the offender.

Speculation about why there should be this c-word difference between the US and some other anglophone countries ranges from the greater strength of the feminist movement in America to the substantial puritan strain that still runs across the nation. In America this offensive term remains just that: deeply derogatory when applied by a man to a woman, and a possible invitation to a fight when used by one man to another. In the UK as in Australia it can, in the right company, be almost a term of rough affection. Not across the Atlantic, though.

As with 'queer' and 'gay', there have been serious attempts to reappropriate 'cunt' and to turn it into a term of celebration rather than abuse or contempt. Inevitably, these tend to focus on the anatomical sense rather than its function as an insult. As far back as 1970 Germaine Greer edited an issue of the underground magazine *Oz*, which advertised itself on the cover as 'Female Energy', but inside which was the greeting 'Welcome to Cuntpower Oz'. Greer wanted not only to remove any shame from the word and the organ but to stress the power of both; in the same year she published one of the key feminist texts of the time and later, *The Female Eunuch*. Greer has always stuck to her guns. During a TV panel discussion in 1991 commemorating the trial of a later edition of *Oz* (the notorious 'School Kids' issue) on charges of obscenity,

Jonathan Dimbleby mentioned the feminist issue as the 'C-Power Oz'. Greer wouldn't put up with this evasion. 'Come on, Jonathan,' she said, 'it was Cunt Power Oz!' Dimbleby managed to get out 'Anyone can say "Cunt Power Oz" . . .' before quickly moving on.

The journalist Deborah Orr described in 'The C-Word', an article which appeared in *Vogue* in 2006, how she'd 'been cunting away myself for several decades now . . . For me, it's not a serious word. It's a word for playing with, but in a not-very-dangerous game . . . Using the c-word, in the right company, is pleasingly wicked and funny. It shocks. It packs a punch. It grabs attention.' In the *New Statesman* in 2011, Laurie Penny was prompted to write 'in defence of the "c" word' after Jeremy Paxman had accidentally said it on *Newsnight*. Penny didn't have quite the casual approach adopted by Orr. She wondered why, 'in a world of 24-hour porn channels, a world with Rihanna's "Rude Boy" playing on the radio and junior pole-dancing kits sold in Tesco, is the word "cunt" still so shocking'. She concluded that, unlike alternatives such as 'pussy' or 'vagina', it was 'an earthy, dank and lusty word with the merest hint of horny threat', and that despite the attempts by feminists to reclaim the word 'as the powerful, vital, visceral sexual signifier that it is, the taboo seems only to have become stronger' (*New Statesman*, 2 February 2011).

So there seems to be no conclusive answer as to the shocking-ness or otherwise of 'cunt'. In fact, it has a peculiar status, with some women valiantly asserting that far from being a bad word it is a powerful, even beautiful one while others claim that it is the very worst word of all. This is an argument that men are, rightfully, wary of entering. In general I'd suggest that the printed 'cunt' is rarely offensive, in that readers – of the *Guardian*, say, or of hard-boiled crime fiction – are prepared for it. Speech is another matter. It depends on who's saying it, who's hearing it, and the context and circumstances. It's odd to reflect on how everyday the word seems to have been in the early Middle Ages, to judge by the street names and people's surnames, and even references in the occasional medical textbook, compared with how over the following centuries it was edged into unrespectability and then into the taboo territory where, for most, it still lurks.

There is no space to do more than comment briefly on a handful of the many, many slang, obscene and euphemistic terms for the vagina. They range from rhyming slang such as 'berk' (Berkshire hunt = cunt) to bluntly descriptive expressions such as 'crack' and 'slit', both dating back several hundred years, to elaborate formulations either in the old-style pornographic manner of 'Cupid's cave' or the contemporary 'lady garden' (first cited in 2001). 'Twat', which dictionaries characterise as low slang, surfaced in the seventeenth century and, like a number of other such expressions, does double duty as a crude anatomical allusion and as an insult. It was used by mistake by Robert Browning in his 1841 verse drama *Pippa Passes*. Browning, wanting a rhyme to make up a short list of ecclesiastical head-gear, wrote: 'Then owls and bats,/cowls and twats,/Monks and nuns . . .' Asked many years later by the editors of the *Oxford English Dictionary* about his use of 'twat', he told them he'd got it from a line in a seventeenth century poem, 'Vanity of Vanities': 'They talk't of his having a Cardinalls Hat,/They'd send him as soon an Old Nuns Twat.' The coarse meaning obviously never crossed Browning's mind. Whether the *OED* editors revealed the true meaning of 'twat' to Browning isn't known but presumably they were aware of it themselves.

While 'twat' connotes a fool, a complete idiot, and operates as a stronger version of 'twit' (to which it is not etymologically related), 'pussy' has since the early twentieth century defined a weak, probably effeminate man and was originally used with the implication of homosexuality. For hundreds of years before that it was applied colloquially to women, usually to stress amiability or at least harmlessness. But the sexual/genital sense always ran alongside it, underground as it were. The word has had wide exposure in the twenty-first century, from the Russian punk group Pussy Riot, members of which were sentenced to jail after staging a protest/performance in Moscow's cathedral in 2012, to Donald Trump's infamous 'grab them by the pussy' comment as recorded in the so-called 'Access Hollywood' tape of

2005 which, like so much else, utterly failed to derail his presidential career.

Pistol's cock

When it comes to slang or offensive terms for the penis it might seem that men would be entitled to feel a little bit of vagina-envy since not only are the p-words less numerous – though there are still hundreds – but they do not really have the power to shock, or even to grab the attention, possessed by their female counterparts. To begin with, there is the monosyllabic triad of 'cock', 'tool' and 'prick', as long-standing, solid and reliable as a three-legged stool. All are words with prior meanings but the *OED* cites them in penile senses around the sixteenth century, though it's likely they were in common circulation well before then. Shakespeare uses all three words: for example, in *Henry IV, Part 2*, ostensibly referring to the character Pistol's temper as if it were a gun about to discharge ('Pistol's cock is up,/And flashing fire will follow'); and in the same play, when Falstaff is recruiting men to serve as cannon-fodder in battle and he remarks of one 'Prick him' (i.e. mark his name down), the reluctant recruit responds, 'I was pricked well enough before, an you could have let me alone.' In the late play *Henry VIII* a porter says, 'or have we some strange Indian with the great tool come to court, the women so besiege us?' though it is possible that the line was written by Shakespeare's collaborator, John Fletcher.

Tool and prick continued to live relatively innocent existences because they had and have so many other useful meanings, and the suggestive ones could be glided over. But cock became problematic a long time ago, for the Americans at least. Its primary sense – the domestic fowl – dates back in English to before the Norman Conquest. From the very beginning, before the time of King Alfred, it stood for strutting maledom. You can think of a 'prick' and imagine a rose-bush or a tiny cut with a needle. You can glimpse the word 'tool' and envisage a spanner. But hear the word 'cock' and what do you see? It's just too blatant for some people. One solution was to change the name altogether. So the domestic fowl, the he-bird, became the rooster, related to the Old English word for the framework of a roof (*hrost*), which in turn became the part of the hen-house where birds perched overnight before adding an '-er' to become the bird itself. But the frequent appearance of the rooster in US blues songs ('I tell you that he keeps all the hens, fighting among themselves' is an added line from Sam Cooke's version of the classic 'Little Red Rooster') shows that the original cock implication never went away. Then there's the cock that means a tap, a pipe for passing water and the gizmo that regulates or stops the flow. No one knows why a tap should have been called a cock hundreds of years ago, though the word tap is also very old. Was it because it looks a bit like the head and crest of the he-bird? Was it because it's a spout for pouring out liquid? Anyway, the associations of the cock were enough to turn it into the faucet, the word still used in the US. The British dropped the cock too, though it survives in the thing that is usually the subject of a sometimes urgent question: 'Where's the stopcock?'

If you're gifted with the name you may want to modify it, at least in the US. Ed Koch, the New York mayor in the late 1970s, made sure he was pronounced with a soft ending, as in 'loch'. Alcox was the family name of the author of the mid-Victorian bestseller *Little Women*, though Louisa May's father had earlier changed it to Alcott. Meanwhile, weather-cocks became weather-vanes, haycocks turned into ricks and cockroaches lost their front halves altogether. Only the first of these words was connected to the bird (because a weather-vane is traditionally fashioned in the form of a cock). The 'cock' in a haycock refers to a quite different sense of the word (pile or heap) while the cock-roach probably comes from the Spanish *cucaracha*. But before laughing at US priggishness it's worth remembering that that country is also the home of the cocktail, a slang term of unknown origin and dating right back to the beginning of the nineteenth century when the writer Washington Irving described it as a 'recondite beverage'.

One slang term that hasn't made so much penile head-way in the US is 'dick' since in America it tends to mean a cop or detective though, as in the UK, it can also characterise an unattractive or unpleasant man, especially one who thinks a lot of himself. The word is simply an alteration of Ric-, the first syllable of earlier versions of Richard such as the old French Ricard or the Latin Ricardus. Dick, in company with Tom and Harry, can stand for the average bloke. The word took on its penis dimension sometime in the later nineteenth century. The 'dickhead' first thrust himself into the limelight in the 1960s, primarily as an idiot though of course it gets its value as an insult from the anatomical bit (compare with 'bell end' originating around the same time). The word isn't taboo in the written media but, if it appears, it is generally muffled by appearing in quotes as if to stress that *we* didn't say this: 'Hamilton was caught on a microphone calling Verstappen a "dickhead" as he watched a replay of the incident' (*The Times*, 12 April 2018). There's also a specialist application. Fans of Philip K. Dick, the influential author of *Blade Runner*, call themselves Dickheads.

Ofcom, which sorts words into the four categories of milder, medium, strong and strongest, rates 'dick', 'prick' and 'cock' in the third category in its 'swear words and body parts' categorisation ('tool' does not appear). This categorisation, which sounds rather akin to curry or chilli strengths, means that the words are generally unacceptable before the magic hour of 9 p.m., where in any case they rarely appear in their anatomical sense, only in the disparaging one. There are distinctions between them, of course. A male might speculate about whether, if he absolutely has to be called one, he'd rather be a cock or a prick instead of a dick or a tool. But the words have more in common than separates them. All can be synonymous with fools, whether of the clever-dick variety or the useful idiot type. In this they follow a long tradition of equating the penis with a kind of cunning stupidity or, when it comes to sex, of taking the intelligence out of the head and putting it down below – 'He unzipped his pants and his brains fell out,' quipped American author Rita Mae Brown in *Venus Envy* (1993). There is too the Yiddish habit of using penis terms to mean idiot: *putz, schmuck, schmo*.

When it comes to the testicles there is arguably only one word that has retained a moderate taboo status, and that is 'bollocks'. The earlier form of 'ballocks' shows that it's a diminutive of 'balls'. It's odd that it should somehow be ruder than 'balls' but it is. 'That's bollocks!' has a more aggressive ring to it than 'That's balls!' while the low-hanging sound of 'bollocks' seems to imitate the thing it describes. Even the appearance of the word – those two o's separated by the penile if double-shafted l's – may help here. Yet the expression 'to get a bollocking' is quite every day, and many newspapers will use it if it appears as part of a quote. For example, *The Times* diary reported on the experience of a tabloid reporter who claimed that a used condom had been found on the Speaker's chair in the Commons. Summoned by the Serjeant-at-Arms, the reporter claimed that 'being bollocked by a man in tights with a sword on his desk was the most surreal experience I've ever had' (*The Times*, 27 April 2018).

The faintly comic 'goolies' were brought back from India by British troops, and derive from a Hindi word (*goli*) meaning ball or bullet. The *OED* cites a first appearance in Eric Partridge's *Slang Dictionary* of 1937 but it was around before that. During the RAF's operations over the North-West Frontier Province of India in the First World War where downed pilots went in fear of castration by the fierce Pathan tribeswomen, they carried a so-called 'goolie chit'. Printed in several languages, the chit, a word also originating in Hindi, offered a reward to anyone returning a British flier, unscathed, with goolies intact.

Shit Happens

THE SEARCH FOR the etymology of a word, its origins in linguistic history, can throw up some funny stuff. Although the true roots are usually there to be discovered with a little digging around, that doesn't stop people coming up with fanciful and even absurd origins, which are sometimes known as folk etymologies. 'Posh', in the sense of high-class, luxurious, is frequently explained as an acronym of the phrase 'port out, starboard home', a reference to the more comfortable cabins given to colonial administrators and their memsahibs as they steamed their leisurely way between Britain and India in the heyday of the British Empire. Travelling on the left side of the boat going out and on the right-hand side coming back home meant protection from the burning rays of the sun south of Suez. Supposedly, the Peninsular & Oriental Steam Navigation Company (still around as P&O Cruises) stamped such tickets with the initials POSH. It's a very satisfying explanation. Unfortunately there's no evidence, in the shape of a surviving POSH-stamped ticket, to support it. Instead, the *Oxford English Dictionary* suggests a connection with an old Romany term, 'posh' signifying money.

Like posh, a ship-bound etymology hangs around the source of 'shit'. This time the word was attributed not to the eastward voyaging of white men and women but to the transport of large quantities of manure. When stored low in the ship, it got wet, started to ferment and gave off methane gas. Exposure to a naked flame detonated several gassy ships in this manner before anyone worked out the reason. After that, the bundles of manure were marked 'Ship High In Transit', a warning to stow the stuff well above the lower decks to safeguard it from water and the production of methane. Thus, the acronym 'shit' from the initial letters of the warning. It's an ingenious if silly piece of word-sourcing, though it does create a dramatic picture: the crewman clambering down into the hold to check on the precious cargo with a flickering lantern or smouldering tobacco pipe in hand. One missed step, one careless spark and it's all over.

It's hard to know where to begin to unpick this folk etymology. Perhaps with the observation that 'Ship High In Transit' scrawled on the side of a bale sounds like quite a modern instruction or that the practice of creating acronyms didn't really exist before the twentieth century. Or with the fact that the word 'shit', in a different spelling and applying to diarrhoea in cattle, can be found in Old English, i.e. the form in which the language was spoken and written before the Norman Conquest of 1066. Or that similar terms have long existed in other northern European languages, as they still do (German *Scheisse* or Swedish *skit*). Or that there are records of old English street names that, in a less priggish age, attested to their nature before the days of sanitary privacy: Sherborne Lane in the City of London was once Shiteburn Lane (i.e. stream of shit) while Schiteburglane in Romford indicated that there was a fortress-like (burg) privy situated in it. Plenty of historical evidence, then, for the longevity of shit. And, if you think about, it's hardly surprising that such a fundamental and inescapable human and animal function should be noted in language in its earliest stages. Shit happens and always has happened.

How offensive is it as an expression? The answer appears to be that for most people in the UK it is hardly offensive at all, and there is plenty of support for this view. First of all is its popularity as an interjection capable of expressing responses across the spectrum: alarm, dismay, surprise, resignation, excitement. Shit!/Oh shit! The first written note of its exclamatory use in the *Oxford English Dictionary* comes from an 1865 US court-martial record in which Private James Sullivan 'did in contemptuous and disrespectful manner reply "Oh, shit, I can't" or words to that effect'. Presumably he wasn't being court-martialled for his language. Most of the examples given in the *Dictionary* are from American sources and it's hard to pinpoint the moment when the word was taken up as an exclamation in Britain, although my feeling is that it was well into the second half of the twentieth century. Of course, before this it had long been in use in its excremental sense as well as to make a disparaging reference to somebody or something unloved. It may be that the exclamatory, almost meaningless deployment of shit falls conveniently between several stools and that this accounts for its popularity: it is not a rather old-fashioned expression such as 'Damn!' or a twee archaism such as 'Drat!' or 'Darn!', not an exasperated oath such as 'Christ!', not the attention-grabber that is 'Fuck!'

In 2005, Alan McArthur and Steve Lowe started a trend by publishing *Is it Just Me or is Everything Shit?: The Encyclopedia of Modern Life*. Things rapidly went downhill. According to a *Times* report in February 2017 the previous year alone saw the publication of no less than ninety-three book titles containing shit. Occasionally the word might be asterisked on the cover, as in *Sh*t My Dad Says* (2010) by Justin Halpern or *Holy Sh*t: A Brief History of Swearing* (2013) by Melissa Mohr, both of which are by American authors and first published in the US. In the UK it usually appears naked and unapologetic as in Frankie Boyle's 2009 autobiography *My Shit Life So Far*. The ubiquity and acceptability of shit in Britain is also demonstrated by the frequency with which it appears in newspaper word searches. Over 4000 examples on *The Times* website, the surprising figure of some 20,000 on the *Daily Telegraph*'s and around 66,000 on the *Guardian*'s. It is not likely to appear in editorial material – 'The government's policies are shit' would lower the sometimes rather schoolmasterly tone of a leader article – but it regularly pops up as part of a quoted remark. And a number of columnists have it in their repertoire.

By contrast US newspapers' websites register occurrences of the word in the very low hundreds. Even this is an advance on the situation half a century ago. During the Chicago trial of some anti-Vietnam War protestors in 1970, one of the defendants described the testimony of a police officer as 'bullshit'. The *New York Times* reporter urged that the word be printed in the paper. The editor suggested that they simply refer to it as 'an obscenity' but the reporter was worried that readers would imagine a worse word than the one spoken. 'Why don't we call it a barnyard epithet?' was the editor's next suggestion, so that is what the paper did. Henceforth 'barnyard epithet' became a euphemism for bullshit. However, times change. In particular the presidency of Donald J. Trump has meant that newspapers and other media outlets have had to reconsider their unwillingness to inflict bad language on their audiences. A scandalous leak from an Oval Office meeting with congressional leaders about immigration in

January 2018 revealed that Trump, referring to Haiti and some African countries, said, 'Why are we having all these people from shithole countries come here?' The racism may have caused a stir but it was the 'shithole' description that sent the news outlets into a tizzy. How to report on this profanity? By not mentioning it at all? By referring to it as a typically Trumpian use of vulgar or offensive language, without spelling out what he actually said? Or would it be better to fall into the asterisk safety-net: s***hole? Or even to go the whole hog and print/say the word in full? Several papers and TV outlets did just that, often with a warning of what was to come. *The New York Times* printed the word for the first time in its history. NPR (National Public Radio) rationed its shitholes to one per hour. The decision was justified in two ways: the use of language was central to the story and it was the President of the United States of America who was saying these things.

The degree of bad language used in a film is one of the criteria applied by the British Board of Film Classification (BBFC) when issuing certificates.* What the guidelines

---

* Until 1984 the BBFC was known . . . as the BBFC. The same initials and words except that the C stood for Censors. In itself, the switch of words from Censors to Classification is a measure of how far attitudes towards censorship have changed. The intention is not to prevent adults watching what they want to watch, but to grade material so that its suitability for particular ages is made clear.

describe as 'mild bad language only' will earn a Parental Guidance (PG) certificate. The BBFC website says that a 'PG film should not unsettle a child aged around eight or older. Unaccompanied children of any age may watch, but parents are advised to consider whether the content may upset younger, or more sensitive, children.' And what constitutes 'mild language'? Some examples are provided: they include bastard, piss, bollocks, crap, slag, tosser, Jesus, Christ – and shit. Similarly, BBC and Channel 4 guidelines on offensive language allow the expression to be used infrequently before the watershed of 9 p.m. if 'justified by the context'.

One of the principal reasons for the linguistic success and acceptability of shit is that the term has been largely divorced from its original excremental sense. It's interesting to note that the great majority of the slang, non-literal applications of shit and various associated phrases emerged in the twentieth century, in other words the age of almost universal hygiene and sanitation. Defecation, like urination, is a private function, something increasingly closeted. In many, perhaps most, historical times and places it was not necessarily a communal act but still one from which it was difficult to avert one's eyes or nose. Now even a two-star hotel might be expected to offer en-suite facilities.

So, as a slang term for a bodily waste product that is, unless you're a coprophile, of passing interest only to its one-time owner or perhaps to a doctor, shit has been blanched, deodorised and repackaged into not much more than an expression of surprise or (mild) approval or disapproval or an intensifier (shit-scared). Only a small number of shit references are literally excremental while the great majority are metaphorical. If we thought more carefully about what the word actually meant, we probably wouldn't use it so much. In illustration, I used to know someone who objected to the word 'shit' and used 'sausages' instead. This prissy substitution was – if you were in the right frame of mind to be offended – somehow worse than the original, perhaps because it made for a rather too specific visualisation. Other euphemistic alternatives are 'shoot' and 'sugar'.

The principal reason for the ubiquity of shit is surely its adaptability, its plasticity. Leave aside its popularity as a straightforward interjection, shit, like 'thing' or 'stuff', can be made to fit almost any context, and indeed virtually any sense, except the most formal and respectable. It can be synonymous with anything – 'The fog was so thick I couldn't see shit' – or with nothing – 'You can ask but I tell you, they'll give you shit.' The word may signify something good or 'shit-hot' as easily as something bad such as 'a shit day'. It can stand for unspecified objects, any material or random circumstances or business or events or personal belongings. Delivered hippyishly it may be a gesture of commiseration: 'That's some tough shit, man.'

But 'Tough shit' all by itself can express just the opposite, no sympathy at all, like 'Tough titty'. And alongside this, the word has a thriving life in drug culture as slang for heroin or marijuana.

To list the things shit can do and be is impressive: you can be in it, in it deep, up the creek made of it and paddleless, as happy as a pig in it, enjoy acting as a stirrer of it, be as thick as it, stumble across a crock of it, find yourself in the middle of an eponymous storm or list, have loads of it, lose it when getting stressed, suffer the consequences after it hits the fan* or when it's dropped from a great height (although if deposited by an eagle it would be welcome since 'the day the eagle shits' = payday in the US military), have it for brains, get your personal stock of it together, shoot it while chatting, be wearing a grin that looks as though you've just eaten it, or alternatively balk at

---

* In his *Dictionary of Slang and Unconventional English*, Eric Partridge dates the expression 'The shit hits the fan' to Canada around 1930. When Yul Brynner was starring in *The King and I* at the London Palladium he ignored the crowds that gathered by the stage door after every performance, not even accepting a bunch of flowers which a woman repeatedly brought him. Exasperated, she slapped him over his shaven head with the bouquet, an action which caused a member of the theatre management to remark that here was 'a unique instance of the fan hitting the shit'. The story has also been told of an encounter between Rex Harrison and a fan after a performance of *My Fair Lady*.

consuming a sandwich made of it even though on another occasion you might sup it off a shingle (US slang: shit on a shingle = minced beef on toast), be warned against doing it on your doorstep or in your own backyard, be instructed to do it or get off the pot, tell the difference between it and Shinola (a one-time US brand of shoe polish), think your own production of it 'don't stink', invoke a famous detective in mock incredulity ('No shit, Sherlock'), not give a . . ., and – finally – use it to signal the end of a list like a demotic version of etc., and shit. Among the various compound terms or expressions where shit can serve as prefix or suffix are: -bird, -canned, -faced, -head, -heel, -hot, -scared, ape-, bat-, bull-, chicken-, dog-, heavy, holy, horse-, (as rare as) rocking horse-, jack-, tough.

The one area where shit retains some excrementally related force is where it's applied, direct and unadulterated, to a man – always a man, surely, never a woman – whose personality or behaviour comes up seriously short. There's a Second World War anecdote relating how Winston Churchill was in the lavatory in the House of Commons when his secretary knocked on the door and said: 'Excuse me, Prime Minister, but the Lord Privy Seal wishes to speak to you.' After a moment's pause Churchill replied: 'Tell His Lordship: I'm sealed on the Privy and can only deal with one shit at a time.' The visitor was Stafford Cripps, whom Churchill saw as a rival, so it's possible that some of this story at least is true. Better documented is the remark by the wife of David Somerset, the 11th Duke of Beaufort, as reported in his obituary in *The Times* on 17 August 2017: 'On one occasion, over dinner with [James] Lees-Milne and Patrick Trevor-Roper, the conversation turned to the difference between a cad, a bounder and a shit. Caroline looked at her husband and said: "I know what a shit is. David's one."'

There's likely to be resentment, envy, anger in the 'shit' description. But there's also an acknowledgement that the individual so described is someone to be reckoned with, even admired in a perverse way for the sheer quality of his shithood. See how Philip Larkin in his poem 'The Life with the Hole in It' bemoans the fact that he's not a successful author living a reclusively luxurious life, not 'the shit in the shuttered chateau/Who does his five hundred words/Then parts out the rest of the day/Between bathing and booze and birds'. Perhaps Larkin's friend Kingsley Amis had some echo of that poem in his mind when he wrote to Larkin about his novelist son Martin in May 1979: 'Did I tell you Martin is spending a year abroad as a TAX EXILE? Last year he earned £38,000. Little shit. 29, he is. Little shit.' There's a distinction between being a shit and being a little shit and yet another one between that and a piece of shit, and if you don't think so then ask yourself which you'd (least) like to be called.

The variant form of shite is what dictionaries call 'regional' English, and is widely used in Scotland and

Ireland, Australia and New Zealand. Robert Burns used it in its literal, excremental sense in the poem 'Grim Grizzel' (1795) in which the eponymous dairy farmer is trying to get her cow to drop its dung exactly where she wants it: ' "Shite, shite, ye bitch," Grim Grizzel roar'd/Till hill and valley rang.' The cow does not comply. The characteristically Irish word gobshite describes a stupid person or a loud-mouthed one. There seems to me a note of contempt in shite that is absent, or not inevitably present, in shit, perhaps because of the emphatic rise in the voice when it's uttered. Shite is always rubbish. Similarly, the adjective shitty and the noun shittiness are never anything but disparaging.

Poop or poo?

A few other linguistic branches on the copro-tree should be noted. Turd is probably as old linguistically as shit in its excremental sense and is cited in the *OED* as emerging around the end of the tenth century. Like so many other bad words, it makes a memorable appearance in Geoffrey Chaucer's 'The Pardoner's Tale'. After the Pardoner – he who preaches against swearing by Christ's body – exposed his shameless sales patter to the other pilgrims, he offers the host or inn-keeper who's in charge of the party the chance of kissing his relics for the price of a groat. The Host's response is robust:

'Thou wouldest make me kiss thine olde breech
  [leggings],
And swear it were a relic of a saint,
Though it were with thy fundament depaint [smeared
  with your arse].
But, by the cross which that Saint Helen fand,
I would I had thy coillons [testicles] in mine hand,
Instead of relics, or of sanctuary.
Let cut them off, I will thee help them carry;
They shall be shrined in a hogge's turd.'

When I studied this Chaucerian text at school for an
exam back in the mid-1960s, most of these lines were
excised as unsuitable for teenage eyes and ears. Such was
the power of the turd and the testicles even when rendered
in Middle English. The word turd doesn't have the plasticity or sheen of shit. It is simply what it is, something ugly
and unwelcome. Its metaphorical life is limited and as an
item it cannot be improved on or glossed away. Two
expressions, probably originating in the US, illustrate this
nicely: 'You can't polish a turd' emerged as phrase sometime in the mid-1970s while the disconcerting 'as welcome
as/sticks out like a turd in a punchbowl' may be slightly
earlier.

Crap is a softer version of shit, that is, it's a more acceptable term. Originally appearing in medieval times and
usually in the plural form of craps, it described leavings or

residue (of grain husks or rendered meat). In the following centuries it gathered up other meanings, including money and the gallows. It wasn't until the mid-nineteenth century that crap emerged in its faecal sense. It can double up for shit in a few phrases (craphouse, craphead) while having some distinct formulations of its own such as crap artist (= bullshitter), craperoo and crapola, both of which signify nonsense. And it has the position of honour in Sturgeon's Law. The science-fiction writer Theodore Sturgeon (1918–85) coined the eponymous law, which usually appears in the following brisk form: 90 per cent of everything is crap.* The excremental crap has nothing to do with the US crap-game or craps, whose linguistic origin is uncertain, and nor is it connected to Thomas Crapper, the Victorian sanitary engineer who earned several royal warrants for his deluxe lavatories. The name is a coincidence.

---

* In fact, Sturgeon used the word crud (originally a dialect version of curd). Somewhere along the way crud became crap. Sturgeon's views may not be quite as damning or disillusioned as they sound. In a feature for the September 1957 issue of the magazine *Venture Science Fiction* and talking of himself in the third person, Sturgeon recalled how he'd had a revelation: 'It came to him that sf [science fiction] is indeed ninety-percent crud, but that also – Eureka! – ninety-percent of everything is crud. All things – cars, books, cheeses, hairstyles, people and pins are, to the expert and discerning eye, crud, except for the acceptable tithe which we each happen to like.'

Shit, crap and turd are the traditional big three in excremental lingo, the first two classified by the *Oxford English Dictionary* as 'coarse slang' and the third as 'not now in polite use'. There are several other expressions such as 'number two', 'jobby', 'poop' and 'doo-doo'. As Jonathon Green points out in *Slang Down the Ages* (1993) it's hardly surprising that, given the importance of excrement in the juvenile mind, expressions used at that stage of life – often by grown-ups to children – should carry over into adulthood, particularly if they are essentially euphemistic, as 'number two' or 'doo-doo'.

The most successful word by far, though, in terms of public frequency in Britain is 'poo'. This doesn't seem to be related to the largely US-based 'poop', which onomatopoeically denoted a short blast of sound, then farting, then the act of defecation or the product. (Poop has several other meanings including the stern of a ship and, in American military slang, information.) Linguistically speaking, poo seems to develop from 'pooh', now a rather fusty exclamation of contempt or dismissal. ('But there was nothing on the back of the door, except the screws and nuts that held the knocker on, so he said "Pooh, pooh!" and closed it with a bang.' Charles Dickens, *A Christmas Carol*, 1843.) But 'pooh', along with related terms such as 'phew' and 'poh', as well as generalised disgust can also signify a bad smell, perhaps evoking the way the nose wrinkles in displeasure. So in the last few decades it has been transferred from the reaction to the thing that provokes it.

The word 'poo' is extraordinarily popular and widespread in the UK. Even if you don't use the term yourself you are likely to hear it and see it pretty often. Keep Britain Tidy has a poster campaign encouraging dog owners to clear up after their pets when out walking: 'There's no such thing as the Dog Poo Fairy' is the tagline below a rather Disneyfied fairy clutching a see-through plastic bag containing not Cinderella's slipper but a dog turd. And the word is comfortably embedded in daily discourse, as this arbitrary selection of newspaper quotes goes to show: UK'S FIRST 'POO BUS' GOES INTO REGULAR SERVICE (*Guardian* headline, 16 March 2015, above an article about the Bio-Bus fuelled by human and household waste and running between Bristol and Bath); WISH POO WERE HERE? MAJORCAN BEACHES ARE FLOODED WITH FAECES AFTER TORRENTIAL RAIN CAUSED SEWAGE PLANT TO BREAK DOWN (*Daily Mail* headline, 20 September 2017); 'Spoiler alert! This restaurant review will end with a poo. In a sense, of course, all restaurant reviews end with a poo' (Giles Coren, *The Times*, 16 August 2014).

While poop is popular in the US and poo thrives in Britain, there's an increasing interchange between the linguistic cousins. The American academic and author, Ben Yagoda, runs a blog called 'Not One-Off Britishisms' (NOOBS), which traces and comments on the growing use of British English terms on his side of the Atlantic. The NOOBS blog is worth looking at, not least because it helps counter the belief that, when it comes to language and the Americans and the British, it's all give and no take. In an item on poo (17 December 2012) he observes that the phrase 'dog poo' is rising in popularity, even using a Google Ngram chart to show it. Yagoda further observes that 'my sense is that my fellow Americans are rather conflicted' on the poo-v.-poop question, citing a feature in the *Huffington Post* that used both forms: ' "Poop. Is there anything it can't do? On Wednesday, The Denver Zoo introduced what is believed to be the world's first poo-powered motorized tuk tuk showcasing The Denver Zoo's very own patent-pending gasification technology." Make up your mind, Huffington Post!'

Lexicographers or dictionary-makers aren't supposed to pass judgement on words. They hunt them down, try to explain where they came from, define them, find examples of their changing usage, as well as providing information about spelling and pronunciation. The furthest a modern dictionary will go is to inform, but not dictate, users' judgement by categorising a term as 'coarse slang' or, sometimes with racially charged terms, as 'derogatory' or 'offensive'. Well, I'm not a lexicographer, professional or otherwise, and this book is called *Bad Words* so I'd like to claim that poo, whether as noun or verb, is a bad word. This is not because it is gross or offensive in the dictionary sense. Rather it is an aesthetic crime, an offence against taste. Poo may be fine, or at least acceptable, when an adult is talking to a three- or four-year-old and for a few years after that. It's more infantile than juvenile. The prevalence of poo now in Britain suggests that somewhere in the national psyche there's a regressive infantile streak. The US poop escapes this charge, I think. There's a comic quality to it, probably based on its onomatopoeic nature as a sudden, mild expulsion of sound – poop! – that makes it childlike rather than just childish. But maybe I'm over-analysing here. Let's move on to . . .

Number one

Number one, micturition, urination, pissing, peeing, weeing, wee-weeing, piddling, widdling, tinkling, having a Jimmy Riddle . . . This isn't an exhaustive list but it contains most of the principal terms for passing water. Why number one? Dictionaries don't offer much enlightenment, referring to it as a nursery or juvenile euphemism. Obviously a number one complements a number two. Perhaps urination has the numerical edge on defecation because it is more frequently performed, and so takes precedence. Perhaps it arises from some instinctive sense that because the front-facing part of one's body is inevitably ahead of the back or rear, anything issuing from it therefore comes first.

The formal terms, urination and the relatively rare micturition, derive from Latin. Among the slang terms, piss, as noun and verb, seems to be by far the oldest, first noted in English in the fourteenth century, and originally coming across with the Normans after the 1066 Conquest. The self-explanatory 'leak' is dignified by having Shakespeare as a first user in *Henry IV, Part 1* (1597), even if he puts the word into the mouth of a working-class – i.e. inevitably comic – character: 'Why they will allow us ne'er a jordan [chamber pot], and then we leak in your chimney.' It's odd that a noun use of leak, as in 'take a leak', wasn't recorded until nearly 350 years later in 1934. But see below for some explanation of why a few words, especially slang ones, take a long time to get into dictionaries.

Other pissing expressions are indeed recorded in the dictionary later on: piddle (first cited as a verb in 1784, as a noun in 1870), pee (a verb in 1788, a noun in 1880), pee-pee (noun only, in 1923), widdle (noun use 1925, verb 1934), wee-wee (probably formed as an echo of pee-pee and first appearing as a verb in 1934, noun in 1937), wee (verb 1934, noun 1968), tinkle (verb 1960, noun 1965). Slash (noun 1950, verb 1973), which I remember being widely used in schooldays, is something of an outlier. It lacks the gentle onomatopoeia of most other terms and its source is obscure, though possibly coming from a Scotch word for a splash of liquid. Whiz takes us back to more childlike forms though perhaps the most distinguished thing about it is that D. H. Lawrence is cited as the first user in his 1929 collection of poems titled *Pansies*: 'I wish I was a gentleman/As full of wet as a watering-can/To whizz in the eye of a police-man.' I have heard whizzer used as slang for lavatory, as in 'go to the whizzer', but can find no documentary or dictionary evidence. A latecomer, possibly deriving from whizz or perhaps a regional term, is wazz (verb 1984, noun 1994).

It's worth noting that the verb form generally comes before, sometimes a long time before, the noun form: on their first appearance the words above tend to describe the action of pissing, rather than the act. Another thing is that the first dated appearance of a word in a dictionary doesn't mean it was 'invented' in that year. Dictionaries are properly slow to act, not giving words all the blessings of research, explanation and definition, until they've become fairly well established in public use. This is especially so with slang and colloquial terms, such as the majority of words in this book. By definition, colloquialisms are spoken before they are written down, and since most dictionaries depend on written evidence (even if that now includes 'unofficial' sources such as blogs), slang terms will be circulating by word of mouth long before they're committed to print, whether actual or electronic. For example, is it plausible that almost a hundred years passed between the verb use of pee in 1788 and its application as a noun in 1880? Between peeing and having a pee? Of course people would have talked about having a pee before 1880, it's just that it wasn't recorded in a form that could be recovered and noted down by a dictionary, in this case the *Oxford English Dictionary*. Significantly, the first citation for the noun pee in the *OED* is 'He actually produced the poe [chamber pot] from under the bed, and made me sit down and do my pee.' It comes from the Victorian pornographic magazine, *The Pearl*, not a publication that would have been left lying around in respectable drawing-rooms in the 1880s and not one that dictionary compilers would have thought of using as a resource before at least the 1980s.

Most of the slang terms to do with urination either have an onomatopoeic quality (piss or tinkle) or are nurs-ery formulations (wee-wee, pee-pee) or both. Piss is the 'strongest' term – 'coarse slang' in the dictionary descrip-tion as opposed to the 'colloquial' tag for widdle, etc. – but it was and is widely acceptable. More than acceptable, in fact, if the word of the King James Bible is to be believed since we're told in the first Book of Kings of God's threat: 'Therefore, behold, I will bring evil upon the house of Jeroboam, and will cut off from Jeroboam him that pisseth against the wall' (1 Kings 14:10).* The term has longevity

---

* The meaning of 'piss against the wall' is obscure here. It does not have its current sense of 'to waste money'. In an age when men routinely pissed against the wall, it may signify simply 'all men'.

both in a literal sense and in metaphorical expressions: from the line in Shakespeare's *The Tempest* (1611), 'Monster, I do smell all horse piss, at which my nose is in great indignation', to a quoted remark in *The Times* (29 September 2017), ' "It will be easier to perpetuate my story when I'm not around," [Hugh Hefner] said in 2011. "Because then nobody will be pissed off that I'm still getting laid." '

As with shit, the sheer number of uses to which piss can be put linguistically is testament to the flexibility and enduring quality of the word. It has given birth to a range of expressions: piss about, piss away (= squander), piss off (doing triple duty to mean 'leave' and 'irritate' and also as the exclamatory 'Piss off!'), piss on (= spoil, as in the Americanism 'piss/rain on someone's parade'), piss up (= mess up). It does good work as part of a phrase: piss against the wall (waste money), piss against the wind/piss up a rope (= US for doing something pointless), piss in someone's pocket (Australian slang for trying to ingratiate oneself with someone). An easy task is a piece of piss, a habitual drunk is a piss-artist or a pisshead, a pisstake is a send-up, piss-elegant is flashy, while the meaning of piss-poor is obvious although piss-proud may not be (having an erection as a result of a full bladder). A small distinction between American and British slang emerges in the sentence 'He's pissed'. In the US it's likely to mean 'He's mad' (i.e. angry) while in the UK it more usually means 'He's drunk'.

To this old word we also owe the useful British phrase 'take the mickey/mick', capable of a mocking upgrade to 'take the Michael'. Sometimes considered to be a shortened form of 'micturate', it's much more plausible that it's a piece of rhyming slang (like Jimmy Riddle = piddle). Michael Bliss may be as imaginary as Jimmy, but if not he gave his name to an expression which is a euphemism for the not very shocking 'taking the piss'.

The smallest room

There are several dozen slang terms for the lavatory or water-closet, ranging from the euphemistic and semi-ironic 'throne room' to the bluntly functional 'shitter/ shithouse', from the twee 'little boys'/girls' room' to the sonorous 'thunderbox'. Some are specific to a particular brand of English. Australia gives us the 'dunny' (from 'dunnekin' and probably deriving ultimately from dung), while America has the 'john'. The most useful term in British English, because it's short, simple and carries no particular social or cultural bias is 'loo'. As often with the simplest and shortest words, mystery hangs around the origins of loo. A shortening of Waterloo, suggested by the 'water' prefix? A shortening of a French phrase, *'Gare de l'eau!'* ('Watch out for the water!'), once uttered in Edinburgh when dirty water was being thrown out of the window? A version of the French word *lieux*, itself a shortened form of *lieux d'aisances* or places of ease (compare the old English expression 'chapel/house of ease')? There are other possible origins for loo, but French seems to be a common factor. Its very obscurity and the absence of any obvious linguistic link to the lavatory itself may account for its popularity. Almost all such terms, from shitter to loo, are filed in the dictionary under 'coarse slang' to 'colloquial'. Not always completely inoffensive, then, but far from taboo.

Even the relatively formal words describing the rooms where people urinate and defecate generate a certain discomfort, as suggested by the way in which definitions have shifted over the centuries. It's as if old terms that signified something different have to be appropriated to mask the essential function of the room, like a kind of linguistic air-freshener. The lavatory, deriving from Latin and once denoting a basin, was somewhere to wash one's hands or feet, as in the contemporary French equivalent *lavabo*, before extending around the middle of the nineteenth century to become the word for a room containing the wherewithal to wash oneself. And when such rooms began to be equipped with a water-closet, the lavatory grew to encompass that item as well. In the days before water was readily available on tap inside a house, 'water-closet' suggested the purpose of the little room – the water was there to wash away the waste – without being too specific about it. The full-length term has disappeared from daily use but survives as the universally understood WC.

Toilet has gone through a similar transformation to lavatory. Deriving from French terms to do with cloth, its meaning extended to cover the dressing-table on which the cloth might be spread. From there, it is applied to all the items required for dressing or doing one's hair or to the cosmetics on the dressing-table. In Alexander Pope's poem *The Rape of the Lock* (1712), Belinda is dressed and made up for the day by her maid. The elaborate cosmetic description begins: 'And now, unveil'd, the toilet stands display'd,/Each silver vase in mystic order laid.' And this cosmetic sense lasted right up to the early twentieth ·century, when doing/making one's toilet – sometimes toilette – meant getting ready for the day. Slightly earlier, and in America, toilet comes to be used in the sense of public conveniences and then to mean a WC or lavatory. This definition has now driven out the earlier ones.

Euphemistic language abounds when it comes to the act of going to the lavatory, as in expressions such as 'spend a penny' or 'make a comfort stop' or 'bathroom break', as well as what is perhaps the ultimate soft-focus question to be asked of visitors just arriving at your home: 'Would you like to wash your hands?'

In British English things are further complicated by the way that different terms are sometimes taken as indicators of class or background. In 1956 Nancy Mitford published a collection of essays called *Noblesse Oblige*, a half-humorous commentary on the English aristocracy and, like anything to do with the English aristocracy, actually taken very seriously. An introductory piece by Alan Ross, a professor of linguistics at Birmingham University, brought two new expressions to the language and made for plenty of anxiety. Blandly titling his article 'An Essay in Sociological Linguistics', Ross claimed that the use of certain words marked out the user as upper class ('U') or middle-class ('non-U'). So serviette, sweet, lounge and saying 'Pardon?' were non-U while napkin, pudding, drawing room and saying 'What?' were U. Some of the distinctions in the book, such as wireless/radio or looking-glass/mirror, have fallen down the rabbit-hole of archaisms. But others have survived, none more so than the distinction between toilet (non-U) and lavatory (U). This is why loo is so useful: it's short, simple and almost free of the odour of class distinction.

Like communal bathrooms and lavatories in hotels, the chamber pot has almost disappeared, more often to be found on an antique stall or serving as a pot planter rather than under the bed. There are a handful of abbreviated or slang terms for this item. 'Jordan' is medieval, used by Shakespeare in the 'leak' quotation from *Henry IV, Part 1* already noted, and a word of unknown origin; the suggestion that it comes from 'Jordan-bottle', a bottle of water brought back from the River Jordan by crusaders or pilgrims and then linguistically transferred to the container used by physicians who routinely examined urine, is a derivation that doesn't, as it were, hold water. Another term, 'jerry', does derive from the name of a vessel, the jeroboam* or large bowl/goblet. 'Jerry', 'slop jar' and 'po' date from the second half of the nineteenth century while 'potty' is twentieth century.

In *A Local Habitation* (1988), a fine memoir of his early life growing up in a working-class district of Leeds between the two world wars, Richard Hoggart describes how as some members of his family became more genteel they became increasingly reluctant to talk about the 'po' or the 'jerry' ('very vulgar') or even the 'chamber pot'. For a time, 'article' became the preferred word before turning into the rather more menacing 'thing' as in: 'You'll find a thing under your bed.' Hoggart, who wrote the classic *The Uses of Literacy* (1957), commented on the po–jerry problem:

---

* For reasons that are obscure, Jeroboam is one of several names taken from Old Testament figures and describing large and very large quantities of wine in a single bottle. Others include the methuselah (6 litres), the balthazar (12 litres) and the nebuchadnezzar (15 litres). The jeroboam was the first to have this style of name and is the baby in the family, containing only 3 litres. Jeroboam was a King of Israel, 'a mighty man of valour' and one who 'made Israel to sin', so perhaps the bottle-size name originated as a joke, with the other biblical names following in imitation.

'It was a lesson in the cultural accretions of language, in how no word is in itself pure or impure, neutral, objective or biased; in how words can become tainted in time with what they indicate and so have to be moved on from.'

WTF

LONG BEFORE THE arrival of the online digital channel BBC Three, there was a late-night satire/chat show with the same name. Running during the winter of 1965–6, *BBC-3* was the successor to the satirical *Not So Much a Programme, More a Way of Life*, which in turn followed the satirical *That Was the Week that Was* (otherwise known as '*TW3*'). All of the shows were produced by Ned Sherrin while David Frost – acerbic, nasal, seemingly anti-establishment – fronted the first two. By the time *BBC-3* aired the reins had been handed to Robert Robinson. Both Frost and Robinson, with their grammar-school backgrounds and occasionally chippy stance, might have been seen as representatives of the new meritocratic Britain of the 1960s. But Robinson, twelve years older than Frost, was avuncular enough to have presented *Points of View*, the long-running television slot where listeners wrote in to air their complaints, and traditional enough to have written an Oxford-based detective story called *Landscape with Dead Dons* when he was still in his twenties. Like the show's title, Robinson's stint on *BBC-3* was a sign that the satire boom was fading or, rather, being nudged aside by the more comfy format of the chat show. Even the off-the-shelf title *BBC-3* sounded a bit tired, whether it was meant to distinguish the programme from the recently established BBC Two channel or to recall the glory days of *That Was the Week that Was*.

But there was one shock still in store. Early in the programme's run on a Saturday evening in November 1965, there was a studio discussion on censorship chaired by Robinson and pitching Kenneth Tynan against Mary McCarthy. Ken Tynan was at the height of his powers, having moved from the *Observer* newspaper on which he had been a feared though venerated theatre critic to the newly established National Theatre, where a wary Laurence Olivier had appointed him as literary manager. Mary McCarthy was an American novelist and commentator whose reputation in England was also at its peak around the mid-1960s, largely because of her bestselling novel *The Group* (1963), which had drawn attention for its unapologetic treatment of sex and contraception among a group of girls graduating from Vassar in the early 1930s.

McCarthy had gone for Tynan in print, and the two were not friends. Perhaps that was the reason they were paired in discussion. A third guest was Denis Norden, best known for his comedy writing partnership with Frank

Muir, and their very popular radio quiz show *My Word!* That night's live broadcast of *BBC-3* is famous for a particular word: it came in Tynan's answer to Robinson's question about whether a play featuring sexual intercourse could be staged at the National Theatre.

Like many people in English theatre at the time, Tynan had been engaged in the campaign against the Lord Chamberlain and his extensive legal authority to censor anything put on the public stage, ranging from disrespectful comments about the royal family to swearwords to suggestive poses. So it wasn't surprising when he replied to Robinson's sex-at-the-National question with 'Oh I think so, certainly.' It was what he went on to say next which sparked furious editorials, motions in Parliament and (supposedly) national outrage. 'I doubt if there are very many rational people in this world to whom the word "fuck" is particularly diabolical or revolting or totally forbidden.'

The discussion continued, with neither Robert Robinson, Denis Norden or the gravel-voiced Mary McCarthy seeming to turn a hair. But at home hundreds of people were reaching for their phones and fountain pens. By the Monday morning the story was front-page news. Tynan might have been right that 'rational people' wouldn't object to the word but the reaction showed that there were plenty of not so rational people out there, quite a few of them writing for and to the *Daily Telegraph* or the

Express (where one commentator claimed that Tynan was responsible for the 'bloodiest outrage' he had ever known).

The hole at the centre of all the newspaper stories was precisely what Tynan had uttered in his soft stuttering tones. There was, of course, no repetition of that word. Almost everyone could guess what the 'something' was but no newspaper was going to confirm it in print just as no broadcaster was going to say it aloud again. How could they, since to do so would have undermined the high moral stance behind the outrage, to say nothing of losing listeners and readers? Tory MPs demanded that Ken Tynan be prosecuted or sacked from his post at the National Theatre. More than a hundred members from both sides of the House added their names to motions attacking both Tynan and the BBC. The Corporation expressed regret about the incident but added that the word had been used in the course of a serious debate. In a characteristically impish way Harold Wilson, the Labour Prime Minister, promised not to use the word in his own television appearances.

Although Tynan received some support, he was not only the target of public vitriol but of plenty of letter writers whose invective sometimes went further than calling him a dirty dog or a blighter and tipped over into threats of violence. The best rebuke – because it was unintentionally apt – came from Mary Whitehouse of the newly formed morality watchdog, the National Viewers' and

Listeners' Association. 'Little boys' language,' the one-time schoolmistress said to an interviewer. 'He wants his bottom smacked.' It was only after Tynan's death and the posthumous publication of his diaries that his own proclivities for spanking and sado-masochistic games came to light. Whitehouse's comment, if he ever saw it, must have given him a particularly satisfactory frisson.

Tynan made his own defence with the statement: 'I used an old English word in a completely neutral way to illustrate a serious point, just as I would have used it in similar conversation with any group of grown-up people. To have censored myself would, in my view, have been rather an insult to the viewers' intelligence.' This was disingenuous. Tynan knew the word was hardly 'neutral' but came loaded with the disapproval, even the taboo of centuries of English speakers. Nor was the use of 'fuck' especially relevant to the question he had been asked by Robert Robinson. Or, rather, the word could easily have been avoided in his answer. The fact was that Tynan had come into the late-night studio intending to strike a blow against censorship and prudery. The word did not slip out in the heat of the moment. He was ready and more than willing to say it. Perhaps he had not anticipated the strength of the backlash. Perhaps he was secretly gratified by it. Probably a bit of both. He enjoyed controversy and attention. Appropriately, his middle name was Peacock, the surname of his (unacknowledged) father, a northern businessman. At the same time, and whatever the calculations behind his use of the word, he was a genuine libertarian who really did believe what he preached.

Yet when Tynan died of emphysema in 1980 at the age of fifty-three, that flash of notoriety on a BBC show was one of the defining occasions recalled in the obituaries. That, and his erotic review *Oh! Calcutta!*, one of the first fruits of the disappearance of the Lord Chamberlain from the British theatre scene at the end of the 1960s. Later revelations from his own diaries and his first and second wives, Elaine Dundy and Kathleen Tynan, as well as dramatisations of his life on stage and television have confirmed the picture of Tynan as a sex-obsessed hedonist and, ultimately, a somewhat melancholy figure. Nevertheless he was a trail-blazer even if that trail consisted of only one word.

It would be eight more years before 'fuck' was again uttered on television, and then by an individual who, like Tynan, was often regarded as a rather dandified and contrary figure though from the other end of the political spectrum. In 1973 a Conservative minister Antony Lambton was exposed in the *News of the World* for his liaisons with prostitutes, or 'call girls' to use the paper's more glamorous euphemism. For a dizzying and delightful moment the country thought it was in for a rerun of the Profumo affair: government panjandrums in sensitive positions (Lord Lambton, like Profumo, was a defence minister), aristocratic nobs, call girls and cover-ups. Peregrine Worsthorne, the deputy editor of another week-end paper, the *Sunday Telegraph*, was asked on a BBC news programme what he thought the public's reaction would be. In Worsthorne's own words: 'After a few prelim-inary platitudes, I concluded by saying that in all proba-bility the public "will not give", and then I paused, and added, "there is only one word for it . . . will not give a fuck." ' On the one hand, Worsthorne thought he'd used the '*mot juste*', given the nature of the scandal; on the other hand, he felt he'd been foolish if only because his position as a conservative commentator was seriously undermined in a way that the liberal Ken Tynan's couldn't have been. As it happened, Worsthorne was right. The public turned out not to care very much, and the Lambton affair fizzled out.

The third person to deploy the word on British TV was Steve Jones, the guitarist with the Sex Pistols, in a notori-ous and bad-tempered interview with Thames Television presenter Bill Grundy in December 1976. What Jones actually said to Grundy, after a certain amount of goad-ing, was 'You dirty fucker', the climax of a short list of insults including 'sod' and 'bastard'. Two things distin-guished this moment. One was that Jones, unlike Tynan and Worsthorne, was not a privately educated Oxbridge intellectual and a member of what would now be called, semi-contemptuously, the elite, but authentically working class. Another and more important consideration was that Grundy's programme wasn't a late-night chat show or serious news broadcast but something which aired live in the early evening when families – with children! – would have been watching. The resulting uproar served to finish Grundy's career while raising the Sex Pistols' profile.

It may have taken a couple of decades from the mid-1970s but 'fuck' slowly bedded itself in as acceptable, then became almost normal. By 1994 a winsome 15-certificated Richard Curtis-scripted romcom – *Four Weddings and a Funeral* – could open with a string of 'fucks' and almost everyone thought they added a bit of tartness to the charm, especially as delivered by Hugh Grant. So WTF? What the fuck happened over the intervening years? Or, more precisely, what happened to fuck? And where was it for all those years, those centuries, before Ken Tynan flourished it on a late-night Saturday TV show in the mid-1960s?

First, let's spool back to a few years before Tynan's late-night, calculated outrage, and the couple of isolated television sightings in the early 1970s. The first extensive public outing of the word occurred in 1960 when Penguin Books was prosecuted for its publication of D. H. Lawrence's novel *Lady Chatterley's Lover*. The failure of the prosecution was a watershed moment in British cultural and social life, and was seen by some to presage the Swinging Sixties. In his poem 'Annus Mirabilis' Philip

Larkin mordantly dated the beginning of sexual intercourse to 1963, 'Between the end of the "Chatterley" ban/
And the Beatles' first LP.' Later in that decade, laws penal-
ising homosexuality or abortion were liberalised, the death
penalty was abolished and, in one of the causes closest to
Ken Tynan's heart, the ability of the Lord Chamberlain's
office to censor plays was removed by the Theatres Act of
1968. So the trial and acquittal of the publishers of *Lady
Chatterley* on obscenity charges doubled as a milestone
and a signpost to what was coming.

D. H. Lawrence (1885–1930) knew that *Chatterley*
would never be published in his lifetime because of its
sexual explicitness and frequent use of four-letter words,
principally 'fuck' and 'cunt' but also 'arse', 'cock', 'shit',
'balls' and 'piss'. The book, printed privately in Italy in
1928 and sent to subscribers in Britain, led an underground existence for many years until 1959 when the
New York Court of Appeals upheld the decision of a
federal judge that the book had literary merit. A similar
defence had recently become possible in Britain under
the Obscene Publications Act, which rules that an
'obscene' work may be published provided that publication is shown to be for 'the public good'. Expert witnesses
could now be called to testify to the merit of a book,
something that hadn't been allowed before. All this
encouraged Penguin to bring the book out in the UK,
even though it knew that a prosecution was almost

inevitable. It was a 'test case by arrangement', intended to clarify the new obscenity laws.

The book, more familiar now from its several television and film versions, describes a passionate affair between Constance Chatterley, an upper-class woman, and Mellors, a gamekeeper on her husband's estate. The setting is the English Midlands in the 1920s. Some of the book's shock value lay in the sexual trampling of class boundaries but the greater part came from Lawrence's description of 'thirteen episodes of sexual intercourse' and the taboo-breaking use of four-letter terms. For the trial, the prosecution called only one witness, a detective inspector who testified that the book had actually been published: that is, he had gone to the Penguin offices and been handed a copy. The defence had lined up an imposing array of writers, academics, literary critics and one liberal Anglican bishop (John Robinson, the Bishop of Woolwich, and later to become more controversial for his 1963 book *Honest to God*) but many of these experts were not required to testify to Lawrence's integrity as an artist and the serious intentions behind the book.

The most famous moment from the case is not an example of Lawrence's four-lettered prose but a couple of rhetorical questions from prosecuting counsel Mervyn Griffith-Jones: 'Is it a book that you would wish to have lying around the house?' he said, and 'Is it a book you would even wish your wife or servants to read?' As the case went on, Griffith-Jones seemed to be more bothered about the adultery and the breaking-down of class distinctions by the lovers than he was by the obscene language. After reading out a passage of dialogue, he posed another question to the jury: 'Is this a realistic conversation between a baronet's wife and her gamekeeper?' The jury of nine men and three women to whom he put these questions included no baronets or their wives but a furniture-maker, a dock worker and a teacher. Despite the judge's hostile summing-up, which caused Penguin books and the defence to think that they'd lost, it took the jury only three hours to return with a 'Not Guilty' verdict. And within a year of its official publication in Britain *Lady Chatterley's Lover* had sold more than two million copies. 'Fuck' had well and truly arrived on the page even if it wasn't yet acceptable when uttered on television.

The underground word

The silliest explanation of the origin of this archetypal four-letter word is that it is some kind of acronym, suggestions ranging from Fornication Under Consent of the King (because once upon a time in Merrie England the king's permission was required for single people to have sex) to File Under Carnal Knowledge (supposedly how Scotland Yard marked rape files). The more straightforward answer is that it's probably a word inherited from the

Germanic speaking peoples of northern Europe, like many other ordinary English words. The *Oxford English Dictionary* cites a number of similar-looking terms from early Dutch and various Scandinavian languages whose meanings vary from 'have sex with' to 'strike' to 'be tossed by the wind'. A contemporary of Shakespeare and an early lexicographer called John Florio included it in an Italian–English dictionary, where he gives some English translations for the Italian *fottere*. Among Florio's equivalent words are 'swive' (used by Chaucer several times, e.g. 'As I have thries in this shorte nyght swyved the milleres doghter') and 'occupy' ('The word "occupy", which was an excellent good word before it was ill-sorted,' says the prostitute Doll Tearsheet in Shakespeare's *Henry IV*). Keeping company in John Florio's list with swive, occupy and others is – fuck.

An indication of the word's long-time power as the jewel in the crown of sexual slang is that, after Florio's time, it seems to drop out of the official written record for the next few hundred years. Presumably almost everybody would have been familiar with the word while quite a few would have been using it in speech, but almost nobody commits it to paper, although it does appear in two eighteenth-century dictionaries. Nathan Bailey in his *Universal Etymological English Dictionary* (1721) resorted to a Latin definition of fuck (*foeminam subagitare*), a quite usual way both at the time and later of sanitising a dangerous word and coming with the patronising implication that such obscene knowledge should be restricted to the highly educated. In fact, the whole point of such words is that they are universally known and available for use. The second reference occurs in John Ash's *New and Complete Dictionary of the English Language* (1775). Ash is a bit more upfront than Bailey; after the bracketed description of fuck as '(a low vulgar word)' he gives this definition: 'To perform the act of generation, to have to do with a woman.' Nathan Bailey, a schoolmaster in Stepney, and John Ash, a minister in Worcestershire, were both Baptists, and it is tempting to explain their inclusion of such a word as a kind of lexical non-conformity – Ash also has 'cunt' (defined as the female pudendum) – but what it more likely shows is that in the eighteenth century 'fuck' hadn't quite achieved the taboo status of later centuries.

Dictionaries apart, where the word does appear it is in a kind of private setting. If it was not the kind of expression that the prosecutor in the *Lady Chatterley* trial could imagine occurring in a dialogue between a baronet's wife and a gamekeeper, it was certainly familiar to an earlier aristocrat. John Wilmot (1647–80), the Earl of Rochester, was the quintessential rake and poet in the court of Charles II. Only a handful of his poems was printed in his lifetime. Generally bawdy or outright obscene, most of what Rochester wrote was meant to be heard by private ears in recitations or read by private eyes in manuscript form. 'A Ramble in St James's Park' begins 'Much wine had passed, with grave discourse/Of who fucks who, and who does worse'. King Charles II was an occasional target: 'Peace is his aim, his gentleness is such/ And love he loves, for he loves fucking much.' And Rochester was the probable author of a short satirical play titled *The Farce of Sodom*, which includes in its cast of characters three 'Maids of Honour' called Fuckadilla, Cunticula and Clitoris. Nearly a hundred years later John Wilkes would write in his parodic poem 'An Essay on Woman' of how 'life can little more supply/Than a few good fucks and then we die'. Wilkes was prosecuted for the work, which had been published in very small quantities, though the reasons were more to do with a political vendetta against him than with supposed obscenity. When 'fuck' and other four-letter terms were actually put into print, they appeared underground, as in Victorian pornography such as *My Secret Life* (*c.*1890) or *Venus in India* (*c.*1900).

So between John Florio's time and the *Chatterley* era the word 'fuck' could be written down and even published but, with dictionary exceptions, not by respectable or approved channels. Yet ingenious authors might hint at it, sometimes surprising authors too. John Donne, in a poem of seduction dating from the early seventeenth century, tries to persuade a woman to go to bed with him using an elaborate metaphor to do with a flea. He begins:

Mark but this flea, and mark in this,
How little that which thou deniest me is;
It suck'd me first, and now sucks thee,
And in this flea our two bloods mingled be.
Thou know'st that this cannot be said
A sin, nor shame, nor loss of maidenhead

Donne goes on pleading with her, ingeniously and absurdly and, it seems, unsuccessfully, at least for the time being. But the seventeenth-century reader of the poem would have seen something different in those opening lines from what would be heard by a listener. Writers and printers in Donne's time and afterwards used what was known as the 'long s' when the letter occurred at the beginning or the middle of a word. This long s is almost indistinguishable from an f, so that the last line quoted above would have looked more like this on the page: 'A fin, nor fhame, nor lofs of maidenhead'. And, more to the point, the third line would have looked like this: 'It fuck'd me first, and now fucks thee'. Coincidence? Not likely, given the subject matter and the author.

In the century after John Donne's, i.e. the eighteenth, 'fuck' stirs and stretches its limbs. That is, it begins to be applied to the world beyond sex. Specifically, as a verb it takes on the meaning of 'ruined', 'spoiled'. In his memoir *The Word Detective* (2016), John Simpson, the former chief editor of the *Oxford English Dictionary*, identifies the text in which this shift in sense becomes apparent, even if the word is not spelled out in full. *The Frisky Songster* (1776), a collection of racy and suggestive lyrics, has the couplet: 'O, says the breeches, I shall be duck'd,/Aye, says the petticoat, I shall be f----d.' The ostensible subject is how a gust of wind blows breeches and petticoat off a washing line and into a well, but of course 'petticoat' also suggests the woman who wears it. By the next century what John Simpson calls 'this lively entrant to the language' was well developed. It could be used as a straightforward insult and for evidence of this there is a very unexpected source.

In *Wuthering Heights* (1847), Emily Brontë has the fiery Heathcliff utter a characteristic curse even if she – or her narrator Mr Lockwood – doesn't report it in full: ' "And you, you worthless – " he broke out as I entered, turning to his daughter-in-law, and employing an epithet as harmless as duck, or sheep, but generally represented by a dash – .' The implication of a duck/fuck* rhyme is obvious, though perhaps given a bit of cover by the addition of 'sheep'. That Brontë meant to depict Heathcliff as a hard

---

* This is far from the only time the two creatures have been coupled in this way. For example, there is the line from *The Frisky Songster* quoted above, and the experts on childhood games and rhymes, Gordon and Iona Opie, note the ditty, 'Mary had a little lamb/She also had a duck/She put them on the mantelpiece/To see if they would fuck.'

swearer is plain enough from his daughter-in-law Cathy Linton's equally fiery reaction: ' "I'll put my trash away, because you can make me if I refuse," answered the young lady, closing her book, and throwing it on a chair. "But I'll not do anything, though you should swear your tongue out, except what I please!" '

Although Emily Brontë's hint at a taboo word seems surprising in itself, the practice of censoring words by substituting dashes or using only initial letters was disliked by her sister Charlotte, who wrote in the preface to an 1850 edition of *Wuthering Heights*, published after Emily's death, that it struck her 'as a proceeding which, however well meant, is weak and futile. I cannot tell what good it does – what feeling it spares – what horror it conceals.' It's true that she's talking about milder words that in the puritanical days of the early Victorian era were often reduced to a single letter followed by a dash, such as 'damn' or 'God', but nevertheless her attitude is very unusual.

After Emily Brontë, it would be surprising if D. H. Lawrence hadn't somehow squeezed the term into one of his pre-*Chatterley* books. And so he did. In his semi-autobiographical novel *Sons and Lovers* (1913), Lawrence writes this: ' "You shouldn't funk [flinch from] your own deeds, man," remonstrated the friend. Then Dawes made a remark which caused Paul to throw half a glass of beer in his face.' Many readers would understand that Dawes has said something punning on the similarity between 'funk' and 'fuck' but Lawrence could not spell this out; had he done so, the publisher would have insisted on its removal.

James Joyce uses the word twice in *Ulysses* (1922) but the book was at first printed in very small numbers and unavailable to a wide readership, the exact opposite of the Penguin edition of *Lady Chatterley's Lover*. In any case, in the general charge-sheet of obscenity against *Ulysses* the author's use of fuck would have been a minor item. Bodley Head produced the 'first unlimited edition' of *Ulysses* in 1938 – one had already appeared in the US in 1934 – so that the general reader could be corrupted by those two appearances: one a curse ('God fuck old Bennett') and the other part of Molly Bloom's unfiltered unpunctuated musings at the end of the book ('I had to hug him after O Lord I wanted to shout out all sorts of things fuck or shit or anything'). But these two Joycean fucks could be easily mislaid or overlooked in a book of more than a quarter of a million words, a book which was almost deliberately made 'difficult' for the general reader by its author. If Joyce's modernist masterpiece wasn't very accessible in literary terms, it was not very accessible in literal ones either. And more than thirty years later it still wasn't that easy to come across *Ulysses*. At sixth form in school in the mid-1960s – yes, the liberated 1960s and some years after the *Chatterley* case and the Beatles' first LP – I had to ask for a copy at the local library where the red-bound book was produced from under the counter.

The word comes out

If one had to plot a kind of recent chronology for the public acceptability of 'fuck' in Britain it would have the appearance of a graph that begins with a gentle incline and then starts to rise steeply around the 1980s. The word is not found in respectable print before the *Lady Chatterley* trial and acquittal of 1960 but is increasingly used thereafter in fiction. It was always much less widespread in the printed news media, a situation which continues to the present day. The first use in a British newspaper* was, unsurprisingly, in the *Guardian* in an article on the *Chatterley* trial, quoting one of the defence witnesses. The decision to use the word wasn't taken lightly, with the newspaper's lawyer warning that 'It is wrong to think that the Chatterley finding "takes the brake off", and that anybody can in future get away with anything.' He added, however, that he thought the *Guardian* could get away with it whereas a tabloid paper such as the *Daily Mirror* could not.

Appropriately, fuck's British film debut was in a 1967 version of James Joyce's *Ulysses* made by the unconventional US director Joseph Strick. Like the book, Strick's

* The first official use, that is. In 1882, a report on a parliamentary speech in *The Times* attributed the following to the Attorney General: 'The speaker then said he felt inclined for a bit of fucking. I think this is very likely.' Not so much a typo, more a mischievous typesetter.

film was an arthouse production and so hardly likely to appeal to the general public, yet it still ran into censorship problems with the BBFC (the British Board of Film Censors, as it then was) mostly because of the obscenities in Molly Bloom's monologue, done as a voiceover. But local authorities could override the national censors and the GLC (Greater London Council) duly gave it a certificate for the capital, and the BBFC soon relented. I remember seeing it at the now defunct Academy Cinema in Oxford Street, the audience probably swollen by the notoriety the film had achieved.

Certainly the situation with Strick's film was unusual, in that the scandal and the attraction lay not so much in any images but in the words uttered on the soundtrack, mostly by Barbara Jefford playing Molly, words that as the director pointed out came entirely from Joyce's original. That was the problem, of course. But from then on it was the US that led the way in filmic bad language. An early example was the gay melodrama *The Boys in the Band* (1970), adapted from a stage play and directed by William Friedkin who would later make *The French Connection* and *The Exorcist*. In Britain *The Boys in the Band* immediately earned itself an X certificate, the precursor to the '18' rating, not only for its unapologetic gay subject matter but because of the sometimes almost epigrammatic quality of its use of obscenity. One line in particular gained wide currency: 'Who do you have to fuck to get a drink around here?' And the film was reputedly the first to use a word that was, if anything, even more taboo at the time: 'Donald, you are a real card-carrying cunt.'

Almost all of the more than 130 films listed on Wikipedia for the highest frequency of 'fuck' are American, and the fact that they date predominantly from the last twenty years shows not that the word has just been discovered but that it's being used increasingly often on screen. Britain lags behind in the fuck-quotient cinema partly because the industry is smaller but also because the UK doesn't specialise much in the kind of street-life or institutional *mise en scène* of, say, Martin Scorsese, where swearing and obscenity are second nature. Costume dramas or uplifting recreations of wartime Britain don't offer the same fertile ground. To find the equivalent of the quota in Scorsese's *The Wolf of Wall Street* (fuck count: 569; uses per minute: 3.16), you would have to turn to a television show such as Armando Iannucci's *The Thick of It*.

The first appearance on British television was, as already noted, by Ken Tynan back in 1965. There is a longer, less steep incline to the 'fuck' graph-line on television, compared with its appearance on the printed page. This can be explained by the belief that 'there are certain things that can be read but not heard', in the words of the director of the Cannes Film Festival who in 1967 was responsible for obliterating twenty-nine subtitles in Joseph Strick's version of *Ulysses*. Reading is private and cinema is public (though what it shows is helpfully certificated), while television sits somewhere in between the two. So it was not until the 1980s or even the 1990s that programmes containing four-letter terms, including fuck, became acceptable on British television, and then only after the nine o'clock watershed and frequently preceded by a warning about 'strong language'.

If such warnings seem less frequent now, it is in no way because the quantity of 'bad words' has diminished but because viewers have become more relaxed – or hardened. Sustained use of the strongest and most 'problematic' language in the description given by the regulator Ofcom will probably merit a warning, but only three words out of the forty-seven terms on its list come into this category ('cunt', 'fuck' and 'motherfucker'). More significantly, the regulators – and the viewers – are much more likely to object to racist or discriminatory language, and this will frequently be apologised for in advance if its appearance can't be avoided, for example in showing an old film or an uneditable piece of news footage. Even in this changing landscape it's interesting to note that the old broadsheet/tabloid division referred to above in press reporting on the *Chatterley* trial seems to apply: greater latitude is given to the minority channels such as BBC Two or Channel 4, rather as if their audiences – supposedly more cerebral or less shockable – are all *Guardian* readers, in spirit if not in fact.

American mainstream television hasn't been given the same licence. Federal law prohibits obscene, indecent and profane content from being broadcast on the radio or TV. That previous sentence is not mine; it is the opening of the Federal Communications Commission's (FCC) own Consumer Guide. The FCC is a powerful body, with teeth. When Bono of U2* accepted a Golden Globe award in 2003 at a ceremony carried live on NBC he blurted out 'This is really, really fucking brilliant.' At first the FCC were grudgingly forgiving, ruling that the adjectival use of the word was 'fleeting' and 'nonsexual', but a year later

---

* One U2 story suggests another. The high-altitude U-2 spyplane was famous in the early 1960s mostly because its shooting down on a CIA reconnaissance mission over the USSR led to a rise in Cold War tension, and the eventual exchange of the captured American pilot for a Russian spy arrested in the US (the subject of Spielberg's film *Bridge of Spies*, 2015). The origins of the U-2 name are straightforward: U for 'Utility', perhaps because labelling it R for reconnaissance would have been a giveaway, and 2 for its place in development programme. But an alternative story is too good to pass up. In this version, the test pilot on the maiden flight got into an argument with the aircraft's designer. The plane had very long wings to give it lift but they also made it hard to land. In the end, after half a dozen attempts, the pilot had to stall the engine to get back on the ground. 'What the hell were you trying to do, kill me?' said the angry pilot to the designer, giving him the finger. 'Well, fuck you.' 'And fuck you too,' retorted the designer. Hence the U-2. Or not.

they reversed their own decision following a public outcry and a perception that broadcasting standards were slipping. In between the two decisions came the TV debut of one of Janet Jackson's breasts in the 'nipplegate' scandal during her duet with Justin Timberlake at the Super Bowl, a 'wardrobe malfunction' that for some seemed to signal the end of the world, and led to a hardening in the FCC's attitude and the imposition of a $550,000 fine. In this changed climate many television stations refused to run Steven Spielberg's *Saving Private Ryan* (1998) on Veterans Day in 2004, even though the film had been shown on the same anniversary in previous years, because they were afraid of a backlash not just against the bloody realism of the battle scenes but against the adult language used by soldiers in combat. As some commentators pointed out, this desire to protect the public was ironic given that at the time the US was involved in two actual wars, in Iraq and Afghanistan.

British viewers whose only exposure to American television is via series such as *The Sopranos* or *The Wire* may be surprised by this squeamishness and prudery. But these are cable shows, paid for by subscription and delivered via privately built hardware. The implication is that, if you pay, you know what you will be getting even if it involves more explicit violence or sex or a profusion of four-letter words, most likely all three. Indeed, that is part of the attraction of the pay-to-view channels. By contrast, anyone with a TV and an aerial can pick up the principal broadcasting services such as NBC or CBS, so their output has a public dimension that doesn't exist in cable or satellite provision. Both the 'national broadcasters' and the cable providers are threatened by the rise in streaming, and so the remit of the FCC will narrow still further. Yet the image of mainstream American TV, and of their media in general, as rather correct and priggish persists, and it is not unusual for a US guest on a British chat-show to venture 'Can I say that?' about some four-letter term or risqué story only to be reassured by the sometimes smug host that, sure, over here you can say what you like. The subtext is: we are liberal and easy-going when it comes to bad language, unlike you uptight Yanks.

But, as noted in the 'Shit Happens' chapter, things are beginning to change and it's partly because of the presidency of Donald J. Trump, and his unique style of public and political engagement. Of course, it would be naive to imagine that bad language started with the gold-plated mogul or that it is confined to the Donald. President Obama's first chief of staff, Rahm Emanuel, was famously foul-mouthed. Obama once joked to a room full of journalists that Emanuel wouldn't be able to celebrate Mother's Day because he was unaccustomed to saying the word 'day' after 'mother'. But usually the cursing occurs behind closed doors, and is not meant to be on the record. Hence the frazzled media response that resulted from an indiscreet phone conversation between a reporter from the *New Yorker* magazine and Anthony Scaramucci, who was the White House communications director for a whole ten days in the summer of 2017. Scaramucci characterised a colleague/rival as 'a fucking paranoid schizophrenic, a paranoiac' and, in reference to another competing presence in the White House, said, 'I'm not Steve Bannon. I'm not trying to suck my own cock.' These on-the-record comments were highly newsworthy. At the same time they were highly offensive, both to the people they were directed at and in themselves. Some newspapers managed to run stories without using any of the objectionable words. But others considered that they were central to the story and included them. CNN opted for a kind of reverse verbal striptease when it came to 'fucking'; at first the television channel displayed the word as 'f*****g' but then it decided to fill in some of the blanks to give 'fu**ing', a response that falls down the gap between timidity and frankness and ends up satisfying no one. Charlotte Brontë wouldn't have approved.

Now back to fuck and its offspring ('fucking', 'fuckwit', etc.) in Britain. They are everywhere. Although bleeped out on television, especially before the 9 p.m. watershed, or asterisked in most newspapers, the tolerance for the word and its place in what one might call public discourse is remarkably high. What was once the ultimate taboo word, at least when uttered in public, has in Britain lost most of its sting. Nothing illustrates that more clearly than the couple of cases from recent political history, mentioned in the Introduction to this book. Both involved senior figures who were reported as saying 'fuck' or 'fucking'. Tony Blair was taken to task for coupling the word with 'Welsh'. Not the swearing but the national hostility caused problems. In Andrew Mitchell's case it was, in addition to an antagonistic attitude towards the police at the Downing Street gate, the use of the word 'pleb' and not the more traditional four-letter expletive that resulted in the loss of his job and subsequently a great deal of money.

Of course, the sudden emergence of fuck from the closet doesn't mean that the word hasn't been used repeatedly in private over the last centuries. The fragments of evidence we pick up from writers such as Emily Brontë and D. H. Lawrence suggest it's always been there, below the respectable surface. Indeed the British may have a particular taste for 'fucking'. Evidence from wartime may not be representative since where you have groups of young men together, especially in times of tension or frustration, the f-graph is likely to spike. Nevertheless expertise and ease in swearing, especially among the Other Ranks (i.e. the non-officers), seem to have been a British speciality during the Second World War. After a German spy had managed to deceive a British unit during the North African campaign because he spoke impeccable

'Other Ranks English', a pamphlet came from the War Office with the warning: 'It should . . . be impressed on all ranks that the use in conversation of "f-----s" and "b-----s" is not necessarily a guarantee of British nationality.'

The American academic and critic, Paul Fussell, who wrote rawly and evocatively about military life from his experience in the Second World War, stressed how among 'the working class fucking had always been a popular intensifier, but in wartime it became precious as a way for millions of conscripts to note, in a licensed way, their bitterness and anger' (*Wartime: Understanding and Behavior in the Second World War*, 1990). In the same book Fussell also has the following story: 'Once, on a misty Scottish airfield, an airman was changing the magneto on the engine of a Wellington bomber. Suddenly his wrench slipped and he flung it on the grass and snarled, "Fuck! The fucking fucker's fucked." The bystanders were all quite well aware that he had stripped a bolt and skinned his knuckles.' The airman could have inserted another 'fucking' as the penultimate word and still made perfect sense, though it would have changed the rhythm of the sentence.

Playing around

There have been attempts to play off the taboo value of 'fuck' in advertising and elsewhere, but the diminishing shock value of the term means that its employment tends to reflect nothing so much as the canny infantilism of the users. If Mary Whitehouse were still around, she'd be calling for their bottoms to be smacked. Giving Ben Stiller the name of Gaylord 'Greg' Focker in *Meet the Parents* (2000) made for a few sniggers, and the innuendo was underlined by the sequel *Meet the Fockers* (2004) but the third film in line, *Little Fockers* (2010), ran the joke into the ground. The UK-based fashion company French Connection had a good old dyslexic time with its initials FCUK/fcuk plastered across T-shirts, shop fronts and billboards. In the four years after the fcuk campaign was launched in 1997, profits tripled. There were perfume lines for women and men (fcuk her, fcuk him) and, naturally enough, a condom ('fcuk safely'), all launched to little whinnies of distaste and complaint – which was the point, of course. In 1999 Conservative Future, the youth wing of the Conservative Party, scrabbled to get its leg over the side of the bandwagon by announcing that it was henceforward to be known as CFUK. Then the grownups stepped in and told it not to be so silly and the Conservative youths dropped the new name. As for the original, after something of a fcuk-lull and a drop in market share, French Connection announced in 2016 that it was bringing back its 'controversial' slogan. The Phat Phuc Noodle Bar in Chelsea is not accidentally named, though when people complained about a similar venue in Glasgow the proprietors pointed out that 'happy' in Vietnamese was spelled 'phuc', a line of argument that was accepted by the Advertising Standards Authority. Occasionally, the plays on fuck may even produce something approaching wit. When KFC suffered a chicken-supply crisis early in 2018 in the UK, it took out full-page newspaper ads with a paragraph of text, beginning 'A chicken restaurant without any chicken. It's not ideal', under a large and empty bargain bucket on which the company's trademark initials had been tweaked to read FCK.

While 'fuck' and 'fucking' continue to engender euphemistic spin-offs such as 'the f-word' and 'f-bomb' and enable advertisers to tease with their f-play, an earlier and less liberal climate produced slurred variants like 'frigging' 'freaking' and 'fugging', the latter used by Norman Mailer to avoid censorship in *The Naked and the Dead* (1948), his classic novel about the war in the Pacific. The story goes that the first-time author was approached by the actress Tallulah Bankhead at a party: 'Oh, hello, you're Norman Mailer. You're the young man that doesn't know how to spell fuck.' The rock band, the Fugs, formed in 1964, gave themselves that name in tribute to Mailer's euphemism.

Now, more than fifty years after Kenneth Tynan's f-bomb on the BBC and the letters of complaint and the questions in Parliament, the changing fortunes of the f-word seem to have mirrored those of 'bloody', infamously deployed by George Bernard Shaw in *Pygmalion* around fifty years before Tynan's time and also followed by the usual apparatus of outrage. Rage dies away, familiarity sets in. There are differences though. 'Bloody' scarcely raises a metaphorical eyebrow now. But 'fucking' may still raise at least one, Roger Moore-style, if used in the wrong company or context. And 'fuck' and its variants have a versatility and centrality that 'bloody' can never match.

Despite bloody's limitations it shares a linguistic peculiarity with 'fuck/ing' as well as its one-time shock-and-awe value. Both can be shoved into the middle of another word to reinforce its sense: 'fan-bloody-tastic', 'un-fucking-believable'. Technically this effect – producing a word-within-another-word like the ham wrapped in a sandwich – is called tmesis, from an ancient Greek word for cutting. And there is a structure to it that even the most careless swearers and expletive-deliverers observe even if they're not aware of it. The f- or b-word cannot be chucked in, willy nilly. It needs to be inserted delicately into the mother word, which should ideally be one of several syllables to maximise the ham-sandwich effect, and the insertion has to come before the stressed syllable: 'absolute-fucking-ly' doesn't work, 'abso-fucking-lutely' does. Incidentally, it's worth noting that stress, in both senses, is an essential feature of swearing. Not only do people swear when they are stressed, but they often lay stress on the swearword in order to stress how stressed they are. A minor illustration of instinctive stressing is the way the word 'damn' caused problems in the 1939 film version of *Gone with the Wind*, perhaps less from the censor's viewpoint than from the feeling that the cinemas audience shouldn't go home with a cuss-word ringing in their ears. The emphasis in Rhett Butler's famous departing line, which Clark Gable delivers to Vivien Leigh, had to be changed so that the stress fell not, as it would naturally, on the final 'damn' but on the earlier 'give': 'Frankly, my dear, I don't give a damn.'

The mother word

If, in recent history, there was a word worse than fuck or fucker it was 'motherfucker'. I say 'was' because at least a couple of other terms, specifically the n-word and arguably 'cunt', are now regarded as more offensive. But this one is still a strong term. Many people are quite happy to talk about 'fuckers' but they will draw the line when it comes to 'motherfuckers'. The reason is the additional level of taboo – incest – which overlies the original obscenity. Though Oedipus was a literal and inadvertent motherfucker, the word is rarely if ever employed in this narrow sense. Instead, the addition of 'mother-' intensifies an insult, which originated in the US around the turn of the twentieth century. Usually referring to an obnoxious person or a formidable problem, 'motherfucker' can flip over like a coin, particularly in black American use, and signify someone or something admirable. Heads or tails? Samuel L. Jackson has talked in interviews on the liberating power of the word, and of its versatility.

But however often Samuel L. Jackson uses it on film – 'I've had it with these motherfucking snakes on this motherfucking plane!' – the word is still stuck in the doghouse as far as general usage is concerned. Kurt Vonnegut's *Slaughterhouse-Five* (1969) may be a modern American classic yet ever since publication the novel has met opposition from those wanting to exclude it from American schools and libraries, partly on the grounds of 'foul language'. In November 1973, a school caretaker in Drake, North Dakota, fed thirty-two paperback copies of Vonnegut's novel into the furnace beneath the school gym. In the view of the school board the book, which had been set as a class assignment by a teacher, was profane. The English teacher was new and had emigrated with his family from California because they were looking for a quieter life away from the city. Critics in the media and from larger places than Drake, North Dakota, recalled Nazi book-burning and the fictional world of Ray Bradbury's *Fahrenheit 451*. Meanwhile the tiny town on the Great Plains hunkered down to endure a media shit-storm as well as the icy winds beginning to sweep down from Canada at the start of winter. The thirty-two paperbacks cannot have warmed the school gym for long. In an essay written later Kurt Vonnegut commented, ironically, on the persuasive power of words and one in particular: 'There is the word "motherfucker" one time in my *Slaughterhouse-Five*, as in "Get out of the road, you dumb motherfucker." Ever since that word was published, way back in 1969, children have been attempting to have intercourse with their mothers. When it will stop no one knows.'

When London's National Theatre staged the New York play *The Motherfucker with the Hat* in 2015 they advertised it on websites and in the press as *The Motherf**ker with the Hat*. The *New York Times* dropped the whole word and substituted a dash, so that any prospective theatregoers left wondering just who or what was wearing a hat can only have concluded it must be something pretty bad. Reputedly, the title was one reason the play didn't do well on Broadway. Not only did the *Motherfucker* put a spoke in the advertising campaign, but even when the producers cast the high-profile Chris Rock – the man once unafraid to pepper his stand-up with 'niggas' – he found himself unable to utter the word in promotional TV interviews. Inevitably, British newspapers avoid 'motherfucker' or subject it to extreme asterisking (for example, the *Daily Mail* has 'm*****f*****' as part of a quote). Even the *Guardian*, reliably upfront in its use of taboo terms, doesn't go overboard for the term, tending to limit its appearance to quoted remarks.

There is a way out, and that is to jettison the second half of the word altogether and leave 'mother' standing by herself, as in 'He's a mean mother'. In a similar way, the moderately offensive 'bullshit' can be modified to 'bull', and no one will blanch. The *Scientist* magazine headlined a 2006 article about the ruthlessness of Mother Nature with A NASTY MOTHER, knowing readers would get the point. According to Jim Dawson, author of *The Compleat Motherfucker: A History of the Mother of All Dirty Words* (2011), the word could be smuggled into Hollywood movies in the old censorious days when even a 'damn' might be questioned. One example he gives is of Barbara Stanwyck in the film *Night Nurse* (1931) spitting out 'You mother' at a neglectful mother, with the word not being intended in a maternal sense. Dawson says that when he saw a new print of the film at Hollywood's Egyptian Theatre in 2006, 'the audience gasped and tittered' because the half-word in an early black-and-white film context had more impact than any number of effusions in *Snakes on a Plane*.

A curious and highly specialised use of the word is too good to let go by. In 2017 there was published a book titled *Chamberpot & Motherfuck: The Price-codes of the Book Trade*. In it, Bruce McKittrick revealed the secret meanings behind the apparently random string of letters sometimes pencilled on the flyleaves of an antiquarian book. They are there to remind the dealer how much he paid for the book in the first place, and encrypted to conceal that knowledge from the customer. The letters stand for digits. A book dealer in Edinburgh employs 'motherfuck', a word with no repeating letters – the same principle lies behind the Playfair encryption code sometimes used in crosswords – and so M can stand for 1, O for 2, etc. with no risk of confusion. A book that cost the dealer £185 would thus, courtesy of 'motherfuck', have MUEKK pencilled in the back. The codeword has the advantage of being easy to remember.

'Get rid of the poof'

JOHN SHOLTO DOUGLAS, the 8th Marquess of
Queensberry (1844–1900), has gone down in history
as the man who gave his name to boxing's Queensberry
Rules (he endorsed but didn't write them) and as the man
who persecuted Oscar Wilde because of the great playwright's relationship with Queensberry's son, Lord Alfred
Douglas, or Bosie as he was known. So infuriated was the
Marquess by his son's association with Wilde that he
finally left his calling card at the latter's London club with
the scribbled addition 'For Oscar Wilde, posing
Somdomite'.* Despite the misspelling, the meaning was
clear and Wilde unwisely launched a libel action against
Queensberry. The trial collapsed and in turn led to Wilde's
prosecution on charges of homosexuality and a two-year

* Queensberry claimed in court that he'd written 'posing as a
Somdomite' because that was a better defence against the libel
charge.

term of imprisonment, followed by exile in Europe and death in Paris in 1900, coincidentally the same year in which Queensberry died. Wilde had long been goaded by his opponent's campaign but it was those two words that pushed him over the edge, as he wrote to a friend: 'Bosie's father has left a card at my club with hideous words on it.'

Hideous words. The lexicon of deprecatory terms for homosexuality and homosexuals is long and occasionally inventive, but the Marquess of Queensberry's choice is notable because of its age and biblical origins. Sodom, in conjunction with its twin city Gomorrah, conjures up visions of vast but vague vices. 'Sodomy' is found in written English towards the end of the thirteenth century, though it seems to refer to any sexual relationship regarded as unnatural rather than just sodomy. The 'sodomite' comes a century later, and the jaunty little 'sod' pops up in the Victorian era. The word was wittily and nastily used in a little jab at Wilde supposedly written by Algernon Charles Swinburne: 'When Oscar came to join his God./ Not earth to earth, but sod to sod,/It was for sinners such as this/Hell was created bottomless.'

Out of the dozens of expressions that have been used throughout history, a number were still in regular circulation until a few years ago and of course will still be found in private contexts, though you are unlikely to encounter them in print or broadcast media. In the order in which they appeared in English they include: bugger (Middle

Ages), poof (1830s), nancy (1880s), queen, fairy (both 1890s), poofter (early twentieth century), queer, pansy, homo, fag/faggot (all 1920s), bent (1950s).

Linguistically, the derivation of most of these is fairly obvious, apart from the long and tangled history of the bugger. This comes into English from medieval French; a *bougre* was a heretic, and he (or she) takes his (or her) name ultimately from the Latin *Bulgarus* or Bulgarian because that's where a sect of heretics originated in the eleventh century. Related groups such as the Albigensians or Cathars set themselves up in opposition to the established church and were duly persecuted to extinction. Catholic propaganda and popular belief attributed forbidden sexual practices to them including bestiality, pederasty, incest and anal sex. So the name for the heretic became the name for someone indulging in one of those practices. But over the centuries the bugger became detached from buggery. From the late seventeenth century it could be used without any sexual connotation as a term of contempt, and then expanded in the late nineteenth century into an expression of pity or exasperated affection, as in 'poor bugger' or 'silly bugger'. French followed the same course: *bougre* now means a chap, a guy, a fellow, sometimes with a pejorative twist; a *bon bougre* is a 'good sort' while a *pauvre bougre* is a 'poor devil'.

A versatile word in English as in French, 'bugger' also applies to a hard task, a knotty problem and a great nuisance. Otherwise it was a quite common oath or swear-word, lying somewhere between 'drat' and 'fuck' on the spectrum of acceptability and offence. There was a brief return to the old sexual sense in the late 1960s while the Sexual Offences Act, legalising consensual sex in private between men over twenty-one, was working its way through Parliament. Lord Arran,* sponsor of the Bill in the House of Lords, took to referring to it as 'William'. Others were more direct, with opponents talking about a 'buggers' charter' designed to protect 'pimps, pansies and queers'. But, in general, bugger and its relations – buggery, buggered – have taken a back seat in the bad-language charabanc, while stronger expressions are sitting at the front. My impression is that users tend to be old(er) and, if this is the case, bugger, etc. will slowly fade from view. The word has never really flourished in either the sexual or the slang sense in the US, where a bugger is more likely to refer to an electronic eavesdropper.

As for the other slang expressions referred to above: poof seems to come from 'puff', a word with several meanings including the now obsolete 'boaster' as well as an expression of distaste (more usually spelled 'poof'). Poofter and pooftah are Australian variants. Fag and faggot in the homosexual

---

* Arran, who was an eccentric and a badger fan, claimed he had two interests in life: 'to stop people buggering badgers, and to stop people badgering buggers.'

sense originated in the US, though quite why they acquired this meaning is unknown. One dictionary of American slang offers a link with cigarettes or fags, since these were initially regarded as less manly smoking choices than cigars and pipes. Another theory links the sexual sense with the traditional English boarding-school fag, the junior boy who performs tasks for an older boy. Both suggestions ignore the primary associations of the word not with the US but with Britain; boarding-school slang doesn't travel well and 'fag' for cigarette was used much earlier in the UK than in the US. Indeed the relative unfamiliarity of the term in this latter sense in America is shown in a story told by Louise Rennison, author of *Angus, Thongs and Full-frontal Snogging* (1999). She was doing a promotional tour in America and mentioned 'lighting a fag'. The journalist interviewing her was shocked: 'Don't you think that's kind of cruel?' American visitors must also be baffled by the traditional British dish of faggots in gravy.

The public airing of these expressions, or at least of the attitude behind them, one combining amusement with disdain, will be familiar to anyone in the UK who listened to the radio, watched television or read the papers in the 1980s and earlier decades. There were several radio and TV stars, including Kenneth Williams, Frankie Howerd and Larry Grayson, who for personal and professional reasons never came out as gay but whose shtick was nudge-and-wink innuendo. Everybody knew, nobody said. In the 1960s radio comedy series *Round the Horne*, Julian and Sandy (Hugh Paddick and Kenneth Williams respectively) emerged in every episode to be quizzed by the bemused straight man Kenneth Horne; not only were Julian and Sandy unmistakably gay – at a time when homosexual acts between men were illegal – but they also employed a handful of terms from Polari, a form of slang that was characteristic of gay subculture (e.g. *bona* for good, *varda* for see). This was a daring move for a show broadcast around Sunday lunchtime, and in an era when families still sat down together to eat a roast dinner with the radio – or wireless – on in the background. In a peculiar example of British doublethink, Julian and Sandy were the most popular creations on *Round the Horne* at the same time as young policemen were acting as agents provocateurs to entrap homosexuals out 'cottaging' in public lavatories.

In TV sitcoms – the natural home for mass-audience camp – what would now be seen as stereotyping or even homophobia wasn't necessarily explicit. The very long-running BBC series *Are You Being Served?* was set in an old-style department store, and it was fuelled by double entendres. No one who saw the show, which also acquired a devoted following in America, is likely to forget the formidable purple-haired Mrs Slocombe of the Ladies Department, as played by Mollie Sugden, and a woman whose main concern in life was the welfare of her cat

Tiddles ('My pussy got soaking wet. I had to dry it out in front of the fire before I left'; 'At 7 o'clock tonight, my pussy's expecting to see a friendly face'). An equally popular figure was the menswear assistant Mr Humphries with his trademark cry of 'I'm free', when asked to serve a customer. In John Inman's hands Mr Humphries became an unthreatening and endearing version of the gay man, more than acceptable to mid-evening television audiences, even if some in the gay community objected to this stereotype of a limp-wristed, mincing character. Like Mollie Sugden, Inman had the knack of delivering his lines with an absolutely straight face, even when the double entendres were stacked high: 'I had just bent down to tighten my nuts, and there was a double yellow line, see. And next thing I knew, there was a policeman behind me. He put a sticker on my helmet and tried to clamp me.'

Yet this gay-but-not-gay act wasn't universally popular within the BBC. While Mrs Slocombe's pussy remarks passed without objection – after all, she's only talking about her cat Tiddles, and anything else is in your dirty mind – Mr Humphries's hand on hip posture and his eagerness to take inside-leg measurements didn't leave much room for ambiguity. A senior BBC official took such a dislike to the character that he told one of the co-writers, David Croft, to 'get rid of the poof'. Croft replied: 'If the poof goes, I go.' The p-word wasn't used on

Are You Being Served?, though one would have heard it elsewhere on television at the time, for example in a *Two Ronnies* sketch ('Have you any proof, you old poof?').

The word certainly appeared in the red tops or tabloid press, as it was then known. The *Sun*, under Kelvin MacKenzie's editorship, was obsessed with 'poofs' and 'poofters' and ran lengthy articles smearing Elton John, the chat-show host Russell Harty and the gay rights campaigner Peter Tatchell among others. This despite the admonitory comment to an earlier editor from Australian proprietor Rupert Murdoch soon after he'd bought the paper in 1969: 'Do you really think our readers are really interested in poofters?' (quoted in Peter Chippindale and Chris Horrie's *Stick It Up Your Punter! The Uncut Story of the Sun Newspaper*, 1990).

Things had evidently changed by the 1980s when MacKenzie was in the editor's chair. Public opinion, which had been gradually growing more tolerant, was negatively swayed by the emergence of HIV/AIDS and newspapers followed suit. Poofters were everywhere, even – perhaps especially – in the Church of England, and they needed to be outed and harried. In 1987 when the Church Synod was agonising over the issue of the clergy and homosexuality, the result of the debate was summarised in MacKenzie's headline: PULPIT POOFS CAN STAY. The drive to 'uncover' gays in public institutions, as well as in show-business, was unceasing. It was reminiscent of earlier

Reds-under-the-bed campaigns in the US. Another *Sun* headline from 1987 trumpeted SIXTY-FIVE MPS ARE POOF-TERS (REVEALS ONE WHO IS). When in 1990 the newspaper was ticked off for its homophobic attitude by the Press Council (predecessor to what is now the Independent Press Standards Organisation), its response was a characteristic two-fingered one: 'We know a great deal more about how ordinary people think, act and speak. Readers of The Sun KNOW and SPEAK and WRITE words like poof and poofter. What is good enough for them is good enough for us.'

It would take another eight years and, in the case of the *Sun*, a different editor altogether for the pendulum to swing back towards tolerance. Although by this time the 'poofter' had largely disappeared from the headlines there was still the itch to expose 'gays', while a belief that a 'gay mafia' was pulling the strings behind the scenes of British public life preoccupied tabloids such as the *Mirror* and the *Sun*'s stablemate, the *News of the World*. But in 1998 after the outing of a couple of ministers in Tony Blair's government, the tone suddenly changed. In an online BBC interview in July 2012 David Yelland, who was *Sun* editor at the time, explained: 'That was the turning point for me as an editor. I immediately felt ashamed that I had allowed the [gay mafia] story in and I wrote an editorial the next day saying that in future the *Sun* would no longer invade the privacy of gay people by outing them.'

But this reversal wasn't entirely a matter of scruple. As Yelland went on to say: 'The gay mafia story felt wrong to me but I also believe it was out of step with the public, who were becoming far more tolerant and accepting of gay people.'

Climate change

Just as the tone and language of the news media influence public opinion – though perhaps not as much as the media like to imagine – so does public opinion operate on what stories are selected, how they're presented and what language is used by them. There's no doubt that, as more and more figures in British public life came out as gay in the closing years of the twentieth century, familiarity grew and, with it, came acceptance. Not universal but enough to mark a real change in the cultural climate. If the reaction to the news is a shrug of indifference, then the news is no longer news. The passing of various 'hate speech' laws in England and Wales from the late 1980s onward also contributed to the shift in public mood. Initially these laws were directed at expressions of racial hatred but in 2008 they were extended to apply to people and groups stirring up hatred on the grounds of religion or sexual orientation. Although there were, and continue to be, complaints about the infringement on liberty and free speech that these laws are supposed to embody, they inevitably have an influence on attitudes and behaviour. And then after a few years have gone by most people look back and wonder what the fuss was about. There would be few votes now for a party campaigning to restore smoking in public places or to abolish compulsory seatbelt wearing in cars, yet laws bringing in both these changes were resisted at the time because they encroached on individual choice and liberty. The 'hate speech' laws are more complex and contested, and do raise genuine issues of freedom of speech, but they have undoubtedly helped to shift the public outlook on homosexuality as well as race and other matters.

This change, both in the media and in the public view, is well illustrated by a story from the *Sun* – once again! – appearing at the beginning of 2018. The attention-grabbing BUS ABUSE was accompanied by a single large-type sentence: 'Will Young claims London bus driver called him a "poofter" and pleads for help to track him down' (9 January 2018). Now the newspaper's tone is one of indignation, not at 'poofters', but that the *Pop Idol* star has been on the receiving end of 'homophobic abuse'. It's significant that the offending headline expression, 'poofter', is fenced off in quote marks – not our word, guv, but someone else's (hate) speech. There are phone line and email details at the paper for anyone who was on the bus and wants to report in and share the outrage. The attitude is shared by the authorities. TfL (Transport for London) responded instantly: 'Hi Will, I am so sorry to see this . . . The behaviour you described is unacceptable.'

For anyone who remembers the Britain of thirty or forty years ago, at least as represented by its newspapers or its bus companies, this 2018 reaction represents a significant and welcome reverse. When once you might be pilloried for being a 'poofter', now you can be pilloried and taken to court for calling someone else a 'poofter'. The BBC executive who once told David Croft to 'get rid of the poof' from *Are You Being Served?* has had his wish fulfilled in the sense that the word no longer has any place in public discourse. Where once TV stars like Kenneth Williams or Frankie Howerd were reluctant to come out, their contemporary equivalents such as Julian Clary or Graham Norton or Paul O'Grady have had no problem at all. In truth, they were never in. The only context in which 'poof' is acceptable now is when it's used for self-mocking self-definition. Thus a staple on Jonathan Ross's BBC One chat-show for several years was the house band who call themselves, with limiting accuracy, 4 Poofs and a Piano.

In a similar way to 'poof' and its variants but much more significantly from a cultural and linguistic point of view, 'queer' has been turned from a term of abuse to a badge of identity. Like several deprecatory terms, 'queer' seems to have originated in the US. For most of its one hundred and more years in the homosexual category, 'queer' was a negative term. Once again, the Marquess of Queensberry comes in handy for linguistic evidence since he wrote a letter to his son Bosie in which he condemned the 'Snob Queers like Rosebery' (Lord Rosebery, briefly Prime Minister in the 1890s, was reputed to be bisexual). With 'queer' the older and mildly pejorative meanings of 'odd', 'peculiar' and 'suspicious' seemed to coexist with the gay sense, so that applying the word was a way of hinting at the subsidiary meaning without explicitly having to state it. Just as displays of homosexual style were either suppressed outright or could only be shown in an approved nudge-and-wink style by licensed entertainers, so too did language become coded or ambiguous. It's another example of the way in which the words we choose to use – or more accurately the ones at our disposal – tell a story by reflecting the culture around us. So for many years 'queer' was legitimate because it both did and didn't mean the thing it seemed to mean.

At the end of *Down and Out in Paris and London* (1933) George Orwell talked about the conclusions he'd come to after many months spent living and working among some of the poorest people in the two capital cities. Chapter 36 begins: 'I want to set down some general remarks about tramps. When one comes to think of it, tramps are a queer product and worth thinking over. It is queer that a tribe of men, tens of thousands in number, should be marching up and down England like so many Wandering Jews.'

Orwell, concerned to stress 'the extraordinarily futile, acutely unpleasant life' of the tramp, apparently means 'queer' in its primary sense of odd, peculiar. Yet his image of a 'tribe of men . . . marching up and down England' can't help but foreshadow the secondary gay sense. This is confirmed when he refers to the fact that destitute men outnumber destitute women very heavily (about ten to one, according to a 1931 statistic which he cites). Consequently, says Orwell, the tramp is 'absolutely without hope of getting a wife, a mistress, or any kind of woman except – very rarely, when he can raise a few shillings – a prostitute'. So, he continues, it 'is obvious what the results of this must be: homosexuality, for instance, and occasional rape cases'. If he merely hinted at the sexual queerness of tramps, Orwell was more explicit when he referred in later life to the London literary scene and its often homosexual cabals, particularly what he termed in print the 'pansy left'.

Even a writer much more in sympathy with gay culture such as Evelyn Waugh seems to elide the odd and gay senses of 'queer', often deliberately. In his most famous novel, *Brideshead Revisited* (1945), 'queer' crops up on around eight occasions. Several of them seem to hint at the gay sense, as when the alcoholic charmer Sebastian is referred to as 'a queer old character'. Others are ambiguous, as when the father of the narrator, Charles Ryder, says to his son: 'Your cousin Melchior was imprudent with his investments and got into a very queer street.* He went to Australia.' More explicit is the language of Anthony Blanche, the campest character in the novel and one based on Brian Howard, a friend of Waugh's from his time at Oxford: 'there were some rather queer fish, my dear, in and out of my little apartment. Who knows better than you my taste for queer fish?' All this suggests that Waugh was playing around with the word, teasingly acknowledging its slang or secondary meaning.

But if 'queer' seems somehow to be held at a distance for most of the twentieth century, it comes into its own around the late 1980s. Rather as 'nigger' or 'nigga' was appropriated by some blacks, particularly in America, so too 'queer' became in parts of the gay community an expression worth not just reclaiming but, as it were, proclaiming. 'Queer theory' emerged in US academic circles and 'queer history' became a course of study in several British universities. In 1999, Channel 4 started a series about the lives of three gay men in Manchester. Notably unapologetic and explicit

---

* 'In queer street' – i.e. in difficulties, especially financial ones – predates the gay sense of queer. 'To queer someone's pitch' – i.e. to spoil their plans – similarly comes from the early nineteenth century and refers to the way a street seller or market trader's 'pitch' or spot could be intruded on by a rival shouting louder, undercutting him, etc. It also had the sense in the theatre of 'upstage'.

for its time, *Queer as Folk* was a play on the northern saying 'there's nowt so queer as folk' as well as the expression 'queer as fuck'.

There are several ways in which 'bad words' can lose their sting. One is when they simply become outdated, as with the oaths and swearing invoking Christ's body, which were common in the medieval era and later. Another is through sheer repetition, with the result that what at first prompted an outcry becomes so every day that it scarcely registers with most people, even if they wouldn't use those expressions themselves; into this category fall words such as 'shit' and 'fuck', discussed at length elsewhere in this book. The third category includes 'nigger' and 'queer', once terms of opprobrium but then taken up by members of the very groups that were being stigmatised. It's not exactly that the words have become domesticated, rather they are like weapons that have been captured and turned against the original users. Even so there's a caveat. (Some) blacks and gays can and do employ 'nigger' and 'queer', but the non-black or non-gay user is likely to run into trouble if heard saying them in a public context.

Bitter sweet

The overarching and acceptable expression now to replace all those older and derogatory terms to do with homosexuality is 'gay'. It's an interesting term because it has within the space of a few years made the transition from the general to the particular, a reversal of the more usual pattern whereby words spread out by moving from a specialist area into general use, as for example with computer terminology. 'Gay' has been around for a long time. In the Middle Ages it signified something bright and colourful, especially clothing, and soon extended to someone cheerful and high-spirited. Geoffrey Chaucer uses it in both senses in *The Canterbury Tales*: the Yeoman, one of the Canterbury pilgrims, is described as wearing both a 'gay bracer' (wristguard) and a 'gay daggere'; another pilgrim, the much-married Wife of Bath, talks of her fourth husband and how 'in her bed he was so fressh and gay . . . /Whan that he wolde han my bele chose' ('When he would have my pretty thing', a euphemism for what she elsewhere calls her 'queynte', itself, as discussed, a euphemism for 'cunt').

Although 'gay' could sometimes suggest being a bit too exuberant or frivolous, and even enjoyed a life on the side as a slang reference to a prostitute ('a gay lady'), it is the more innocent sense of 'cheerful' that prevails from the medieval period until well into the twentieth century. For example, there was certainly no alternative meaning in the mind of Harry Graham who wrote the lyrics for the operetta *The Maid of the Mountains*, which premiered in Manchester in 1916 and included a number called

'Bachelor Gay'. It begins: 'A bachelor gay am I, though I suffer from Cupid's dart/But never I vow will I say die in spite of an aching heart.' But a few years later Noël Coward composed his operetta *Bitter Sweet* (1929), which celebrates the 1890s, and included a song titled '(We All Wear a) Green Carnation'. A handful of lines run: 'Art is our inspiration,/And as we are the reason for the "Nineties" being gay,/We all wear a green carnation.' As with 'queer' in other contexts there may be some elision between the standard sense and the more covert one in Coward's lyrics, but the *OED* offers it as early evidence for the homosexual sense of gay.

An even earlier one comes in a 1923 story by Gertrude Stein, 'Miss Furr and Miss Skeene'. Closer to a poem than a conventional piece of prose, it makes repeated use of 'gay' to describe the life and style of the two women of the title who seemingly live together for a time before going their separate ways. A sample passage reads: 'They stayed in a place and were gay there, both of them stayed there, they stayed together there, they were gay there, they were regularly gay there.' Stein's repetition of the word, some 130 times in the space of a few pages, invests it with a peculiar – and faintly monotonous – power.

Later references in the 1930s and 1940s are unmistakeable, even if they suggest it's still a coded word. Once again America is the primary source. One writer in the early 1940s offers the advice that if you want to find out whether a stranger travelling on the train* from Boston to New York is homosexual then you should casually drop the question 'Are there any gay spots in Boston?' putting a slight emphasis on 'gay'; the stranger will understand that the reference is to 'homosexual resorts'.

Despite all this it was still quite feasible to use 'gay' in its old sense. Evelyn Waugh has already been quoted for his ambiguous deployment of 'queer' in *Brideshead Revisited*, yet he uses 'gay' several times in the same novel and never with any inkling of the newer meaning ('returning home, [I] found Sebastian there and the sense of tragedy vanished, for he was gay and free as when I first met him.'). So when did people first realise they had to be a little bit careful about the application of gay? Even to answer that question you'd have to be in your sixties or older, because the shift seems to have occurred sometime during the late 1960s or early 1970s. That's when the word came out in its current sense. The Gay Liberation Front emerged in New York in 1969. But such is the osmotic

---

* One of Alfred Hitchcock's most distinguished films from his mid-American period was *Strangers on a Train* (1951). It concerns two young men who, during a chance encounter on a train, discuss the idea of 'exchanging' murders so that each should have no apparent motive for killing the victim. The relationship between the two, played by Farley Granger and Robert Walker, has rightly been characterised as homoerotic and the film praised as a 'queer film classic'.

way in which new words and new meanings seep into public consciousness that it is impossible to pin down a moment or even a period of a couple of years on one side of which 'being gay' meant one thing in general usage and, on the other side, something else.

In his highly entertaining and revealing book *A Very English Scandal* (2016), John Preston records the following conversation in February 1965 in the House of Commons dining room between Liberal MPs Jeremy Thorpe and Peter Bessell. Bessell, pretending to have homosexual leanings, is trying to pin down the rumours about Thorpe's own sexuality, a very sensitive subject given that a) homosexuality was still illegal and b) Thorpe was a prospective leader of the Liberal Party. After a bit of waltzing round the subject, Thorpe asks Bessell whether he'd describe himself as 50/50:

"No," said Bessell hurriedly. "I would say more like 80/20."

"Do you mean 80 or 20 per cent gay?" Thorpe asked.

'Bessell had never heard the expression "gay" before and it took him a moment or two to work out what Thorpe meant.

"I mean 80 per cent for girls," he said.

"Really? It's the other way with me," said Thorpe. "I'm 80 per cent gay."

When Russell T. Davies, who also wrote the innovative *Queer as Folk* for Channel 4, adapted the book for the BBC in 2018 he added the line from Peter Bessell: 'Gosh, I'm not sure that word's ever been said within these walls before, not in that context.' The record of what Thorpe and Bessell discussed presumably comes from Bessell, and assuming it is accurate this moment in the Commons dining room early in 1965 is a useful indication of the shifting sense of 'gay'.

Years after the 1979 trial (and acquittal) of Jeremy Thorpe on the charges of incitement and conspiracy to murder his lover Norman Scott, there was resistance to the new application of 'gay'. As late as 1990 the *Sun*, huffing and puffing at Press Council strictures on homophobia, raised a semantic objection in an editorial: 'Incidentally, our dictionary defines gay as carefree, merry, brilliant. Does the Press Council approve of homosexuals appropriating such a fine old word?' The comment is ridiculous, of course, but the paper was far from alone in feeling that some kind of hijacking or appropriation was involved in this fresh application of gay. At the root of this, I think, was a feeling that gays didn't deserve to be, well, gay. Maybe they couldn't help being like that but, if so, they ought at least to be long-faced about it. Grudgingly, resisters might even concede that homosexuals had the right to be out, but did they have to be so proud – and cheerful – about it as well? For the *Sun* and other hold-outs, gay turned from a 'fine old word' into a bad one.

Yet the disconnection between 'gay' and 'gayness', in the older senses, and the reality of homosexual life, especially in the years before the law was changed but in the years immediately afterwards too, had hardly escaped other observers, including some who were in a much better position than tabloid pontificators to judge the appropriateness of the term. From the beginning they at least were alert to its potential ironies. *The Boys in the Band*, Matt Crowley's ground-breaking gay play first staged off-Broadway in 1968, contained the line very near the end: 'You show me a happy homosexual and I'll show you a gay corpse.' When Clive Barnes, the make-or-break reviewer for the *New York Times*, went back to look at the play again the following year his piece was headed: 'THE BOYS IN THE BAND' IS STILL A SAD GAY ROMP. In fact, what is most apparent now is the assumption threaded through the play that gay life wasn't – couldn't be – really gay in the old sense. Whatever else it might be, homosexuality was not something which made for a happy life. Being gay was at best, to use the title of Noël Coward's operetta, a bittersweet business. That this now seems a dated, almost patronising assumption is a sign of how far things have changed.

One of the great conveniences of 'gay' is that it is gender neutral. The slang and/or derogatory terms for gay women are few in number compared to the male ones: 'lez/lezza' was the usual abbreviation for lesbian, a word apparently not in use before the early twentieth century, in addition to the forthright 'dike/dyke' (1940s) and 'butch' (1950s) to describe a masculine woman. And for a more markedly masculine woman 'bull dyke' and 'diesel dyke', both originating in the US, would do. If gay hasn't quite swept these terms away, any more than it has swept 'homo', 'poofter' and 'fairy' away, it has nevertheless driven such old and disparaging expressions to the margins, and given everyone, whether straight or gay, a word that (almost) everyone can agree on.

'The nastiest word in the English language'

ANTHONY A. WILLIAMS was only the fourth person to hold the post of Mayor of Washington, DC, when he was voted into office at the end of 1998. Only the fourth because until the early 1970s, and the passing of a Home Rule Act that took control out of the hands of the United States Congress, the citizens of the most powerful city in the world had no say over who governed them directly from day to day. Like his predecessors as Mayor, Williams was black but within a few weeks of his inauguration there were questions about whether, in the headline phrase of a column in the *Washington Post*, he was 'black enough'.

Williams had earned a name for efficiency as the District of Columbia's Chief Financial Officer but some saw him as too willing to cut jobs and budgets in a city with a substantial black majority population. Nor can his critics have been pacified or reassured when, on his first day in office, he appointed four white men to senior positions. One of the four was David Howard, a key organiser during the mayoral campaign, who now found himself running an agency that responded to residents' complaints about public services, a kind of ombudsman. David Howard had a budget for the job but, mindful of economic constraints, he made a precautionary remark to several associates during a meeting in January 1999. He said that he would have to be 'niggardly' over how he deployed the budget.

Niggardly.

An adjective deriving from niggard, meaning 'miser'. Niggard, a noun that probably originates in an old Scandinavian tongue. Niggard and niggardly, a couple of related words that have been in the English language for more than five centuries and which now sound dated, even affected. A pair of words that, unfortunately for the Washington ombudsman, are quite close in sound and spelling to the abusive term 'nigger', which, as we will see below, has an entirely different etymological root. The n-word – a term that was once a more or less stand-ard piece of slang in the USA, and beyond, but which is now highly offensive and even taboo. According to one of the prosecutors in the O. J. Simpson murder trial, it is 'the dirtiest, filthiest, nastiest word in the English language'. So toxic or radioactive has the n-word turned that it is capable of contaminating any other term that comes close to it, for example a term that has a similar sound or look.

A few days after David Howard had commented on how his Washington agency would have to be careful with money, rumours began to circulate that he had used the notorious n-word. In fact, Howard must have realised his mistake the moment 'niggardly' was out of his mouth. Whatever precise reactions – looks? sounds of surprise? – he got from the others in his office it was enough to make him apologise on the spot and say that he would never even think of making a racist remark. Howard's awareness of a minority position may have been heightened by the fact that he was a prominent member of the Washington gay community.

But he felt compromised enough by the uproar which followed to resign within ten days, saying that he could no longer do his job effectively. Mayor Williams, perhaps conscious of those earlier accusations of 'disloyalty' to the black community, at once accepted the resignation. The Mayor knew that David Howard never intended any insult, that he had in effect been misunderstood, but he still criticised his aide's carelessness. 'I liken it to, here we are in a refinery and you shouldn't smoke in a refinery,' he said. 'I think what David did was get caught smoking in a refinery, which would result in an explosion.' For his part, Howard was generous in accepting the rebuke, pointing out that it was his decision to quit and saying that a white person 'doesn't have to think about race every day. An African American does.'

This was long before Twitter but the storm in Washington spread across the US via radio, TV and the newspapers. It was a gift to the anti-political-correctness brigade. It encouraged mocking speculation about what word or phrase would be the next to turn toxic because it seemed to contain a racial innuendo (spic 'n' span? chink in the armour?). Although almost every commentator defended the use of niggardly and, either directly or by implication, attacked the excessive sensitivity or the straightforward ignorance of those who'd kicked up a fuss, there was a universal reluctance to actually use the word that was so close to niggard. Instead it was referred to as a 'racial epithet' or a 'slur'. So the entire controversy unfolded without the word 'nigger' ever being used in any public forum, let alone by the inadvertent offender.

Julian Bond, then the chairman of the NAACP (National Association for the Advancement of Colored People), opted for the direct approach when he said, 'You hate to think you have to censor your language to meet other people's lack of understanding. David Howard should not have quit. Mayor Williams should bring him back – and order dictionaries issued to all staff who need them.' The Mayor did have second thoughts. Within a few days of Howard's resignation he referred to having acted in haste by accepting it, and both men started to talk about a new post in Washington local government. In future, Howard said, he'd use the word 'parsimonious'.

This was not to be the last word on niggardly, however. Shortly after the Washington incident, a black student at the University of Wisconsin complained that her professor had several times employed the term – in a discussion on a Chaucer poem – even though he was aware it offended her. He then used her reaction as a springboard for a debate with his class on the implications of language. The furore that resulted ended in the repeal of the university's faculty speech code, an already contentious attempt to control and discipline 'offensive speech'. The outcome was different in a North Carolina school where a teacher was reprimanded and sent on sensitivity training when a parent complained about her use of the word in class, also in a literary discussion. (If the word has a natural place, it is surely in a literary discussion.)

After such exposure, can niggardly ever be uttered aloud again? Yes – or yes probably – but only if the speaker were sure of their audience. Sure that listeners wouldn't take offence. Sure that they could understand the proper, long-standing meaning of the word. Which tends to cut down the potential audiences. And, after all, it takes a certain kind of person to think of using niggardly as well as a certain kind of audience to listen to it. In the niggardly affair there were claims that political correctness was killing off words, although it would be more true to say that an obscure word was being brought out of the shadows. The uproar most likely made more people aware of it than at any time in history. Equally likely, a few of those people would have used it for a time as an insult. Niggard and niggardly are insulting by definition, of course, but now the words came with racist stickers that have nothing to do with dictionaries and etymology. These terms, with their medieval English pedigrees, turned dangerous. Neither can any longer be used innocently, as David Howard had believed he was speaking with innocent intent in his Washington office. If you do use the term, at least if you hold a public post (teacher, administrator, politician), then you are culpably naive. You should know better.

Not all of the consequences of the niggardly storm were negative. It's likely that it was one of the inspirations behind Philip Roth's novel *The Human Stain* (2000). At the start of the narrative the principal character, a university professor, loses his job because of a careless use of the term 'spooks', referring to a couple of persistent absentees to class. ('Does anyone know these people? Do they exist or are they spooks?') He forgets that spooks is an old disparaging term for blacks, which these students happen to be.

The furore over niggardly reflects the extreme toxicity in America of the n-word, a euphemistic formulation that was first recorded in 1985. But before glancing at the history of the word itself, it's worth noting that the term is now almost as contentious and taboo in the United Kingdom as it is in the United States. In July 2017, Anne Marie Morris, the MP for Newton Abbot in Devon, was recorded as saying during the launch of a report into the future of the UK's financial sector after Brexit: 'Now I'm sure there will be many people who'll challenge that, but my response and my request is look at the detail, it isn't all doom and gloom. Now we get to the real nigger in the woodpile,* which is, in two years what happens if there is no deal?' (quoted in the *Guardian*, 11 July 2017). There was general uproar and on the orders of the Prime Minister, Theresa May, she had the whip withdrawn, the parliamentary equivalent of excommunication. Even those who objected more to the response to the MP's words, rather than what she said, conceded that she'd been 'dim' or 'stupid' in her careless use of an old and racist metaphor. A few years earlier Lord Dixon-Smith, a Conservative member of the House of Lords, used the phrase during a debate about housing and was gently admonished by a fellow Tory: 'My Lords, before my noble friend sits down, he used a phrase about a woodpile. If your Lordships'

---

* The meaning of the phrase – referring to a concealed and unwelcome complication in a situation – is plain but the origin isn't completely clear. It may relate to fugitive slaves escaping from the American deep south and hiding in piles of wood, possibly as the lumber was being transported north by railroad.

House were happy, I think it would perhaps be helpful if the wording of the phrase were revised.' Lord Dixon-Smith replied: 'I apologise, my Lords. I left my brains behind. I apologise to the House.' Later he said: 'It was common parlance when I was younger, put it that way.' The then Tory leader, David Cameron, faced calls for the peer to be disciplined.

And Then There Were None

'Nigger' derives from negro or neger, and comes via French and Spanish ultimately from the Latin *niger* (black). On its first recorded appearance more than four hundred years ago, and for at least a couple of centuries thereafter, it seems to have been a neutral term. From the middle of the nineteenth century, it became a term of abuse or contempt when uttered by white people (though not necessarily when said by blacks). Sometimes it was used descriptively or metaphorically, rather than as an insult, but it was still used and it went on being used for a long time. That is, the word could be spoken or written in some contexts without apparent embarrassment or discomfort. Agatha Christie has a character in one of her Hercule Poirot novels say, 'He worked you like a nigger – and who pocketed all the fat fees?' (*One, Two, Buckle My Shoe*, 1940), and such uses are far from infrequent in writing at the time and after. In current editions of the Christie novel the wording is changed to 'He worked you like a dog – and who pocketed all the fat fees?'

The word was not confined to the page. Michael Anderson, the director of the classic British war film *The Dam Busters* (1955), was such a stickler for accuracy that he refused to contemplate any change to 'Nigger', the name of the black Labrador belonging to Wing Commander Guy Gibson and the mascot of Gibson's dam-busting 617 Squadron. The dog was far from incidental to the action: its death in a road accident shortly before the raid gave Richard Todd, playing Gibson, the opportunity to show a stiff upper lip as he contemplated the now useless dog lead, and 'Nigger' was the codeword used to signal the success of the operation. Yet the name was (slightly) problematic in Britain even in the mid-1950s and the dog was turned into Trigger for the film's American release. In a proposed remake, to be directed by Peter Jackson and scripted by Stephen Fry but yet to go into production, the dog is to be called Digger. When the original film was shown on Film 4 on the seventy-fifth anniversary of the raid it was preceded by a 'warning' about the language and fidelity to history.

The *Shorter Oxford English Dictionary*, first published in 1933 but frequently revised and reprinted, glosses the n-word in its 1968 edition as 'Colloq[uial] and usu[ally] contempt' (i.e. in contemptuous use). But contemporary English dictionaries don't just signal the attitude behind the word, they highlight its poisonous freight. 'Strongly racially offensive when used by a white person in reference to a black person,' says the current online edition of the *OED*, while the 13th edition of *Chambers Dictionary* (2014) says 'offensive, often taboo'.

Unsurprisingly, given the country's charged racial history, the shift in the n-word from a kind of rough acceptability to a state of offensiveness and then to outright taboo occurred earlier in the US than in Britain. In 1936 the body that administered the segregated 'Negro public schools' in Washington warned against the 'adoption of any textbook, basic or supplementary, magazine, or periodical known to make use of the term N----- in its publication.' This was directed at black authors and publishers, since 'white authors . . . making use of such material have [already] been refused for adoption in our public schools'.

The problems with this word come together in an almost inextricable knot in Mark Twain's *Huckleberry Finn* (1884), a novel which rightly has a central place in American literary culture (Ernest Hemingway said, 'American writing comes from that. There was nothing before. There has been nothing as good since'). But the novel has also long been the country's most problematic classic. The reason is not the friendship between young Huck Finn, escaping down the Mississippi River on a raft from a violent drunken father, and the runaway slave Jim, who becomes a substitute father to the poor but resourceful white boy. It is the repeated use of 'nigger' in the novel, on more than two hundred occasions by one reckoning. Twain was the opposite of a racist and he frequently deploys the word ironically to expose the shallowness, insensitivity and unthinking double standards of the white characters, as when Huck's Aunt Sally asks if anyone was hurt in a steamboat explosion and Huck himself replies, 'No'm. Killed a nigger,' to which Sally says, 'Well, it's lucky; because sometimes people do get hurt.'

Despite its impeccable credentials, *Huckleberry Finn* has caused problems since its publication.* At first, this

---

* Even before *Huckleberry Finn* was published, advance copies of the book had to be hurriedly withdrawn. Twain, dissatisfied with the way his previous books had been published and promoted, set up his own company to sell the book by subscription, employing door-to-door salesmen. A Chicago salesman with an early copy of the book spotted an unfortunate emendation to one of the woodcut illustrations: Uncle Silas, with Aunt Sally at his side, is addressing Huck. He is also sporting a discreet erection. No one knew who was responsible or the motive for the addition. Panic followed the discovery. Production was halted, the offending plate removed, and weeks lost before a cleaned-up edition was available. The story got about, with the *New York World* describing how a 'mere stroke of the awl would suffice to give the [wood]cut an indecent character never intended by the author or engraver'. The delay meant that the book missed its scheduled publication for Christmas 1884. Even so Twain and Huck most likely benefited from the extra publicity.

deeply moral novel was taken to task for its (lack of) morality. A ban by the public library in Concord, Massachusetts, in 1885 provoked a gleeful letter from Twain: 'They have expelled Huck from their library as "trash and suitable only for the slums." That will sell 25,000 copies for us sure.' More absurdly, Brooklyn Public Library banned the book in 1902 with the comment that 'Huck was a deceitful boy; that he not only itched but scratched' and that he said 'sweat' when he should have said 'perspiration'. Rumbles about the low-life characters and the demotic language growled across the next half century. But the real trouble started in 1957 when the New York City Board of Education removed it from its approved list of textbooks because it was 'racially offensive'. Ever since, the inclusion of *Huckleberry Finn* in school libraries has been 'challenged' in some states by parents in accordance with their right to keep what they regard as unsuitable material away from their children. The book has been banned outright. And it has been issued in versions that have been toned down or bowdlerised, most recently in a 2011 edition, which substituted 'slave' for 'nigger', and also replaced 'injun' with 'Indian', and 'half-breed' with 'half-blood'. The editor, Twain scholar Alan Gribben, explained that in reading sections of the text aloud to students he had 'found himself recoiling from uttering the racial slurs in the words of the young protagonists'. Gribben and his edition were attacked but his intention was not so much to censor as to make *Huckleberry Finn* easier to get at. In this he was acting similarly to Thomas Bowdler who in the early nineteenth century produced a cleaned-up edition of Shakespeare – that is, one without the oaths, suggestive puns and sexual innuendo – which would be suitable for consumption by the whole family.

Another classic work, Joseph Conrad's *The Nigger of the 'Narcissus'* (1896), hasn't attracted so much attention. This story of a merchant ship and its crew, including the single black member James Wait, on a voyage from Bombay to London is seen as Conrad's first significant work. In the US it was published as *The Children of the Sea: A Tale of the Forecastle*, a change of title insisted on by the American publishers not because of any racial sensitivity but because they believed that a book featuring a black man in the title would not sell. In 2009 a Netherlands-based publisher issued an 'accessible' version of the novel titled *The N-word of the Narcissus*. The publicity around the change drew attention to the project but there was more mockery than approval.

The taboo attaching to 'nigger' came much later in Britain, as suggested by the title tweaks and changes that affected one of Agatha Christie's best known whodunnits. *And Then There Were None* was serialised under that title in the US in 1939 while it was issued almost simultaneously in the UK as *Ten Little Niggers*. The famous story of ten strangers lured to an isolated island off the Devon coast where they are murdered one by one also appeared in later versions as *Ten Little Indians*, arguably a slightly less offensive variant on the original. All three titles come from the old children's rhyme that is central to the plot. In addition, in the British edition the action took place on Nigger Island (in fact, Burgh Island, which Christie also used as the setting for the Hercule Poirot novel *Evil Under the Sun*), so called because of the head-like profile of the island. This is changed in current editions to Soldier Island.

In retrospect it seems astonishing that Christie's bestseller continued to be issued in the UK under its first title until at least the late 1970s. Yet a fairly casual attitude towards race and stereotyping was widespread in Britain during that era. Earlier in the same decade Alan Coren, the editor of *Punch*, produced weekly bulletins purportedly written by Idi Amin, the murderous leader of Uganda. Although these spoofed a figure who'd become a major irritant to the British government, part of their widespread appeal was that it legitimated laughter at supposed ethnic ignorance ('Accommerdation apart, we offerin' a lot of interestin' sights in Kampala and environs, such as watchin' de changin' of de guard, which is where de incomin' lot turnin' up every mornin' at eleven a.m. an' shootin' de outgoin' lot'). It wasn't until 1978 that *The Black and White Minstrel Show*, in which white male singers performed American country songs while facially made up as blacks, was finally removed from the BBC Saturday night schedule. Little more than ten years before, in 1965, Laurence Olivier put on film his celebrated stage version of *Othello*, blacking both his face *and body*,* adopting a deep voice and donning a 'a wig of kinky black hair' to play the lead part. The film reviewer in the *New York Times* compared Olivier's *Othello* to 'an end man in an American minstrel show' adding that 'You almost wait for him to whip a banjo out from his flowing, white garments or start banging a tambourine.' As late as 1990 Michael Gambon blacked up to play the part at Scarborough Theatre. All this suggests that, compared to their US counterparts, the British media were slow to appreciate the change in attitudes towards racist language and stereotyping.

Indeed, in America, even a favourable reference to the long-discredited practice of 'black-facing' will cause problems, as NBC's Megyn Kelly discovered when she remarked on her morning show in October 2018: 'What is racism? Because, truly, you do get into trouble if you are a white person who puts on blackface on Halloween, or a

---

* It was Raymond Chandler who said, in a throwaway comment in his essay 'The Simple Art of Murder' (1950), that putting on all-over black body make-up for *Othello* was the mark of a ham actor. But then there was always quite a bit of ham in Olivier.

black person who puts on whiteface for Halloween. Back when I was a kid, that was like, OK, as long as you were dressing up as like a character . . . I can't keep up with the number of normal people we're offending just by being normal people' (quoted on Slate.com, 25 October 2018). Kelly, formerly an anchor on the right-wing Fox News who shifted to the more centrist NBC after a spat with Donald Trump during the 2015–16 presidential campaign (see the 'PC Snowflake' chapter), later apologised on air but even so her already uncertain tenure at the channel became even shakier.

Can we borrow that word?

The n-word has sometimes been appropriated to apply to whites or other groups, usually because of their down-trodden or impoverished status. 'Woman is the Nigger of the World' is the title of a John Lennon and Yoko Ono song from a 1972 album. 'White nigger' was a slur, one among many, used about the Irish by British troops during the Troubles. A trip to Belfast in 1978 was the prompt for Elvis Costello to write 'Oliver's Army', which includes the lines 'Only takes one itchy trigger,/One more widow, one less white nigger.' The expression ('a renegade and a white nigger') was used in 1969 about a Protestant editor of the *Irish Times* in a discussion between the British Ambassador to Ireland and a member of the

Times's board, though in this instance its meaning is closer to an 'Uncle Tom': that is, it was considered that the editor wasn't respecting the racial/cultural/national divide but was siding with the enemy's cause, the Irish Civil Rights movement of the late 1960s. There was consternation after this came to light in 2003 when the Ambassador's letter to London recounting the conversation was released under the thirty-year rule.*

Another, less glaring example of appropriation is the white deployment of 'nigger' as a sign of the user's hip coolness, of his maverick vibe. The self-identification of some whites with blacks and black culture dates back at least to 1957 when Norman Mailer wrote an essay titled 'The White Negro: superficial reflections on the hipster'. The *Oxford English Dictionary* quotes from a 1971 book, *Positively Black* by Roger Abrahams: 'Hippies and other recent Bohemian groups have openly proclaimed themselves "white niggers"

---

* Records of cabinet meetings and other government business are confidential documents and only transferred to the National Archives after thirty years – the thirty-year rule. At this point most material is released to the public. But with the government deciding to release two years' worth of files every year since 2013, by 2022 the thirty-year rule will have turned into the twenty-year rule. Not everything is revealed. One of six files relating to the Profumo scandal of 1963 remains sealed at the National Archives in Kew and will not be made public until at least 2046, prompting intense speculation about what can possibly be in it.

by which they seem to mean that, like blacks, they represent an alternative to the lifestyle of majority-group American culture.' But this borrowing or theft of a disparaging term hasn't gone unchallenged.

Ageing white enfant terrible Quentin Tarantino has been involved in a decades-long feud with the black film director Spike Lee over the way in which Tarantino peppers his films with the word, rising to a peak of over 110 occurrences in the schlock slavery-fest *Django Unchained* (2012). Incidentally, it was this film that prompted the Sinn Fein president Gerry Adams to tweet 'Watching Django Unchained – A Ballymurphy Nigger!', a tweet quickly deleted but not before he'd drawn criticism for likening the plight of republicans in Northern Ireland to that of blacks in the USA. Over the years Tarantino has defended himself in characteristically aggressive style against charges that he overuses the word. For those interested, a full account can be found in an article by Rich Juzwiak on the Gawker website ('The Complete History of Quentin Tarantino Saying "Nigger"', 21 December 2015). Tarantino's probable motives, as catalogued by Juzwiak, seem convincing enough to apply to other white and professedly non-racist users of the n-word: it provokes taboo laughs, it is connected with 'a not entirely well-reasoned sense of activism', and (in Tarantino's case particularly) it fuels his reputation as 'a renegade artist'.

It may be that some contemporary white liberals simply enjoy the transgressive frisson of using the word, or putting it into the mouths of others, and that in doing this they imagine themselves to be appropriating the term from the wrong users (i.e. white racists) and sanitising it with a wrapper of irony or good intentions. Unfortunately, it's a see-through wrapper. The irony and the good intentions are lost. All that anyone sees, hears and remembers is 'nigger'.

There has long been a gap – more accurately, an abyss – between the acceptability of the term as used by white people and its deployment by blacks. Lucius Harper was the managing editor of the *Chicago Defender*, a weekly paper founded in 1905 and directed primarily at African-Americans. He observed as long ago as 1939: '[Nigger] is a common expression among the ordinary Negroes and is used frequently in conversation between them. It carries no odium or sting when used by themselves, but they object keenly to whites using it because it conveys the spirit of hate, discrimination and prejudice.' If Lucius Harper had been around three-quarters of a century later and watching a late-night British TV show he might have expressed himself less formally but would have had no reason to change his opinion.

The African-American comedian Chris Rock, appearing with Kate Winslet, Liam Gallagher and Idris Elba on BBC's *The Graham Norton Show* in October 2017, told a story about 'being at a club with Eddie Murphy . . . This girl comes up to Eddie and goes, "Eddie Murphy, I love you so much." It's a white girl. "I've never kissed a black man in my life. Can I please kiss you? Please, I just want to be able to say I've kissed a black man." Of course, Eddie's got this big entourage of thirty. And Eddie goes, "OK, OK. Let's get this straight. You can't start at the top. You gotta kiss some of these broke niggers first." ' The comment provoked plenty of Twitter comment, some of it negative with one user accurately observing 'imagine the shit storm if Liam Gallagher said it'. But Norton and his guests as well as his audience thought the story was hilarious. The BBC was evidently OK with the use of the n-word: the programme is pre-recorded so it could have been bleeped or muted, as Rock's use of 'fuck' in the same show was muted on the iPlayer catch-up service.

It was Chris Rock who in 1996 performed a stand-up riff-rant on 'Niggas vs. Black People'. Far from the most outrageous comment in the set was Rock's remark that 'niggas love to keep it real – real dumb'. The whole piece was an attack on one section of the US black minority and their low expectations, self-excuses and general ignorance, an attack which would have cause riots if uttered by a non-black comedian. Indeed, it's possible that the same routine performed now, more than twenty years later and in a climate that is in some respects less liberal, would provoke real trouble for the performer whatever his colour. Chris Rock said in an interview on CBS in February 2005: 'By the way, I've never done that joke again, ever, and I probably never will. Cause some people that were racist thought they had license to say n-----. So, I'm done with that routine.'

But the implication of the word, especially when written or pronounced as nigga, has been turned on its head in the world of rap or hip-hop. The trail leads from NGA (Niggaz Wit Attitudes), one of the most significant groups in the gangsta rap scene in the late 1980s, to a present-day rapper such as Nicki Minaj who uses 'nigga' over thirty times in her number 'Lookin Ass' (originally titled 'Lookin Ass Nigga'). A word that in its nigger spelling originally defined, deprecated and confined the people it was describing is now a badge of honour – and a brand. The difference between the two spellings was explained by rapper Tupac Shakur in an interview: 'Niggers was the ones on the rope, hanging off the thing; niggas is the ones with gold ropes, hanging out at clubs.'

To adopt a language that is more technical but less colourful than Tupac's, what's occurring here is a process that linguistics calls 'semantic bleaching' in which a word or expression loses its earlier force or shock value and becomes acceptable or at least more widely usable. In the right hands, nigga isn't very different from the standard American 'guy'. And the non-standard spelling signals a non-acceptance of mainstream, orthodox ways of doing things. Or 'wayz' in hip-hop (like 'chainz', 'boyz', 'gunz' and 'gangstaz').

Nevertheless, in the wrong hands but in the 'right' spelling (i.e. ending in -er rather than -a), this remains arguably the most toxic term in *Bad Words*. Any non-black user of the n-word, even if they are deploying it in the most controlled circumstances, had better be prepared for a firestorm. Lawrence Rosen, a white professor of anthropology at Princeton University, set out to provoke a response on the first day of his 2018 lecture series, 'Cultural Freedoms: Hate Speech, Blasphemy, and Pornography', by asking his class: 'What is worse, a white man punching a black man, or a white man calling a black man a n***er?' He repeated the term several times, to the discomfort of the students, some of whom walked out. The professor refused to apologise, saying he meant to shock; he was defended by the (black) chairwoman of his department who claimed that he was aiming to teach his students to argue why hate speech should or should not be protected without using the argument 'because it made me feel bad'. Presumably Professor Rosen felt that he failed for he cancelled the planned course a few days later. It doesn't seem that he received any answer to his initial question. This suggests that there are very few, if any, occasions on which a speaker can legitimately use the n-word.

When the black deputy district attorney, Christopher Darden, described it as 'the dirtiest, filthiest, nastiest word in the English language' during the protracted trial of O. J. Simpson for the murder of his wife Nicole, he wasn't merely making a rhetorical point or grandstanding. Simpson's defence counsel wanted to cite several instances in which one of the first (white) detectives to arrive on the murder scene was alleged in the past to have used the word 'nigger'. The prosecution saw this as an attempt to imply police prejudice and to influence the predominantly black jury because as Darden said, after his 'filthiest, nastiest' description, '[Hearing the word] will do one thing. It will upset the black jurors. It will say, Whose side are you on, "the man" or "the brothers"? . . . It'll blind the jury. It'll blind the truth. They won't be able to discern what's true and what's not.' According to the *New York Times* (14 January 1995), the prosecutor's voice was trembling when he said that the n-word was so vile he would not utter it.

Yet at the same time as the O. J. Simpson trial was taking place, and elsewhere in Los Angeles, rappers were making waves, headlines and money by deploying the very term – indistinguishable in its two spellings to most ears – that was causing an unprecedented scene in the courtroom. If the n-word is the most poisonous of terms, it is also among the most ambivalent.

Till Death Us Do Part

There is a handful of other expressions that don't have the prominence of the n-word but are still offensive. 'Coon' is short for raccoon, the North American animal whose name derives – as is usual for animals and flora unique to the US – from an American Indian term (the Algonquin *aroughcun*). Early in the nineteenth century a coon signified a sly fellow as well as being a nickname for a member of the old Whig party* of the United States, which at one time used the raccoon for its emblem, while the first cited use of the word to apply to a black person comes in 1862. 'Coon' had some currency in British English. It was even used by the otherwise right-on Ken Tynan – he of the infamous first utterance of the f-word on British television – when in a cutting review of Orson Welles's stage performance as *Othello* in 1951 he wrote that 'Citizen Kane' had become 'Citizen Coon'. 'Spade', deriving from the playing-card suit, originated in the US in the 1920s, while at about the same time 'wog' (a shortened form of golliwog) became popular in British English, where it often signified any non-white foreigner.

* The Whig party was the opposition to the Democrats in the earlier part of the nineteenth century. The Republican Party or GOP (Grand Old Party) did not appear until shortly before the Civil War.

Indeed, to the English mind, 'wog' might signify any foreigner at all. During a 1949 debate in Parliament on colonial affairs a Labour member, decrying the way in which some Conservatives talked about the many indigenous peoples still under British rule, said 'The hon. Gentleman and his Friends think they are all "wogs." Indeed, the right hon. Member for Woodford (Mr. Churchill) thinks that the "wogs" start at Calais.' Half ironic at the expense of British insularity while at the same time hinting at the sense of Anglo-Saxon superiority, the 'wogs start at Calais' phrase might have been found before 1949; it was certainly in use until quite recently. In Australia and New Zealand 'wog' may be used about any foreigner or immigrant, especially one from southern Europe or the Middle East. The expression never had much currency in the US though the CIA talked about the 'wog factor' to account for unfamiliar motivations and actions that couldn't be understood by the Western (or the CIA) mind. The word was erroneously explained away as an acronym for 'Western Oriental Gentleman'.

As with other racist terminology, Britain lagged behind America in finding itself uncomfortable with the words listed above. And it wasn't only a matter of words. Robertson's Jam retired the golliwog image from the labels on their jams only in 2002. For nearly a century the firm encouraged children to send in tokens from the jars in exchange for an enamelled badge of golly doing a variety of things such as footballing, playing cricket or golfing, or – to mark the 1937 coronation of George VI – wearing a union jack jacket and saluting proudly. In an echo of that, though the original image was patronising and imperial rather than patronising and racist, the manufacturers of Camp Coffee changed the illustration on their distinctive bottles of liquid coffee as recently as 2006. The coffee, created in the late Victorian era for soldiers in India, provided a quick alternative to grinding beans and brewing up in the field – hence the name. The original illustration depicted a seated Gordon Highlander wielding a cup of coffee above his kilted lap while to his left stood a Sikh batman holding a tray on which was a jug and a jar of Camp (presumably featuring the scene of the Highlander and the Sikh in infinite recession). Some years before the end of the twentieth century it must have occurred to the manufacturers that this looked not charmingly retro but embarrassingly regressive. The servant was deprived of his tray but was left standing, waiting. It required the turn of a new century for the picture to be changed again to show the Sikh and the Scotsman sitting side by side, both enjoying a cup of Camp. The manufacturers refused to say whether complaints of racism had produced the new image of 2006. The headline in the *Daily Mail* was CAMP COFFEE FORCED TO CHANGE LABEL BY THE PC BRIGADES (11 September 2006).

Attempts to tackle racism and racist language through satire were liable to backfire. *Till Death Us Do Part* ran for ten years on the BBC, bridging the 1960s and 1970s. The creation of Johnny Speight, it featured the East End Garnett family, headed by Alf, a working-class Conservative with racist views and reactionary politics, and played by Warren Mitchell. He was in perpetual conflict with his socialist son-in-law, played by Tony Booth, in later life famous for his activism on behalf of the Labour Party, his tabloid love-life and for being the father of Cherie Blair. Alf's casual comments about 'coons, wogs and pakis' were satirically intended, but it wasn't always evident that the audience was laughing at him. Warren Mitchell remembered a fellow Tottenham supporter congratulating him on 'having a go' at immigrants and replying, 'Actually, we're having a go at idiots like you.' Yet part of that long-running programme's popularity was surely due to the fact that more than a few viewers did agree with Alf Garnett, or at least experienced relief that here on the BBC was someone saying things that weren't quite polite, respectable or sanctioned. Outside the comparatively sanitised world of television, from the 1970s onwards comedians such as Jim Davidson and Bernard Manning regularly used racist – and sexist and homophobic – language in their shows in pubs, clubs and theatres. The language was all of a piece with the material. Davidson guyed an imagined and slow-witted West Indian called

Chalky, complete with accent, while Manning said that visiting Bradford made him feel 'like a fucking spot on a domino' (a very mild example of his humour).

Now, as shown by the examples given earlier, there is extreme sensitivity over the use of the n-word. No doubt it can occasionally go too far or simply be wrong-headed as in the furore over use of a term such as 'niggardly' or 'guerrilla'. But in general, here is a taboo to cheer for.

Culture Wars

W E LIVE IN a confusing time when the line between politics and culture has become blurred while political and cultural divisions have grown stronger. The line-blurring means that it is often possible to make (generally correct) assumptions about people's political beliefs or their voting intentions from the positions they hold on various topics that, on the face of it, have no direct political component. Meanwhile, the growing division means that those occupying different or opposing political and cultural positions regard each other with suspicion, even contempt. This is a trend that is most marked in America but it is detectable in many other democracies. If you know what someone thinks and feels about abortion or climate change or, in the US, about gun control or 'creationism', then you can make a fair guess at whether they are to the right or to the left, or in American terms Republican or Democrat, even if by British standards mainstream Democrats would hardly qualify as left of centre. There are more political parties in Britain but the centre-right/centre-left division still holds, and once again it is frequently possible to infer an individual's views on, say, global warming or the European Union from their political preferences.

The increase in suspicion and contempt between the various political/cultural groups has become especially marked since the Brexit vote in the United Kingdom and the election of Donald Trump in the United States, both occurring in 2016 and both results putting severe strain on the 'united' claim enshrined in the name of each nation. And, correspondingly, as the language used to describe the other side and their beliefs turns more grating or strident, so the gap becomes ever wider. A characteristic headline to an article by James Delingpole in the *Spectator*, LEFTISTS, LIBERALS AND WARMISTS BEHAVE LIKE A DIFFERENT SPECIES (5 December 2015), shows how certain terms can be lumped together because one position (being left of centre) necessitates another (belief in climate change). As it happens, global warming is a good place to examine the increasingly vicious spiral in which language is employed to diminish and demonise the opposition – the very situation in which words, hitherto innocent as it were, may turn bad.

What is largely forgotten now is that climate science and the belief that human activity is contributing negatively to the world's weather was once an apolitical question. It was a Republican president, Richard Nixon, who established the Environmental Protection Agency in 1970. It was Margaret Thatcher who in 1989 delivered a speech to the UN General Assembly in which she spoke of global warming as one of the most serious threats facing humanity. Forty and more years ago there was a cross-party consensus that climate change was real and that measures should be taken to ameliorate its worst effects. Then the cause was taken up by politicians who are in American terms to the left of centre, figures such as Al Gore, the US Vice President during Bill Clinton's administration.

The issue became politicised and it remains politicised. Because the climate problem is, in the end, a worldwide problem it follows that the only solutions to it must be transnational ones, since here is a crisis beyond the reach, means and capacity of any single government. If anything is more despised and feared by the hard right than a meddling government, it is a meddling super-government or a transnational set-up such as the UN. It doesn't help that some of those preaching most loudly about climate change are perceived as hypocrites, flying around the world delivering lectures on how everyone else should stop flying round the world. It hardly helps that some of the earliest, direst predictions of disaster either didn't come true quickly enough or didn't come true at all. In the late 1960s and early 1970s, most of the talk was of overpopulation and of global cooling, with forecasts of another ice age.

In some quarters, and particularly on the right, scepticism became cynicism became outright hostility to the whole notion of 'climate change', a euphemistic expression often preferred to 'global warming'. Because the great majority of climate scientists agree that warming is happening, something must therefore be done to undermine the scientists. There are various tactics. Point to minor flaws in their arguments; impute outright dishonesty to their motives; if all else fails, impugn them as 'experts', members of an 'elite', pillars of the scientific 'establishment' (words discussed elsewhere in this section). The real interest of these out-of-touch individuals, it is claimed, is in keeping the bandwagon rolling, in maintaining the status quo and preserving their privileged positions in universities and other establishments, positions that they usually hold at the taxpayer's expense. At the same time, the opinion of the sceptical or maverick scientist who doesn't agree with the majority of his peers – even though he must by definition also be an 'expert' – is held up as refutation of the whole global warming nonsense. In the same way an irrelevant item of anecdotal counter-evidence such as an especially cold winter or a mild summer is seized on as part of their 'Warming? What warming?' campaign. Incidentally, I put 'he' a couple of sentences ago because the climate-change denial business is a male-dominated one. And an irony overlooked in all the talk about the vested interest of the experts and their well-funded establishments is the way in which the sceptics' side has been bankrolled by companies and individuals with a strong stake in preserving things as they are. Oil companies have spent many millions of dollars in the past two or three decades in public relations, in the effort to downplay the evidence and influence lawmakers, just as tobacco companies did in relation to cancer in an earlier era.

The language around climate change can contain some ironies too. A sceptic might like to be equated with the 'contrarian', a term especially employed – about himself – by the late Christopher Hitchens. Who would refuse the role of the gadfly who battles orthodox opinion or practice, waging a sometimes lonely campaign against entrenched interests? There's a romantic tinge to this, as there was to the Brexiteer label, which emerged during the campaign to get the UK out of Europe. Brexiteer sounds a bit like buccaneer, an adventurous, outgoing word, and so unlike everything represented by those dreary Remainers who just wanted – natch – for nothing to change, ever. By contrast the contrarian strikes out for himself, dares to say the unsayable, speaks truth to power, etc. This ignores the fact that some very powerful forces and resources may underlie the lone 'contrarian' position.

There are surprisingly few disparaging terms from the 'contrarian' side to describe those who believe in climate change. 'Alarmist' is one but it doesn't carry much of a sting, particularly if there is something about which to be alarmed. 'Warmist' is better, and first put in an appearance in the mainstream media in a 1989 *New York Times* column: 'Those who accept the global-warming theory are said to take the warmist position.' It's regularly used by British journalists such as Christopher Booker and Delingpole as a sneer against climate-change believers. Perhaps they enjoy the rather limp quality of the word and imagine it transfers to the believers; warmness, like tepidity, is a passionless halfway house.

The verbal arrows in the believers' quiver are a little more varied. 'Sceptic' is favoured by some on both sides, though even here there's a feeling that labelling disbelievers as sceptics gives them too much credence and a cloak of respectability. After all, scepticism is one of the hallmarks of the real scientist, and the great majority of the disbelievers aren't real scientists. In fact, they distrust, even detest, real scientists.

Climate-change believers have a more powerful verbal sword known as the 'denier' but it can be two-edged. The word goes back to the Middle Ages where it usually appears in a theological context ('deniers of Christ Jesus'). In the late twentieth century it took on a dark hue to characterise those who claim that the Jewish Holocaust never took place or was, at the worst, an exaggeration of historical reality. In this context it is a highly charged word, carrying the implication that anyone who maintains the Holocaust did not happen is either deluded or unprincipled and, in either case, almost certainly motivated by anti-Semitism. So the transference of 'denier' to those who are sceptical about climate change inevitably comes with a lot of disreputable baggage. That is the point, of course, or part of it. The word nudges an audience into equating Holocaust-deniers and climate-change deniers, both of them groups who wilfully turn their backs on the facts, often for self-serving or sinister reasons. Some scientists and campaigners believe that using 'denier' simply widens the gap between the two sides, although attempts to provide alternatives such as 'delayer' or 'disinformer' haven't worked.

Others think that denier is legitimate. Spencer Weart, a senior US scientist, wrote: 'At some point they were no longer skeptics – people who would try to see every side of a case – but deniers, that is, people whose only interest was in casting doubt upon what other scientists agreed was true.' But the mission of denierism – yes, the word exists – to change the terms of the debate seems to be having some effect. The news agency Associated Press issued this directive in 2015: 'To describe those who don't accept climate science or dispute the world is warming from man-made forces, use *climate change doubters* or *those who reject mainstream climate science*. Avoid use of *skeptics* or *deniers*.' In the US the Republican Party as a whole long ago turned its back on even a minimal belief in climate change or, more precisely, started to regard it as a non-subject. Now it seems to exist in the realm of 'fake news'. Well before he stood for the presidency Donald Trump was tweeting, on 6 December 2013, 'Ice storm rolls from Texas to Tennessee – I'm in Los Angeles and it's freezing. Global warming is a total, and very expensive, hoax!'

All of this may seem so much name-calling about name-calling, as the world all the while floats further and further away on that melting ice-floe from the things that really matter. But words themselves also matter. Terms like 'hoax', 'denier', 'sceptic' and 'warmist' creep into public consciousness where they often serve as a substitute for any real knowledge or thought, especially in a difficult and contentious area such as climate change. Words influence politicians and spin-doctors, or rather they influence what those people believe will most effectively fire up their base. Remember TAKE BACK CONTROL or MAKE AMERICA GREAT AGAIN?

Linguistic tussling occurs in other areas apart from climate change. Indeed, the debate about abortion is a much longer running one. Particularly as conducted in the United States, it arouses deep passions on both sides. From the early 1970s anti-abortion campaigners regularly referred to their campaign as being one for the 'right to life', avoiding the negative associations of being perceived as 'anti-'. Those in favour of making abortion legally available then termed themselves 'pro-choice'. The verbal tit-for-tat prompted the other side to call itself 'pro-life', with each act of renaming meant to cast a negative, unfavourable light on the opposition. The media tended to avoid either term, and aiming for neutrality described people as 'anti-abortion' or 'abortion rights advocates'. Given that these are quite cumbersome expressions, it's not surprising that pro-choice and pro-life are still widely used. Yet they don't really balance out. As Andrea Tyler, linguistics professor at Georgetown University, pointed out: 'By positioning themselves as "pro-life", this group essentially won the war of words. These labels set up particular frames. It doesn't seem like a good thing to be anti-choice. But it's worse to be anti-life. So there's an inequality in the frames when you say pro-life and pro-choice. Being the opposite of pro-choice is not as bad as being the opposite of pro-life.' Another and only slightly less contentious issue in America concerns what children should be taught in schools about the origins of life. Here, the 'creationists', who believe in the literal truth of the divine creation of the Earth, now prefer to talk euphemistically about 'intelligent design' or ID. This hints at divine intervention rather than making direct reference to it, and has a respectable, pseudo-scientific air.

'Enough of experts'

A common thread running through the fierce arguments on climate change, creationism and, to a lesser extent, abortion is the degree of respect or even basic attention that should be paid to the expert. How far should the average person, the non-expert, trust what the meteorologist, the geologist, the doctor has to say? Less and less, it seems. In the twenty-first century the expert has been prised off the pedestal.

For many centuries the 'expert' lived an innocent life, even an admired one. As an adjective it goes all the way back to the fourteenth century, signifying someone with experience: Chaucer talks of those 'that be expert in love'. The meaning with which we're more familiar – an individual with a specialist knowledge or skill – emerges in the nineteenth century. The expert potters happily on through the twentieth century, approvingly used of those who've mastered skills high and low from rocketry to growing house plants. Then something happened on 6 June 2016 that would cast experts and expertise into the outer darkness. Michael Gove, cabinet minister and ardent campaigner for Brexit, was being interviewed by Faisal Islam, the Sky political editor, during the run-up to the referendum, which saw the UK vote by a small majority to leave the EU. Islam put it to Gove that there were many prestigious organisations and people, including the leaders of the CBI, NHS and TUC, that questioned the arguments for leaving. Gove replied: 'I think that the people of this country have had enough of experts—,' at which point the interviewer broke in with an incredulous query, 'Had enough of experts?' Gove struggled to complete the rest of his statement, which continued 'with organisations from acronyms saying – from organisations with acronyms – saying that they know what is best and getting it consistently wrong, because these people – these people – are the same ones who got consistently wrong.'

It didn't matter that the Brexiteer's position was a little more nuanced than an outright rejection of experts and expertise, or that he appeared to be specifically referencing the economic experts' failure to foresee the financial crash of 2008. It didn't matter that Gove later said he'd meant to apply the comment not to doctors and physicists but to 'a sub-class of experts, particularly economists, pollsters, social scientists'. It didn't matter, much, that he made an ill-advised aside a few days later in a radio interview when he compared the experts warning against Brexit to Nazis who smeared Albert Einstein's scientific theorising, a comment which didn't make sense and which he soon retracted. What remained was that ten-word take-away from that Sky interview: 'the people of this country have had enough of experts.'

It struck a chord. Indeed, if anything uttered by Michael Gove is ever to appear in a dictionary of quotations one suspects it would probably be this sentence. Gove's remark was eagerly grabbed by the Leave side and used to lambast any qualified person or organisation that had the temerity to express doubts about Brexit. After citing the Roman politician and orator Cicero, Jacob Rees-Mogg commented on BBC's *Newsnight*: 'I think the suspicion of experts goes back into antiquity and it's a very healthy thing to have. Experts, soothsayers, and astrologers are in much the same category.' Sympathetic commentators piled in with other examples of when the experts had got it wrong, and found plenty of ammunition to hand both before and after the referendum. Some of them went back decades and cited a famous 1981 letter to *The Times*, signed by 364 economists and protesting against Mrs Thatcher's monetarist economic policies – policies which led eventually to the boom of the late 1980s. Thirty years later, the alarmist but expert predictions of what would happen if the nation voted to leave the EU – steeply rising unemployment and costs, stagnant wages, the sky falling – have been derided because they haven't happened. Or, more precisely, didn't happen straightaway. Above all, the election of Donald Trump later in the referendum year of 2016 showed, in embarrassing reality, that experts could sometimes get things completely arse-about-face.

As with the global warming debate, where the deniers have their own smallish stable of experts to call on, the Brexiteers too have their own approved speakers and

commentators. Some of them are, by unfortunate necessity, experts. Indeed, the Bruges Group, an association
long dedicated to battling the centralising tendencies of
the European Union, teasingly headlined an autumnal
2017 meeting in Manchester as 'Jacob Rees-Mogg MP
and expert friends'. To distinguish between their kind of
expert and the others, the programme promised that Rees-
Mogg would 'talk alongside like-minded genuine experts
on Brexit'. So that's the way to tell them apart. Our lot are
the 'genuine experts'; theirs are just . . . experts.

Of course, economists, political pundits, pollsters and
other authorities have frequently got things wrong in the
past and the non-experts, i.e. everybody else, have
frequently enjoyed the discomfiture of those same experts
or have simply been angry at their failures. The Central
Intelligence Agency didn't foresee two of the most conse-
quential developments of the last thirty years: the rapid
collapse of the Soviet Union in the 1990s and the surge in
terrorist activity, which culminated in the Twin Towers
attack of 9/11. Professional economists have been equally
hapless. Alongside the *Times* letter protesting at Mrs
Thatcher's monetarist policies in 1981, another oft-cited
expert failure is the way in which the financial crash of
2008 seemed to take everyone by surprise. Even the
Queen, on a visit to the London School of Economics in
the same year, described it as 'awful' and enquired, 'Why
did nobody notice it?'

Political affairs and predictions appear more of a minefield than secret intelligence or the economy. In the 1948 US presidential election the challenger, Thomas Dewey, was regarded as so certain to win that one Chicago paper went to press with the banner headline DEWEY DEFEATS TRUMAN, a copy of which was jubilantly held up on his victorious trip back to the White House by the actual winner: Harry S. Truman. In the UK the 1992 election was almost universally expected to result in a Labour victory, after thirteen years of Conservative rule and the defenestration of Mrs Thatcher by her own party, yet the Tories won by a clear majority under John Major. This seemed like a harbinger of several United Kingdom elections in the early twenty-first century in which expectations, predictions and forecasts were generally proved wrong, sometimes wildly so. As if to prove no one learns from history, Hillary Clinton, assured of victory by pollsters and pundits in November 2016, didn't switch on her television until several states had declared their results; meanwhile she signed a copy of *Time* magazine, which was prematurely commemorating her victory over Donald Trump.

Predictions about scientific development can be equally wide of the mark, either by underestimating the potential of innovations or by overestimating it. Nothing is easier than to compile a jokey list of quotes about the non-future of the railway, the telephone, the automobile, etc., and to put it side-by-side with plausible-seeming scenarios from the 1960s about how, one day, after consuming our breakfasts in pill form we'd be using nuclear-powered vacuum cleaners at home and commuting to work using monorail or jetpacks.

Although doubt about expertise goes back to antiquity, according to Jacob Rees-Mogg, the last few years do seem to have crystallised a real hostility, even contempt for the 'expert', especially in the realms of politics, economics and social policy. To be an expert is something not to flaunt but to hide. Not quite as dangerous as being a member of the elite – another bad word for a very bad thing – but still quite bad enough. The rise of populist parties across Europe shows that this is not a phenomenon confined to the UK and the US but it is particularly marked on both sides of the Atlantic, where the politician who plays bash-the-expert knows he has a reliable crowd-pleaser.

In part this relates to a long tradition of anti-intellectualism in Britain, and especially in England. Claus Moser (1922–2015) arrived in England as a refugee from Berlin in 1936, one of that generation of displaced European Jewry that contributed so much to British life in the second half of the twentieth century. Moser was a distinguished statistician, an economist and academic, an experts' expert. He said of his adoptive country: 'Intellectuals are viewed with suspicion. Cleverness is not wholly admired. The very phrase "too clever by half" does not appear in other languages.' Moser put this down to Britain's imperial past when, it seemed to him, the qualities required to run a quarter of the world were 'moral character and leadership' rather than an overall educated population.

The word 'intellectual' may, in English, be a slur all by itself, implying remoteness from everyday concerns, an 'ivory tower' mentality, impracticality to the point of hopeless unrealism. It is telling that the least derogatory synonym for intellectual is 'highbrow', first emerging in English in the later nineteenth century and a fitting term for that sometimes earnest cultural era, but a word that in its occasional contemporary use conveys a kind of baffled derision ('Glyndebourne 2015 hopes to bring highbrow opera to the masses', *Daily Telegraph*, 25 August 2014). Also suggesting quizzical affection is that odd word 'boffin', origin unknown, which emerged in the Second World War to characterise backroom scientists and technicians.

English hostility to the intellectual likely predates the heyday of the empire, the Victorian era and the public-school inculcation of 'character and leadership'. The John Bull image of the Englishman, rough, bluff, suspicious of foreigners (especially Mr Frog) but imbued with a certain common sense, was already established in the eighteenth century. Fear of revolution and the intellectual theorising that might lead to it was one of the things that made the English grateful for the wide Channel, which kept some clear grey water between them and France. This national scepticism about theory, at every social level, combines with an anti-authority streak, a bolshy reluctance to be directed or pushed around, which is something experts and intellectuals naturally feel it is their prerogative to do. Or so goes the slightly sentimentalised picture of England and Englishness, popularised by the English themselves. Scotland, with its traditional high regard for education, does not figure much in the anti-intellectual picture. Nor do the Welsh or the Northern Irish have much to say. Perhaps they have their own bolshy attitude towards, and problems with, an overbearing authority, in the shape of England.

In the US a similar hostility is shown to the intellectual by terms like 'smart Alec', first noted in later nineteenth century, and 'egghead'. There is no truth in the colourful claim, put about by the science-fiction author Philip K. Dick, that the egghead (*Eierkopf*) had a particular currency in Germany during the Nazi period because when street thugs beat up defenceless individuals 'their skulls cracked readily against the pavement'. The expression has been around in the US since the early twentieth century and had an extensive outing during the presidential campaign of 1952 when the Democratic candidate Adlai Stevenson was defeated in a landslide by the Republican politician and Second World War Supreme Commander Dwight D. Eisenhower. Stevenson's bald dome together with his intellectual manner led to his supporters being called 'eggheads'. At one time it seems to have implied being 'liberal and politically minded' but it is easy to see how that would slip into a term of abuse. At the very least it suggests someone who's out of touch, as Adlai Stevenson humorously conceded when, on being asked to define the term, he replied that an egghead is someone 'who calls Marilyn Monroe Mrs Arthur Miller'. Ever since, if the American egghead does pop his shiny dome above the parapet it is only to receive a sharp rap from the populist egg-spoon. In Britain, by contrast, the expression is regarded ambiguously enough to be used as the title of a long-running BBC quiz show.

There are many reasons for the rejection of expertise and the denigration of the expert. One is, as suggested above, the undeniable fact that experts are often wrong, sometimes disastrously so, and especially in predictive fields. Another is that almost everybody lives in an online world where a variety of opinions on almost anything is available on one's own personal screen, opinions ranging from the deeply reasoned to the profoundly unhinged.* It

---

* A handful of US sportsmen retreated to the Middle Ages in 2017 by following basketball star Kyrie Irving who claimed in a podcast that the earth was flat. Irving later said he was just 'trolling', but at least one teacher said he was unable to persuade his students that a star they admired was wrong. To them their teacher was just part of the round-earth conspiracy.

is much easier to find validation for non-expert views that are unorthodox or frowned on by authorities, and few would claim there's anything wrong with that. But it is easy too to find validation for views and beliefs that are dangerous or close to criminal. A long-running instance, and one which is having a significant medico-social effect because it has led to a sharp uptick in measles cases, is the false belief that the MMR vaccine causes autism in children. Here suspicion of the state combines with a disbelief in expert medical opinion to make people 'protect' their own children – ironically by not protecting them against measles – at the expense of society at large. Its extreme form is embodied in the US meme showing a relaxed mother outside her rural homestead cradling a baby in her left arm while a rifle dangles from her right with the caption: 'Why yes, this is my unvaccinated child. I certainly hope you don't have a problem with that.'

Expertise is often couched in language that is difficult or specialist, making it harder to understand and easier to dismiss. When he was Shadow Chancellor of the Exchequer in the 1990s, Gordon Brown earned ridicule for a pre-election speech in which he proclaimed: 'Our new economic approach is rooted in ideas which stress the importance of macro-economics, post neo-classical endogenous growth theory and the symbiotic relationships between growth and investment, and people and infrastructure.' The 'endogenous growth' bit was laid at the door of Brown's special adviser, Ed Balls, leading to a quip from Michael Heseltine: 'It's not Brown's, it's Balls.' It's no coincidence that the most successful campaigning slogans of the last few years have been the simple, plain-speaking ones – TAKE BACK CONTROL, MAKE AMERICA GREAT AGAIN – the polar opposites of the expert-speak.

A further explanation for the downgrading or outright dismissal of the expert lies in a decades-long cultural change that has prioritised feelings and personal experience, often at the expense of reason or perspective. When it comes to opinions and beliefs, we're all on a level playing field. Doctors and other health professionals are much more circumspect than they once were in telling their patients what they 'should' do, let alone what they 'must' do. And any attempt by the government to edge people towards healthier living – for example, by introducing a 'sugar tax' – is met with bleating about the 'nanny state'. And at the root of the expert-bashing there may, I think, be nothing much more than a grudging suspicion of cleverness. It's the old back-of-the-class syndrome, familiar to any teacher. In 2017 the Vatican banned the sale of cigarettes in Vatican City, a move welcomed by the World Health Organization, which added that smoking kills more than seven million people a year. But according to a Nigel Farage tweet: 'The World Health Organisation is just another club of "clever people" who want to bully us and tell us what to do. Ignore.' Clever people, eh? Who needs 'em?

Elite pigs

When George Orwell finished his satire *Animal Farm* in 1943 he knew he would have difficulty getting it published because it presented a hostile, even cynical, view of Stalin and the Soviet Union, then a key part of the anti-Nazi wartime alliance. The book was rejected by at least four publishers, including Faber & Faber. The Faber editor who wrote the rejection letter was T. S. Eliot, arguably the greatest English-language poet of the first half of the twentieth century and a man who to many at the time, and since, seemed to embody the highest cultural ideals. They didn't extend, however, to complete freedom of expression for Orwell. Softening the blow of rejection, Eliot said that the book was a 'distinguished piece of writing' while 'the fable is very skilfully handled' but overall he felt it was a negative piece. At some level Eliot obviously sympathised with the *Animal Farm* pigs (i.e. the leaders in the Soviet political hierarchy) and saw nothing wrong with the way those animals had stepped into the shoes of the humans who once controlled the farm. 'And after all,' he argued in the letter, 'your pigs are far more intelligent than the other animals, and therefore the best qualified to run the farm – in fact, there couldn't have been an Animal Farm at all without them: so that what was needed (someone might argue), was not more communism but more public-spirited pigs.'

T. S. Eliot had no problem with the idea of an elite, whether composed of pigs or other intelligent animals. Orwell's attitude was more ambivalent. His final book, *Nineteen Eighty-Four*, is famously the story of Winston Smith's rebellion against Big Brother and the vicious totalitarian system that controls Airstrip One (Britain). But even after Winston is arrested, interrogated and tortured he feels a peculiar love for his torturer, the all-commanding O'Brien who is the representative of the power elite in the novel. Winston desperately wants to rejects his threats and pleas but always the 'peculiar reverence for O'Brien, which nothing seemed able to destroy, flooded Winston's heart again. How intelligent, he thought, how intelligent!' The Eton-educated Orwell felt uncomfortable in the class into which he was born, which was by almost any definition the elite class. The grudging, ambiguous admiration Winston Smith shows is also the best response Orwell was able to register for the intellectual, the egghead and the elite.

In the many years since Orwell's death, attitudes towards the elite have become clearer in a negative fashion: less admiration, less ambiguity, more grudge. In its current sense of the 'choice part' or the 'best', elite has had a place in British English for two centuries. For most of that time it has implied a certain respect, perhaps undercut with wariness. Even now the word can convey approval but such applications tend to be adjectival and restricted to areas that aren't contentious, as in elite troops, elite rowers, elite sportswomen. When the word is coupled with the definite article – the elite – the trouble really starts. It is quite rare to come across the term in an uncritical context: 'The cosmopolitan elite must learn humility' (*Daily Telegraph*, 7 November 2017); 'our blame-dodging, report-compiling, bureaucracy-bloating managerial elite' (*Daily Mail*, 20 February 2018); 'If the elite ever cared about the have-nots, that didn't last long' (*Guardian*, 26 February 2018); 'Elite must recognise the danger of inequalities they help to produce' (*The Times*, 4 July 2017).

The rhetoric of politicians is filled with elite-bashing. Boris Johnson claimed in a newspaper article that the 'elites of Europe' want Britain to remain in the EU so they can hang on to power (April 2016). Theresa May in a Lord Mayor's Banquet speech referred to how communities 'see the emergence of a new global elite who sometimes seem to play by a different set of rules and whose lives are far removed from their everyday existence' (November 2016). Nigel Farage asserted on LBC that 'I am getting tired and bored with this constant negativity we're getting from the global elites' (October 2017). Jacob Rees-Mogg told TalkRadio: 'The elite are consistently trying to push more Europe down people's throats and they don't want it' (January 2018). Donald Trump's presidential campaign was largely devoted to knocking an elite whose whereabouts was variously located in the media, the judiciary, the

Washington bubble, Hollywood or a swamp, targets that he continued to attack as president. An odd yet telling aspect of all this is that the rhetoric at present comes mostly from the right whereas traditional anti-elitism has tended to originate on the left.

Another odd aspect, and one frequently commented on, is that many of the principal anti-elitists would not so long ago have been regarded as archetypal members of that despised club, whether membership is bestowed via birth or wealth or education or achievement or position or, more simply, through some vague cultural aura that clings to the elitists. Nigel Farage was privately educated at Dulwich College before he started work as a commodities trader at the London Metal Exchange. Boris Johnson and Jacob Rees-Mogg both went to Eton before proceeding smoothly to Oxford University, as did Theresa May. Johnson described the £250,000 he was receiving for his weekly columns in the *Daily Telegraph* as 'chicken feed', a supposedly frivolous remark which prompted a union leader to describe him as being 'wired to another planet', in other words the kind of person attacked in Theresa May's speech. Rees-Mogg's wealth, acquired partly through his investment activities, is estimated at around £100 million. Meanwhile, who is to know what Donald Trump's monetary value is? Probably not as much as he'd like us to think it is but certainly more than that of 99.9 per cent of those American citizens who voted for him.

If accused of being members of the elite themselves, politicians and public figures such as the ones above grow indignant and deny the charge. Their defence is that they are the true democrats, speaking up for ordinary people against cliques and small special-interest groups that assume they know best. This populist banner has always been one that politicians – and demagogues – have been quick to unfurl but it's been waved more frequently and frantically in recent years. Yet, as the historian Michael Burleigh points out, the truth lies elsewhere: 'Even a cursory acquaintance with these populist movements suggests that the idea of a "people's insurgency" against elites and experts is a fairytale, and one that usefully masks divergences of class and economic self-interest – financier Jacob Rees-Mogg being a case in point. In reality, renegade members of that class have simply adopted "the people" in the way a regiment acquires a goat as a mascot' (*The Times*, 29 May 2018).

It's apparent that, as a bad word, elite has a much wider remit than egghead. Indeed cleverness or intellectualism is incidental to elitism. 'The elite' is useful as a piece of abuse while remaining more or less useless as a descriptive term because it casts its net so wide. Therein perhaps lies its power. Someone may be born in privileged circumstances, may be privately educated, well-off and hold high office, even the highest office in government – and yet, it seems, not be part of an elite. Another person may have none of those early advantages of birth or privilege and yet because they occupy a senior position in, say, the British Civil Service or in the European Union or the US State Department, they can be regarded as a quintessential member of the elite. Just the simple fact of living in a big city may be enough to qualify you as a member of the 'metropolitan elite', while possession of certain views, particularly on gay marriage or immigration, could put you in the category of the 'liberal elite'.

'Elite' has taken on some of the negative connotations of words such as 'foreigner' or 'alien', in that it tends now to characterise a minority whose concerns and ambitions – indeed, whose entire culture – are perceived as antagonistic to the concerns and interests of the majority. In this view, the elite is not seen as actually 'foreign' (though some of them may be) but as having an allegiance to some transnational system or cause, such as global capitalism or world government, rather than to the nation state of which they are nominal citizens. Again, in words from a speech by Theresa May, this time to a Conservative Party Conference soon after she had become Prime Minister, 'But if you believe you're a citizen of the world, you're a citizen of nowhere. You don't understand what the very word "citizenship" means' (October 2016).

This suspicion about the true nature and motivation of elites combines with an uneasy sense that 'they', the elite, have the real power, that they are pulling the strings and that they will do anything to ensure they go on pulling them. How else to explain the constantly sceptical and watchful tone used in references to 'the elite'? How else to explain the ever-present fears on both sides of the Atlantic that the 'will of the people', as represented by the UK vote to leave the European Union or the US vote for Donald Trump, is about to be subverted or snatched away by the conspiratorial machinations of Civil Service mandarins or the 'Deep State', in Britain and America respectively.

There is no doubt that the 'elite' has risen in recent years, if not in actuality then certainly in the public consciousness. A glance at the archive of *The Times* shows that the word appeared only on some fifty occasions in 2000; now it crops up in the same newspaper several times every day. As a term, it is much more slippery than 'expert'. Out of necessity expertise must be tied to a particular field, such as rocket science or climatology or psephology, whether the expert is believed or not. But the elite aren't tied convincingly to anything, except an amorphous notion of power, privilege and a presumption that 'they' know best.

In the end it may be most convenient to see the elite/ non-elite divide as a cultural one. In Theresa May's terms, the question is: are you a citizen of somewhere or nowhere? In US terms, are you red state or blue state?* Dave Barry,

* Blue is the colour associated with the Democratic Party as red is with the Republicans, a reversal of the standard European linkage of blue with right-leaning parties and red with left-leaning ones.

writing in the *Washington Post* as long ago as 2004, riffed humorously but accurately on how if you're from a Democratic blue state then you will regard red-state residents as 'ignorant racist fascist knuckle-dragging NASCAR-obsessed cousin-marrying roadkill-eating tobacco-juice-dribbling gun-fondling religious fanatic rednecks'; meanwhile if you're from a Republican red state then to you 'all blue-state residents are godless unpatriotic pierced-nose Volvo-driving France-loving left-wing communist latte-sucking tofu-chomping holistic-wacko neurotic vegan weenie perverts'.

It would be wrong to let the elite slip away without glancing at the word so often attached to it: liberal. The word is old and, in the sense of 'generous', has been in use since the Middle Ages. Even the sense with which we're most familiar – 'open-minded', 'tolerant' – dates back two hundred and fifty years. At around the same time, and not coincidentally in the era of the French Revolution and the American War of Independence, the word takes on a political hue. So to be a liberal is to be a supporter of individual rights and civil liberties. The nineteenth and twentieth centuries saw the establishment of Liberal parties in many democracies; in Britain the Liberal Party was the official counterpart to the Conservatives until the Labour Party became the principal opposition in the 1920s. The capital-L Liberal may be used as an insult, just as Tory or Labour can be insults in the mouths of their opponents, but it is the lowercase liberal who seems to excite a particular derision and contempt in some segments of the right. It's not just the word itself but the beliefs and attitudes that are supposedly associated with it: open borders, internationalism, gender equality, social tolerance, gay marriage, abortion rights, green politics, etc. Then there are lifestyle choices that almost automatically brand the chooser as liberal, whether it's living in Islington (or San Francisco) or buying organic food or having a hybrid car. The fact that these things tend to be costly reinforces the common sneer from the right that liberals are self-interested hypocrites: they are sceptical of capitalism but do well out of the system; they are keen on unrestricted immigration because it's handy to have a Polish plumber or an East European nanny for their (privately educated) children; they pontificate on green issues but install wood-burning stoves in their (second) homes.

In the British press, largely right of centre, liberals offer a target that is much broader than communist or socialist, because the word has less to do with politics and more with culture. Paul Dacre, the former influential editor of the *Daily Mail*, once said, 'No day is too busy or too short not to find time to tweak the noses of the liberalocracy' (*Mail Online*, 10 November 2008). And the following remark from the *Daily Express* can stand for thousands of similar ones: 'And no amount of liberal guilt-tripping and social engineering will change the fact that this is still a largely white-faced country' (13 March 2018). The situation in America is, from a liberal point of view, worse since the term has been regarded suspiciously for much longer. As with communist or Red during the days of the Cold War, 'liberal' is a trigger word. From the US comes the abusive 'libtard', a combination of liberal and retard.

The establishment

In September 1955 the journalist Henry Fairlie wrote an influential column for the *Spectator* magazine, one that popularised a new word in the English language. Fairlie's subject was the spies Donald Maclean and Guy Burgess. The two had defected to the Soviet Union in 1951 but it was some years before the British government conceded that they had been agents in the pay of a foreign power. Fairlie commented on how the 'establishment' had facilitated their treachery by refusing to take seriously the possibility they were spies. In particular he blamed the Foreign Office, which by 'its traditions and its methods of recruitment . . . makes it inevitable that the members of the Foreign Service will be men (and the Foreign Service is one of the bastions of masculine English society) who . . . "know all the right people."' No one could deny that Burgess and Maclean were quintessential examples of the 'right people'. Naturally, the argument went, they were never rumbled by those who'd been to the same schools and universities, who instinctively helped each other to get on and who, when difficulties arose, helped each other out.

In the same column Henry Fairlie told another story, which shines a more subtle light on the workings of what he termed the establishment and which is actually more interesting than the ruckus about Burgess and Maclean. Maurice Edelman, a Labour Member of Parliament and later a novelist, had been commissioned by an American magazine to write an article on Princess Margaret to cele-brate her twenty-fifth birthday in 1955. The finished arti-cle contained a single sentence that, without being disre-spectful, could be construed as a criticism of the Princess. Following protocol, Edelman submitted his article to the Palace. The next that he heard about it was when he was summoned to the House of Commons by Clement Attlee, the Labour leader of the Opposition. With the offending article on the desk in front of him, Attlee told Edelman that, while he might have expected many members of the Labour Party to write such an article, Edelman was not of them. The Leader of the Opposition requested that it should not be published. The Princess Margaret article never appeared. Fairlie commented: 'Many things are interesting about this story – not least the delightful picture of Mr Attlee in his most headmasterly mood ("I had hoped, Edelman, to make you a prefect, but now, well, you know . . .") but the more one considers it, the more one realises that the events which occurred did not depend on any formal relationships, but on subtle social relationships. That was the "establishment" at work.'

The story has a historical charm now. Everything about it is redolent of an earlier, more hierarchical era from the idea that a single sentence, mildly critical of a member of the royal family, would be enough to cause an article to be voluntarily withdrawn, to the intervention of a Labour Party leader and his more-in-sorrow-than-in-anger remark to a backbencher, to the deference shown by both left-of-centre politicians towards the Palace. All of this, in Fairlie's view, exemplifies the establishment at work. Helpfully he identifies some of its leading members, men such as the Prime Minister, the Archbishop of Canterbury, the Earl Marshal (the person responsible for organising major state occasions such as a coronation) and 'such lesser mortals as the chairman of the Arts Council, the Director-General of the BBC, and even the editor of The Times Literary Supplement'.

Henry Fairlie is often credited with inventing the 'establishment' to describe these upper circles of power but the word had been around in this sense since the early twentieth century. What Fairlie did was to crystallise a sense that everybody at the top knew each other, and that they shared an outlook that was dedicated to maintaining the status quo and was inclined to secrecy. Old school ties, shared universities, membership of the same clubs, and, often, family friendships and intermarriages enabled them to communicate indirectly and informally, as in the encounter between Clement Attlee and Maurice Edelman. Within a few years the word was familiar enough to be used (ironically) as the name of a Soho club co-founded by Peter Cook, and dedicated to political satire. The Establishment Club – 'the only good title that I ever thought of,' Cook said – lasted from 1961 to 1964, and by an additional irony attracted so many celebrities and famous figures that it effectively became part of the establishment which it was ridiculing.*

As an abstract notion rather than a place, the establishment still had some play in the decades following the 1950s even though most people looking at Fairlie's list now would put a red pencil through several of the

---

* In the same year that the Establishment Club opened, the Prime Minister Harold Macmillan went to the Fortune Theatre to see *Beyond the Fringe*, the new satirical revue written by and starring Peter Cook, Dudley Moore, Alan Bennett and Jonathan Miller. Macmillan was the epitome of the Establishment, and was tempted to the theatre by the prospect of seeing Cook's acclaimed impersonation of him. No doubt he wanted to show he was a good sport. The PM's smile became fixed, however, when Cook started to improvise by announcing that 'when I've got a spare evening there's nothing I like better than to wander over to a theatre and sit there listening to a group of sappy, urgent, vibrant young satirists, with a stupid great grin spread all over my silly old face'.

powerful individuals and institutions he mentions, from the Earl Marshal to the Archbishop of Canterbury or the Foreign Office. Yet an establishment may still exist even as its composition changes. The financial meltdown of 2008 and the general sense that the individuals responsible for it hadn't been held to account while ordinary people suffered the consequences led to a renewed focus on the upper echelons of power, whether financial or political or social.

In 2014 the left-wing commentator Owen Jones produced *The Establishment* (subtitled *And how they got away with it*) while in 2018 Aeron Davies, a University of London professor, published *Reckless Opportunists: Elites at the End of the Establishment*. Jones's and Davies's establishment(s) are very different from the one identified by Henry Fairlie in the mid-1950s – less old-school-tie, less Oxbridge, less clubby – but they are still made up of people and institutions in whose hands are concentrated wealth, power and influence. Owen Jones pointed, for example, to the friendship between David Cameron when he was Prime Minister and Rebekah Brooks, a senior executive at Rupert Murdoch's News International (now News UK), as an illustration of the unhealthy link between government and sections of the media, one that was to be thoroughly exposed after the phone-hacking scandal and the Leveson Inquiry of 2011–12. For Aeron Davies, the establishment is no longer bound together by shared class or background but by allegiance to neo-liberal ideas such as small government, low taxes, deregulation and globalisation. But establishment-knocking isn't confined to the left. In an echo of the way that members of the elite can attack others for being elitists, so too can establishment-bashers be members of the establishment. Attacking those wanting to reverse the Brexit vote, the columnist Dominic Lawson – the Oxford-educated son of Nigel Lawson, Chancellor of the Exchequer in Margaret Thatcher's government, and one-time editor of the *Spectator* and then the *Sunday Telegraph* – writes, 'This is the underlying explanation – prejudice might be a better word – of the social democratic establishment who still can't accept defeat' (*Sunday Times*). Lawson is, of course, picking on a particular segment of the establishment, the 'social democratic' Europhile centrist one, but he would probably not deny that he himself is part of another significant establishment wing, that of the Eurosceptic right. And also that, just as with many of his opponents, he has an 'establishment' experience of education, privilege, and influence through his journalistic career.

So the point is not so much that the establishment changes its components, but that it persists in some form or other and that the majority of references to it are negative. By implication, it operates below the surface, having a stultifying effect on society at large, and occasionally a malign one. The word has more traction in Britain than the US, although the *New York Times* carried the headline on 9 November 2016: DONALD TRUMP IS ELECTED PRESI-DENT IN STUNNING REPUDIATION OF THE ESTABLISHMENT. The word still carries some of the upper-class associations it had when popularised by Henry Fairlie, and it lacks the dismissive smack of the 'elite'. For that reason, despite occasional exceptions as in the Dominic Lawson quote above, it figures less often in the populist rhetoric of politicians and others who are themselves often part of the establishment.

Another term, a four-letter one and the polar opposite of elite and establishment, ought to be glanced at before leaving the subject. As noted at the beginning of this book, when the Conservative chief whip Andrew Mitchell had a sweary confrontation with the police tasked with security at the entrance to Downing Street in 2012, it was not his repeated use of the f-word that scuppered his career and caused him to lose a lot of money in a libel trial. It was rather, in the words of the trial judge, Mitchell's uttering of the 'politically toxic word pleb' in relation to the police guardians. The Latin term takes us back to ancient Rome and the city's firm distinction between the classes, most importantly the well-born governing elite or patricians and the unprivileged commoners or plebeians. From at least the sixteenth century the word has been used not only historically in reference to Rome but to describe 'ordinary people' of any period. Like other words relating to birth and class, it is easily slips from its function as a straightforward piece of social categorisation and takes on derogatory connotations: to be plebeian is to be uncultured, unsophisticated, vulgar, crude. The shortened form of 'pleb' sounds like the insult which it is. The first citation in the *OED* is for 1795 and the illustrative snippet of dialogue from a play by the Irish dramatist John O'Keefe sets the tone: 'You're under my roof, you pleb.' From that day to this, no one has had a good word to say for the pleb.

Proletarian, a term with a not dissimilar meaning to plebeian and also deriving ultimately from Latin, was the favoured Marxist term for the working classes. The linguistic origins of the word reflected the fact that members of the Roman proletariat were expected to serve the state only by providing it with their offspring, themselves destined to work and not much else, and so the civilian equivalent of 'cannon fodder'. Also like pleb, proletarian was after its Marxist adoption soon cut in half so that prole became a disdainful way of referring to the common people. George Orwell uses it extensively in *Nineteen Eighty-Four* to describe the great majority of the population who aren't members of the ruling party. And it occasionally appears in other outlets that are, presumably, not regularly perused by proles but which often trumpet, perhaps paradoxically, their respect for the 'will of the people' in elections and referendums ('He [Donald

Trump] tells it like it is – and the proles love it.' *Spectator*, 5 December 2015). The even more pejorative, and specialised term, lumpenproletariat was sometimes used to characterise the underclass beneath the labouring class, *lumpen* being German for 'rag'.

Other People

A T THE END of 2007 there was a rather rarefied kind of
strike in the US, when film and TV writers laid down
their pens, turned off their screens or drew the dust-covers
over their typewriters in search of more money from the
studios. There were rallies, speeches and demonstrations,
including one in Washington Square in New York. Quite by
chance, I stumbled into this en route to somewhere else and
stayed to listen for a while, clutching some leaflets pushed on
me together with a white and black badge from the WGA
(Writers Guild of America). My first thought was that writers
here really know how to organise and get unionised, and
then to wonder just what proportion of New York screen-
writers the Washington Square group represented. Was it a
tenth, a quarter, a half? I don't remember anything much else
about it now except for the one speaker who started his
speech by gazing from the rostrum at the sizeable crowd
assembled below. 'Wow,' he said, 'I don't think I've seen so
many Jews gathered in one place since *Schindler's List.*' There

was some appreciative laughter. There were no gasps or tuts of disapproval. The speaker must have been Jewish – he wouldn't have got away with it otherwise. And, as he observed, many of the crowd in Washington Square were Jewish too – they had to be, for him to be allowed to get away with it.

As with other contentious or outright taboo terms from 'queer' to 'nigger', the licence to use 'Jew' in a way that may be taken disparagingly in the early twenty-first century is only given to those who are, as it were, insiders. But the use of 'Jew' – one might almost say the accusation of 'Jew' – by non-Jews, whether in the form of an insinuation or a slur or an outright incitement to hatred, has endured for millennia. According to the dictionaries, the word became a 'term of opprobrium' in the early seventeenth century, which might imply that earlier it had been simply a neutral ethnic or religious marker. History tells us otherwise. In the Middle Ages there was added to the original charge of 'killers of Christ' a malign stereotype, which has proved almost impossible to root out: one of greed and deviousness, springing in part from the fact that one of the few historical practices permitted to Jews was the business of money-lending, something technically forbidden to Christians under canon law.

The Holocaust didn't put a stop to anti-Semitism in the West but it did put a kind of brake on it in the sense that overt displays became unrespectable, tasteless. Yet anybody familiar with popular British writers of the first half of the twentieth century will have encountered their reflexive anti-Jewish slurs. As Jonathon Green says in his memoir *Odd Job Man* (2014), talking of his childhood enthusiasm for 'Sapper', the nom de plume of thriller writer H. C. McNeile and creator of Bulldog Drummond: 'Sapper's Jews, like Agatha Christie's Jews and the Jews of nearly every popular writer prior to Auschwitz are de facto bad. It is possible that this was not conscious anti-Semitism as such, merely a given in a world in which P.C. still referred only to a member of the police.'

And it wasn't just the pot-boiling, populist writers either. Through Graham Greene's novels written before the Second World War there runs a thread of mild anti-Semitism ('He had been a Jew once, but a hairdresser and a surgeon had altered that', *Brighton Rock*, 1938), while his pre-war film reviews in the *Spectator* also contain casual references to 'tasteless Semitic opulence' or 'the dark alien executive tipping his cigar ash behind the glass partition in Wardour Street'.* Some of the most notorious slurs are

---

* One of Greene's film reviews for another pre-war periodical didn't pass as unremarked as his anti-Semitic slurs. In *Night and Day* he commented unwisely and too honestly on nine-year-old Shirley Temple, star of the 1937 film *Wee Willie Winkie*, and Twentieth Century Fox's highest paid and most profitable asset. Greene's remarks on the child star's 'dubious coquetry' and on her 'admirers – middle-aged men and clergymen' provoked a storm. The studio sued author and magazine for libel, and won. The cost of the action contributed to financial pressures that closed down the magazine.

an integral part of the work of one of the twentieth century's most elevated writers, T. S. Eliot. The degree of his anti-Semitism, and how far it strayed outside the 'norm' for the period, has been the subject of debate, but there is no blinking away lines such as 'The rats are underneath the piles./The Jew is underneath the lot' from the short poem 'Burbank with a Baedeker: Bleistein with a Cigar' published in 1920.

As suggested, since the 1940s direct and hostile references to Jews and Jewishness have become if not quite taboo then outside the range of polite and acceptable discourse. There are ways round this, usually involving a stress on the foreignness, the alien quality, the otherness, of a person or a group. For example, why not draw attention to their original name as a way of indicating, unsubtly, that they're not one of us? This is what Donald Trump did to satirist and television presenter Jon Stewart in 2013, with the tweet 'I promise you that I'm much smarter than Jonathan Leibowitz – I mean Jon Stewart @TheDailyShow.' To which Stewart responded: 'Many people don't know this, but Donald Trump's real name is Fuckface Von Clownstick. I wish you would embrace the Von Clownstick heritage.'

Another, marginally less obvious way of conveying the same prejudice is to fall back on old tropes concerning rootless, cosmopolitan figures who owe allegiance to nothing and nobody but themselves, the kind of language familiar from Hitlerian propaganda. And also the kind of language used by Theresa May in her first speech to the Conservative Party Conference after she'd become Prime Minister in 2016, and mentioned earlier in the discussion of 'elite'. Reinforcing her Brexit credentials, Mrs May talked of how 'too many people in positions of power behave as though they have more in common with international elites than with people down the road, the people they employ, the people they pass on the street. But if you believe you are a citizen of the world, you are a citizen of nowhere. You don't understand what the very word citizenship means.' Vince Cable of the Liberal Democrats claimed that the speech could have been taken straight out of *Mein Kampf*. Well, not quite perhaps. But the speech did cause some discomfort even among Conservative supporters – or at least the ethnic and more liberally minded ones – because it seemed to echo, unintentionally, the old charges levelled against one race in particular.

A more explicit example surfaced in the summer of 2018 during the long-running row about the influence of anti-Semitism in the Labour Party. Old actions and utterances of the leader Jeremy Corbyn, in particular, were being trawled over for evidence; the results were telling. For example, in 2013, according to the *Guardian*, Corbyn praised Manuel Hassassian, the Palestinian ambassador, for an 'incredibly powerful' account of the history of

Palestine given during a speech at a parliamentary meeting. Corbyn, speaking at a different venue, managed to be both patronising and dismissive when he commented: 'This [the Palestinian ambassador's speech] was dutifully recorded by the, thankfully silent, Zionists who were in the audience on that occasion, and then came up and berated him afterwards for what he had said. They clearly have two problems. One is that they don't want to study history, and secondly, having lived in this country for a very long time, probably all their lives, don't understand English irony either. Manuel does understand English irony, and uses it very effectively. So I think they needed two lessons, which we can perhaps help them with' (*Guardian*, 24 August 2018).

The key requirement in such attacks, of which May's was a mild example and Corbyn's a more unabashed one, is that the group or nation or race in question be perceived as different from us, as not sharing our values, heritage, speech, taste in food, sense of humour, etc. Of course, all such differences between different nations and races are real, they do exist. The trick, though, for the politician or demagogue or tabloid columnist or online agitator is to play them up so that the differences become the only things that matter, and that those differences are (occasionally) a source of amusement or scorn but (more usually) of hostility. So distinguishing features turn into something strange, even abhorrent, and otherness becomes a means of validating ourselves, without the bother of any reasoning or further explanation. We are here. They are over there. Enough said.

Old non-ethnic nouns and adjectives indicative of 'otherness' and dating from the Middle Ages or earlier tended to start life in a fairly neutral state but quickly slipped until they became equated with what was undesirable and even frightening. The composition of the word 'outlandish', originally from Old English, indicates its primary meaning of 'not from this land', 'not indigenous', but it soon meant 'odd' or 'outrageous'. Similarly, 'foreign' at first denoted what was merely 'outside' before it became 'distant' and 'deriving from another country', and therefore 'unfamiliar' and 'strange'. 'Strange' itself once meant no more than 'of another country', then turned into 'unfamiliar' and 'weird'.

There could hardly be terms of higher condemnation than the trio of barbarian/barbarous/barbaric, coming from ancient Greek, and originally applied by the Athenians to non-Greek speakers. Yet the origin of the words is relatively innocuous. Those foreigners who didn't enjoy the blessings of the Greek way of life and its language couldn't be easily understood. They babbled away in their own languages, and it's likely that 'barbarian' started life as no more than an onomatopoeic and patronising imitation of all that babble. Using ridicule turns 'We don't understand them, we must be stupid' into 'They don't understand us, they must be stupid'. Fear and ignorance lie behind much national and ethnic name-calling. But like other types of bad language, nationalist and ethnic name-calling can also be valuable, because it reinforces one's sense of belonging and – let's admit it – may be enjoyable in itself.

When it comes to insult-by-nationality or insult-by-ethnic-group, there are two categories. The first is when the name by itself of the country or the ethnic group is used in a disparaging way. Into this category comes the traditional association of certain countries or races with certain traits. A curious aspect is that these traits are sometimes considered admirable but, when pushed too far, are then held up as being typical of 'that' country, 'that' race, and used as a stick with which to beat them. The English stiff upper lip equates to emotional coldness. So it is with the Scots and a frugality, which can easily be interpreted as meanness, or the German liking for order and system, which becomes a submissive readiness to obey authority, or French sophistication and *savoir faire*, which turns into sex-mad libidinousness.

Sometimes the nationality forms part of a disparaging phrase, as in 'French leave' (desertion), 'the English vice' (usually linked to spanking and flagellation), 'Dutch courage' (confidence gained only through intoxication), 'Irish screwdriver' (a hammer), 'Greek gift' (something given with treacherous intent), 'Mexican firing squad' (in which the shooters are arranged in a circle and so synonymous with a disastrous arrangement). A small handful of terms turn the name into a verb or a verbal phrase: to welsh, to default on one's debts or obligations, supposedly derives from Welsh; the historical 'to turn Turk' was to become a renegade, i.e. to defect from Christianity; bugger, as mentioned, probably derives ultimately from a medieval sect of Bulgarian heretics. However disparaging these terms, the great majority are historical and some hundreds of years old.

The second category is the disparaging nickname or racial slur, as in 'paddy', 'chink', 'wop', 'spic', 'limey', 'pom', 'kraut', 'yank', etc. Dictionaries usually categorise such words as 'offensive slang' but most of them are far from being taboo. Almost every English speaker uses some at some point, and a few terms are acceptable in tabloidese, as when the *Sun* once reminded its readers that 'the Filthy Frogs' had 'tried to conquer Europe until we put down Napoleon at Waterloo'. Even the more decorous press is happy to use a handful of such expressions as long as they appear between quotation marks: 'Starc hopes his understudy, Jackson Bird, "takes five wickets and sticks it up the Poms"' (*The Times*, 25 December 2017).* The unacknowledged rule in the British media seems

---

* 'Pom' seems to be a shortened form of pomegranate, a jokey reference from the early twentieth century to British incomers to Australia, who were Pummy Grants (assisted immigrants).

to be that if a nation is a near European neighbour or a (white) sporting adversary, then it is acceptable to employ a casual or mildly disparaging expression but that the use of, say, Paki or Chink is out of bounds, and indeed could lead to trouble, legal and otherwise.

When nations become adversaries the use of stereotypes, nicknames and slurs is legitimised. Accordingly, as 1914 approached, Fritz, Hun, Kraut and Boche grew in (un)popularity in the English-speaking world, even though all these words had surfaced before the First World War. The only ones that really persisted into the Second World War and, indeed, into the present day are Kraut, from the German fondness for cabbage (= *Kraut*), and Jerry. Though not affectionate, Jerry – possibly no more than a diminutive form of 'German' – is far from a fizzing or guttural monosyllable such as Fritz or Kraut. The Nazis and Hitler fall into a different category, although they have aspects of a national stereotype, and are discussed further on.

Despite the onset of war, there were fewer slang terms for the Italians, perhaps reflecting the fact that they were regarded as a less fearsome class of enemy than the Germans. The reductive 'Eyetie' (i.e. I-talian) was used by the British, Australians and Americans, with 'wop', still in use and still derogatory, more of a US speciality (possibly deriving from an Italian dialect term, *guappo*, meaning bold and showy). There was also an older term, 'macaroni', an example of how 'national' foods can be applied reductively to a country's citizens. When it came to the third member of the Axis, Prime Minister Tojo's name was used, particularly by Australians, to refer to a Japanese soldier or airman though 'Jap' was the standard disparaging expression among the Allies. 'Nip' was common too and derived from Nippon, a shortened form of *Nippon-koku* (land of the origin of the sun). But in general when one puts the wartime slang terms for troops side by side – Aussie, Kiwi, Canuck (for Canadian), Ivan (for Russian), Jerry, Yank, Tommy* – they have a roughly equivalent linguistic status as familiar and casual words.

It's when racial hostility is added to nationalism that the language may become vitriolic. Second World War references, particularly among the Americans, to the Japanese as 'monkey-men' recall the Nazi classification of *Untermenschen* (literally 'subhumans') for those races that they regarded as racially inferior. Widely popularised during the Korean War and in the Vietnam War, 'gook' and 'slitty eyes' entered the lexicon of abuse just as later, during the Iraq War, did terms such as 'camel jockey', 'towelhead' and 'raghead'. In this linguistic

---

* While Yank is a colloquialism for any American (civilian or military) Tommy specifies a soldier and derives from 'Thomas Atkins', the name used in the army from the early nineteenth century as an example in specimen forms.

willingness to deprive the enemy of his human status or to reduce him to a single feature, be it the shape of the eyes or an item of clothing, we can see a parallel with McLurg's Law. This cynical but largely accurate observation, supposedly created by a long-dead British editor, lays down proximity as the most important consideration when it comes to deciding what is newsworthy. According to McLurg's Law, things matter less in inverse relationship to the distance they take place from London. In other words, it takes only one death next door to make the headlines but many multiples of that on the other side of the world. So insults and insulting terms seem to become easier to make and more intense in nature the further away geographically – and culturally – the insulter is from the insultee. The process of belittling other nations when relations between them are difficult even if they are not at war could be seen in the vogue for anti-Irish jokes in the UK during the height of the Troubles in the 1970s and 1980s, or the prevalence of anti-Mexican jokes in the US.

'Don't mention the war!'

In January 2018 Peter Ammon, the outgoing German Ambassador to the UK, gave a valedictory interview to the *Guardian* in which he bemoaned Britain's decision to leave the European Union. He speculated on the extent to which the country's self-image as a lone defender of liberty in the early days of the Second World War had influenced the referendum vote three-quarters of a century later. 'Obviously every state is defined by its history, and some define themselves by what their father did in the war, and it gives them great personal pride,' said Dr Ammon. 'History is always full of ambiguities and ups and downs, but if you focus only on how Britain stood alone in the war, how it stood against dominating Germany, well, it is a nice story, but does not solve any problem of today.'

The Ambassador's remarks provoked a predictable response in predictable quarters: GERMAN AMBASSADOR MOCKS BRITONS FOR BEING OBSESSED WITH WINNING WORLD WAR TWO (*Daily Express* headline, 30 January 2018); DON'T MENTION THE WAR! SNEERING GERMAN AMBASSADOR SAYS 'BREXITEERS ARE OBSESSED BY WWII LEGACY' (*Sun* headline, 30 January 2018).

The tone of the interview, as reproduced in the *Guardian*, was regretful rather than mocking, and there was no sign of the 'sneering' detected by the *Sun*. But what about the charge that when it comes to remembering the Second World War Britain is 'obsessed', even if that's not exactly the word used by the Ambassador?

Also in January 2018 the British Academy Film Awards (run by BAFTA) released its lists of nominations for best film, screenplay, director, etc. Among the five titles in the 'best film' category were *Dunkirk* and *Darkest Hour*. These two films were the only ones on the list with a historical basis. They also happened to share the same narrow slice of history: those few weeks in early 1940 when Britain stood alone against the threat of Nazi tyranny. Of course, the link between films that were conceived a long time ago – in the case of *Dunkirk* as far back as the mid-1990s – and present-day events is a coincidence. But people naturally look for parallels and echoes, however accidental. One conservative commentator was quick to make the connection. Writing in the *Spectator* in February 2018, Charles Moore said: 'Anyway, regardless of the film's [*Darkest Hour*'s] historical accuracy, its great current merit is that it is – possibly by accident – superb Brexit propaganda. The message is that it is sometimes both possible and necessary, if continental Europe is going one way, for Britain to go the other.'

Britain's wartime stand makes for a convenient signpost, and for those unable to make out what the sign says then Winston Churchill is always there to point the way. Whenever Britain's relations with Europe are especially fractious, that is to say most of the time, then invocations of the war and of Churchill grow more frequent. Before that key referendum vote of June 2016, the spirit of Churchill was summoned up to determine which way he would have voted: in or out of Europe? Depending on the sympathies of the speaker or writer, and of their reading of Churchill's views, then the great man was declared more than half a century after his death to be a fervent Leaver – or an ardent Remainer. It was all a bit reminiscent of the 'What would Jesus do?' poser. Discussing what could happen after Brexit at a Tory Conference fringe event in 2017, the MP David Jones concluded: 'If necessary, as Churchill once said, very well then, alone.' It's the kind of thing Churchill might have said but Jones seems to be remembering instead a famous cartoon by David Low published in the *Evening Standard* on the 18 June 1940, after the fall of France and the Dunkirk evacuation. A solitary British Tommy stands in front of a raging sea, waving his fist defiantly at the enemy aircraft advancing across a darkening sky. The caption below reads 'Very well, alone.'

Yet the furious debate surrounding Brexit is hardly the first occasion on which Britain's wartime experience, or aspects of it, have been invoked. Phrases from the beginning to the end are still alive and well in English. The phoney war, the eight months after the declaration of war in September 1939, is recalled to describe any lull before any storm. 'Dunkirk spirit' surfaces in the 1950s, carrying the implication not of disaster but of a plucky pulling through, a characteristically British victory snaffled from the jaws of defeat. The term 'blitz' was rapidly appropriated from the German (*Blitzkrieg* = lightning war) and became anglicised, almost cosily so. In a similarly positive transformation, the suffering of London and other big cities under the German bombers was re-imagined as the crucible in which the national character was forged, class barriers were dissolved and a common purpose discovered. All these nostalgic half-memories would be summoned up fondly in future years. The famous slogan 'Keep Calm and Carry On' was never actually used during the war – the authorities feared it would rub people up the wrong way – but it has had a thriving afterlife in the twenty-first century. And the code name of the most significant military operation of the era as far as Britain was concerned, D-Day (the D signifies nothing more than 'day') in June 1944, has been co-opted to stand for any watershed moment ever since.

Few people will need reminding that the 'Don't mention the war!' tag in the *Sun* headline comes from the 1970s TV series *Fawlty Towers*, and the episode when hapless hotel-owner Basil Fawlty (John Cleese) instructs his staff not to mention the war in the presence of some German guests, only to make constant references to the Nazis himself. This continual harping back to the Second World War – sometimes reluctant, sometimes boastful, yet with an obsessive dimension to it – seems to be the default position of the English. So one could argue that the outgoing German Ambassador did indeed have a point when he commented on Britain's 'focus' on its solitary stance at the beginning of the war.

Even as the war threw up a slew of words and phrases that bring a comforting glow to the British breast, so too did it produce a clutch of terms that have persisted and qualify as 'bad words'. Arguably, the most hostile expression to come out of that era is Nazi, a shortened form of *Nationalsozialist*, and emerging as early as 1930 in *The Times*. Associated terms such as Nazism, Nazidom and Nazification appeared soon afterwards and had negative connotations in English long before the outbreak of war in 1939. Nazi wasn't a term used or liked by the Nazis about themselves but initially by their German opponents. It may have been suggested by a diminutive of the name Ignatius, common in Bavaria where this little 'Nazi' denotes a clumsy individual. This loaded word has had an enduring afterlife not only to characterise a type of totalitarianism or racism, in particular anti-Semitism, but also as a convenient, expressive piece of shorthand applied to any person or behaviour that the user wants to condemn or stigmatise. Such specific uses are intentionally unpleasant: for example, 'grammar Nazi' for someone who is strict on others' linguistic mistakes, and feminazi, popular on right-wing radio in the US as a slur against feminists. The term has an obvious historical value and can be useful in describing neo-Nazi groups that ape the ideology and style of the original *Nationalsozialist* party. But elsewhere the application of 'Nazi' tends to stop debate – though it may easily start an argument – and can be linked to Godwin's Law, named after Mike Godwin, a US lawyer and editor who pronounced: 'As an online discussion grows longer, the probability of a comparison involving Nazis or Hitler approaches one.'*

From out of the apparatus of repression and terror that was employed by the Nazis, the other linguistic expression with the most frightening resonance is Gestapo (formed from the initial letters of *Geheime Staatspolizei* or secret state police initially set up by Hermann Göring). As with Nazi, the term is easily appropriated to describe actions or attitudes that are regarded as high-handed or dictatorial: 'A primary school was accused of running a "mealtime Gestapo" after inspecting children's lunchboxes for unhealthy food' (*Daily Telegraph*, 16 March 2009); 'The breast is best Gestapo: The "natural childcare" zealots who make women feel like failures' (*Daily Mail*, 7 May 2009). Yet well before the end of the war the word could be used to describe the kind of authority you didn't like, even if that authority was home-grown. In 1944 George Bernard Shaw wrote of 'The municipal statesman [who] sends his

---

* Godwin's Law is described in the *Oxford English Dictionary* as a 'facetious aphorism'. In an article written for *Tablet* magazine in 2010 and reflecting on eighteen years of the law's existence, its creator said that his intention was ultimately serious: 'Although deliberately framed as if it were a law of nature or of mathematics, its purpose has always been rhetorical and pedagogical: I wanted folks who glibly compared someone else to Hitler or to Nazis to think a bit harder about the Holocaust.'

sanitary Gestapo into an unhealthy private house and prosecutes the tenant.'

Surprisingly Winston Churchill made a rare blunder in public speaking when he claimed in a party political broadcast during the election campaign of June 1945 that the introduction of socialism into Britain would require some form of Gestapo, 'no doubt very humanely directed in the first instance'. He was talking about the Labour Party under the leadership of Clement Attlee, the Deputy Prime Minister in the wartime coalition headed by Churchill himself. This was such a fall from elevated oratory to naked scare-mongering that, according to polls, it caused 'disappointment and real distress' among listeners. Churchill lost the post-war election not because of the 'Gestapo' remark but for an array of much more profound reasons. Yet it could still be said that Hermann Göring's secret police did make their own very minor contribution to something they'd failed to achieve during the course of the war, Churchill's ousting from No. 10 in the July of 1945.

The Nazi high command offered a roster of characters whose names quickly became bywords for criminality, mania and deceit, and so entered the lexicon of bad words. The principal one, of course, was Adolf Hitler, fascination with whom seems only to grow the further we get from 1945. Yet from the early 1930s both the man himself and his attributes, whether physical (such as the moustache) or psychological (such as dictatorial tendencies), were embedded in English vocabulary. The novelist Aldous Huxley was referring to Germany as 'Hitlerian' in 1934. 'Little Hitler' was soon an established insult for an interfering or officious man. Even though there was occasional admiration during the 1930s among some British for what Hitler was doing in Germany – bringing order, guaranteeing full employment, building autobahns, etc. – the outbreak of war turned him into villain-in-chief. Indeed, it became and remains possible to attach almost anything negative to his name, from book-burning to crackpot theories about Aryan supremacy to pathological anti-Semitism, imperial hubris, aggressive nationalism, rabid oratory, warmongering, and much more. In keeping with Mike Godwin's law, the mere invocation of the Führer's name is sufficient to tar any opposition and shut down argument. If he was in favour of something, it must be bad: 'Hitler was a vegetarian too, you know.' If he didn't like something, it must be good: 'You don't like people smoking around you? Hitler didn't either.' The way in which a man who has been dead for three-quarters of a century is regularly wheeled out as evidence for/against any old argument is sometimes derisively referred to as *reductio ad Hitlerum* (pseudo-Latin along the lines of *reductio ad absurdum*). As insults, therefore, Hitler or Hitlerian or Hitler-like are broad church words, capacious but not illuminating.

Joseph Goebbels, Hitler's minister for propaganda from 1933 and the Chancellor of Germany for the single day and night between Hitler's suicide and his own on 1 May 1945, used his control of the media to push Nazi interests and ideology. His principal propaganda technique was to repeat assertions or lies until people were conditioned to accept them. In our present-day era of unreliable reports and fake news it's hardly a surprise that Goebbels has been called back from the dead: in a 2017 episode of *The Simpsons*, a character says of Kellyanne Conway (at the time of writing a senior member of Donald Trump's White House and the creator of the Orwellian phrase 'alternative facts'), 'I think it's inspiring how now a woman can be Joseph Goebbels.'

In contrast to the derision and hatred justifiably heaped on Hitler and his entourage, the Soviet leader Joseph Stalin was more ambiguously treated. Once Hitler made the fatal misstep of invading Russia in 1941, the Soviets became allies of the West, warily regarded but absolutely essential to the eventual defeat of Nazidom. Iosif Dzhugashvili, who early assumed the name of Stalin ('[man of] steel') as a kind of nom de guerre, was referred to as Uncle Joe among the Allies. The nickname was avuncular but his embrace was as much feared as loved, and the warm feelings towards him and the USSR did not outlast the end of the war. When Stalin or Stalinist is invoked now it is almost always in a negative context, implying brutish and repressive action: 'So what happens after Britain leaves the EU? Will the latter adopt a Stalinist approach and airbrush us out?' (*Sunday Times*, 16 July 2017).

Airbrushing opponents and dissidents out of history was a Soviet practice under Stalin, and it is central to George Orwell's dystopia, *Nineteen Eighty-Four*. Stalin looms large in the book, though never by name. In the same way as Orwell drew upon the resonance of Churchill's first name when creating the heroic but ultimately defeated Winston Smith, so he used the sinisterly reassuring figure of Joseph Stalin in his creation of Big Brother. Orwell didn't actually invent the expression – it had been employed earlier by James Joyce and H. G. Wells among others – but he fixed it in the public consciousness as a synonym for an omniscient, overbearing authority, one which may be protective but is ultimately punitive.

It is curious how the deeply ambiguous figure of Big Brother, who in the novel never appears as anything but an image (and who may not even exist), has shifted from a terrifying threat to something cosily familiar. This isn't so much because people like the experience of being continuously surveilled, though some may do, or because surveillance is a reality in many town centres now, but because of the global popularity of the TV reality show. *Big Brother* originated in the Netherlands and was named out of Orwell's novel. Apart from the continuous surveillance of the inhabitants of the Big Brother House, certain features of the show's format such as the regime of tasks and rewards and the confessional 'Diary Room' seem loosely modelled on the grim world that Orwell conjured up. It is curious, too, that what is arguably the most terrifying feature of *Nineteen Eighty-Four* – the place known as Room 101 where those who are being tortured in the Ministry of Love confront their most primal fears – should have been taken for the title of another very popular TV programme, hosted by a comedian. Orwell, with his sensitivity for the way in which language can be distorted for propaganda purposes, might have been amused at the style in which two of his most fearsome creations have been bleached of almost all of their negative connotations. From bad words to bland, entertaining ones.

Fascists and the antifa

Of the three principal Western dictators involved in the Second World War – Stalin, Hitler and Mussolini – it is the Italian *Duce* who gets off relatively lightly when his name is invoked as a term of abuse. He is associated with bombast and grandiose buildings rather than racism and genocide. Yet it was Mussolini who brought back to life two of the most enduring bad words, fascism and fascist, even if their early connotations were positive ones. In ancient Rome, *fasces* was the Latin term for a bundle of rods wrapped round an axe, a symbol of authority carried by the attendants of the Roman lictors or magistrates. In the Italy of the nineteenth century, *fasci*, the plural form of *fascio* (bundle), signified a 'league' or 'union', though one with distinct political overtones. Then Benito Mussolini adopted the term when in 1919 he formed the paramilitary *Fasci di Combattimento* (League of Combat), soon to become the *Partito Nazionale Fascista* (National Fascist Party), which gained power in 1922 under that name. The bundle of rods containing the axe had a dual symbolic purpose: it represented not only naked power but also the idea that strength comes through unity, since a bundle of sticks is much harder to snap than a single one. Part of the appeal to Mussolini was that it was another reminder of ancient Rome, a glorious imperium to which he was determined his country should return, and the Italian fascist counterpart to the Nazi notion of a 'Greater Germany'.

Mussolini, like Hitler, had his enthusiasts in Britain and other democracies before and during the 1930s. Winston Churchill met Mussolini in 1927 in Rome and commented on the dictator's 'gentle and simple bearing' as well as how his fascist movement 'has rendered a service to the whole world' by being a bulwark against Russia and 'the cancerous growth of Bolshevism'. The movement's name was explicitly taken up when Oswald Mosley founded the British Union of Fascists in 1932, though he later hedged his bets by changing the name of the party to the British Union of Fascists and National Socialists; the BUF flag, previously adorned with the Italianate fasces, now featured a single lightning bolt, reminiscent of SS insignia. Yet, once war broke out, fascism, like Nazism, was discredited overnight in the democracies, except among a few die-hards such as Mosley, and the word turned rancid. Mussolini was shot in 1945 but fascism lived on elsewhere. Two European quasi-dictatorships – Spain under General Francisco Franco and Portugal under António Salazar – were characterised as fascist, even if some cavilled at the word, until the deaths of their leaders (Salazar in 1970, Franco in 1975) led eventually to the emergence of modern social democracies. In other parts of the world right up until the 1980s, and especially among the military juntas of South America, several regimes were given the fascist label.

Nazism and fascism are ideologies sharing so much that they might be visualised as lying one on top of the other rather than as overlapping. Dictionary definitions of each will include all or most of the following features: authoritarianism, nationalism, militarism, anti-communism, social uniformity, a belief in (one's own) racial superiority and a corresponding conviction of other races' inferiority, and acceptance of a repressive state apparatus. Similarly, the fascist and the Nazi are hard to distinguish. Yet, of the two terms, fascism/ist seems to have the broader sweep, to be more inclusive. All Nazis are fascists but not all fascists are Nazis. As insults, as bad words, they work slightly differently. To call someone a 'Nazi' is, as already suggested, to close the argument down. It's like flinging a rock, with the thrower venting their aggression and hoping to wound, an action performed without thought. To describe someone as a 'fascist' is more akin to flinging mud than a stone. Yes, aggression and the desire to hurt are still driving forces, but there's sometimes a touch, though no more than a touch, of thought behind the abuse.

Whenever a far-right party gains ground in a European election, something that has occurred often of late, there are anxious headlines and op-ed pieces asking whether fascism is on its way back. The campaign by and election of Donald Trump provoked a rash of alarmed articles in the US media penned by respectable figures: THE MANY WAYS DONALD TRUMP IS A FASCIST (headline to an article in the *Chicago Sun-Times*, 9 March 2016, by Robert Reich, Labor Secretary in Bill Clinton's administration); HOW FASCIST IS DONALD TRUMP? THERE'S ACTUALLY A FORMULA FOR THAT (headline to a *Washington Post* article, 21 October 2016, by John McNeill of Georgetown University, in which he awarded 'Benito' [Mussolini] points on a scale of one to four for Trump's Hyper-nationalism, Leader Cult, etc.). If some of this speculation was overheated, then Trump has repeatedly fanned the flames. He hardly helped himself during the campaign by equivocating when it came to the endorsement of David Duke, one-time Grand Wizard of the Ku Klux Klan and someone whose views are hard to distinguish from fascism/Nazism. Examples of the Donald's pandering to the extreme right are common, as when in the summer of 2017, in response to a violent clash between white supremacists and the 'antifa' movement in Charlottesville, Virginia, he commented: 'You had a group on one side that was bad. You had a group on the other side that was also very violent. Nobody wants to say that. I'll say it right now.' It is hard to imagine any other post-war Republican president, including Richard Nixon and Ronald Reagan, making remarks that hint at a moral equivalence between white supremacists and their opponents.

All this is to say that the terms 'fascism' and 'fascist', as a hand-wringing topic, as an alarm bell, as a slur, have had a powerful boost in the last few years. The current antifa – i.e. anti-fascist – movement, which campaigns aggressively against racism and the extreme right, has been around for a decade or so but really took off during the US presidential election of 2016. In parallel but on the opposite side of the argument (or riotous assembly), the alt-right movement has also been enjoying its time in the sun. As its full name – 'alternative right' – indicates, the alt-right offers a more radical view of politics than traditional conservatism. That's a polite way of putting it. The group is a white nationalist bandwagon. Both the alt-right and antifa have internet origins, and in geeky conspirato-rial style the names tend to obscure rather than clarify what they're about.

The antifa, a rough coalition of anarchists, communists, anti-capitalists and anti-racists, has a taste for direct, disruptive action and an impatience with 'centrist' poli-tics. Accordingly, it has provoked criticism from other left-wing groups on the grounds that it is alienating public opinion and setting back progressive causes. From the right there have been accusations that such a movement itself has fascist tendencies, in that it wants to silence opposition and quickly resorts to violence. Once again, Donald Trump contributed to the notion of moral equiv-alence by coining the word 'alt-left' to describe those who'd been protesting against the alt-right in Charlottesville. And the often successful attempts to 'no-platform' controversial speakers at university events have fed this narrative, with the anti-antifas, to coin another word, claiming that universities are failing in their basic obligation to ensure freedom of speech and toler-ance for all opinions, including those opinions that them-selves promote intolerance or worse. It is easy enough to fall into a 'You're a fascist', 'No, you're the real fascist' routine.

In short, 'fascist' and 'fascism' tend to be applied indis-criminately. Old and battered these terms may be, but like much-travelled items of luggage they come with a variety of labels attached, some serious, some almost frivolous. 'Clerical fascism' dates back to the early years of fascism in Italy and describes the close relationship between Mussolini's brand of politics and elements in the Catholic Church. Franco's regime in Spain is often referred to as an example of clerical fascism. 'Body fascism', emerging in the late 1970s along with the fashion for jogging and healthy eating, indicates an excessive preoccupation with (someone else's) shape and appearance, and usually boils down to a 'belief' that women should aspire to skinniness and men to washboard abs. 'Eco fascism' or 'green fascism' are pejorative expressions used against environmentalists whose aims are regarded as 'totalitarian'.

The fascism+ formula which has caught on most securely in recent years is Islamofascism. This word, first appearing in the late 1990s, equates Islamic extremism with historical fascism. Inevitably, Islamofascism entered the mainstream after the attacks of 9/11. It is more than a reflex slur, although some have objected to the term on the grounds that it is unhistorical or racist, or because it demonises an entire religion. Those who use it, and they are politically on both the right and the left, argue that there are plausible parallels between the Islamic extremism and fascism: these include a hostility to progress coupled with a harking back to long-lost realms (the Roman Empire, the Caliphate); hostility towards female equality; the elevation of machismo, especially as embodied in the leader; hostility towards knowledge (book-burning, destruction of monuments); and anti-Semitism. Both are described as 'death cults', calling for the complete destruction of the enemy and valuing suicidal sacrifice.

A coinage such as Islamofascism is, as it were, at the serious end of fascist spectrum and can be argued about. But casual fascist name-calling has also been appropriated by writers and media outlets, most of which are right of centre. Often it takes the form of objections to laws or guidelines that are perceived as interfering or moralistic, as when the general public is 'told' how much exercise to take, how much (not) to drink or eat, and so on. This is coupled with mocking reference to the 'nanny state' or to the apparent absurdities of 'health and safety' regulations (usually guyed as 'elf 'n' safety') and is often found with its trusty companion 'political correctness gone mad'. The smoking ban in public places, which came into force throughout the UK in the course of 2006–7, provoked cries of outrage at the do-gooding, liberty-infringing tendencies of central government. The cries continue: 'The neurotic and fascistic anti-smokers of Action on Smoking and Health (ASH) said at the time what they always say: this is as far as we want to go. And, as ever, they were lying. They are now supporting bans on smoking in beer gardens and the outside seating areas of restaurants' (Rod Liddle, *Spectator*, 8 July 2017). More generally, remarks about 'health fascism' represent an anti-nanny-state bleat: 'I don't care what the health fascists say. I absolutely refuse to do something, or not, purely because they tell me that it is good for me' (Dr Robert Lefever, *Daily Mail*, 19 March 2012).

Even if one could object to such examples of 'fascism' or 'fascist' as unhistorical or exaggerated or simply tasteless, there is a grain of accuracy in their use since an element of coercion and moral superiority underlies all of them. But the use of 'fascist' can reach strained or ridiculous levels when the word is applied to anyone who's regarded as precise or pedantic – an expert, in short. Tom Whipple, the Science Editor of *The Times*, wrote an article following the death of a man from a single blow, pointing out how in real life even a 'one punch assault' can lead to death or cause serious brain injury. Whipple contrasted that reality with the absurdity of an action film when a Jason Bourne can take repeated blows to the head yet walk away afterwards, victorious and towelling off a little sweat. He began the piece, 'Many a film director has experienced the wrath of the physics fascists. Show a laser slowly inching its way towards James Bond's crotch and scientists will tediously ruin the tension by pointing out that you can't see lasers side on' and concluded it, 'Films should stop thinking they can get away with it. It is time to mobilise the righteous pedantry of the physiology fascists' (*The Times*, 3 September 2016). Tom Whipple has a significant point, yet when 'fascist' is so widely if humorously applied the word has little value any more.

Commies, pinkos *et al.*

For much of the twentieth century the traditional opponent for fascism was communism. On the 'my enemy's enemy' principle, the anti-communist or anti-Bolshevik instincts of the great majority of British politicians and opinion-formers caused many of them to look on fascism more favourably than they might have done otherwise. It wasn't only Winston Churchill who, back in the 1920s, saw Mussolini's style of fascism as a means of strengthening the West against 'the cancerous growth of Bolshevism'. David Lloyd George, who had been Prime Minister for the last two years of the First World War, was still professing his admiration for Hitler in the mid-1930s and beyond. In a speech to the House of Commons in 1934 he said: 'In a very short time, perhaps in a year, perhaps in two, the Conservative elements in this country will be looking to Germany as the bulwark against communism in Europe.' In September of the same year during a visit to Germany in which Lloyd George was accompanied by his grown-up children, Hitler complimented him on his leadership during the First World War – 'It was you who galvanised the people into a will to victory' – and stressed the dangers of Bolshevism. In response the Welsh wizard described the Führer as 'the greatest German of the age'.

This is a reminder that while 'fascist' became a widely accepted term of abuse only once war broke out in 1939, the Bolshevik and the communist have been reviled for much longer. Now, just as the system which gave them birth has withered, so both expressions have faded as items of abuse. In the 1920s and early 1930s, Bolshevism/ Bolshevik seems to have been the preferred usage. Bolshevik (literally 'member of the majority') was the title of the Social-Democratic Party which was renamed the Communist Party after the Russian Revolution in 1917. That curiously cosy and diminutive term Bolshy – now 'bolshy' – appeared in English immediately following the Revolution. D. H. Lawrence wrote in a letter of 1918: 'The railway people, when one travels, seem rather independent and Bolshy.' The term sounds dated now but occurs occasionally. If there is still a critical note to it, there's also respect for the independence of mind and spirit that bolshiness demonstrates. Writing admiringly about the *New Musical Express*, a *Guardian* writer asked: 'Which unfortunate had been dealt a kicking in the reviews section by one of its bolshy star writers?'

As the precise historical resonance of Bolshevism receded, 'communism' took over linguistically as something to be feared, detested and condemned, especially in the United States and after 1945. The word had already been in existence for more than a century to describe both the general political theory that advocated the abolition of private property and the pooling of resources and labour ('communism') and the specific Marxist doctrine calling for the overthrow of capitalism and a classless society ('Communism'). In practice the lower- and upper-case versions of the word seem to have been used without much distinction. During the nineteenth century Communism was frequently linked to anarchism – also a doctrine, and so Anarchism – as threats to the established order. But it was only when an avowedly communist state took shape after the 1917 Russian Revolution that this newly powerful ideology was equated with a 'cancer' and 'disease', a mortal danger against which fascism might be a 'bulwark'. And so began the long two-part struggle: for much of the first half of the twentieth century, between fascism and communism; for much of the second half, between capitalism and communism.

'Commie' was an early and derogatory US coinage, and the word has enjoyed a long life. The Soviet Union is gone and the communist system generally discredited, but there are still Reds under the bed, certainly as far as right-wing US media outlets are concerned: 'Just when you think you've seen everything, you meet the Commie cadet – the graduate of West Point who is a devotee of Communism' (*National Review*, October 2017); BARACK OBAMA'S COMMIE ANNOUNCEMENT (2008 headline in the *Weekly Standard* above an article pointing out that when Obama was elected to the Illinois State Senate in 1996 he received the endorsement of the state's Marxist New Party). The word has less traction in the UK but is still found, usually in right-wing outlets and especially when they are trying to dig the dirt: CORBYN COMMIE CLEAN, the *Sun* headline (20 February 2018) to a story proclaiming 'Theresa May demands Jeremy Corbyn come clean about his links with Communist Cold War spies'.

The identification of the colour red with revolution and so with Soviet Communism predates 1917. When Giuseppe Garibaldi, one of the founding fathers of modern Italy, visited London in 1864 the population turned out in huge numbers to welcome the revolutionary liberator. The *Spectator* noted that while 'England is not Red ... she does sympathise heartily with Garibaldi's immediate end' and that the city recognised 'in an Italian Red a grandeur which lifts [London] out of its sordid daily life into a higher atmosphere'. Garibaldi's followers were known as Redshirts because they wore the *camicia rossa*. But the romantic and revolutionary bloom to the colour had been lost by the time of the Russian Revolution. Anxiety about the contagious effects of Bolshevism, especially on organised labour, spread across the Atlantic and produced what was later known as the 'First Red Scare' in the US.

When it came to insulting or denigrating the enemy, the word 'red', with its intimations of blood and aggression, had a vividness that the communist or commie couldn't match. Those evocative three letters were ripe for phrase-making: 'the red menace'; 'the red peril' (analogous to 'the yellow peril' of a slightly earlier period); 'reds under the bed'; 'better dead than red', which was reversed by those who opposed all-out hostility to communism and the possibility of an ensuing nuclear war to 'better red than dead'. American life, especially in its popular culture, was shot through with subversives and Red scares and fears in the period after the Second World War. Now the Soviets were enemies, not allies. Stalin was no longer Uncle Joe but a brutal dictator.

In the early 1950s Senator Joseph McCarthy, riding the wave of what became known as the 'Second Red Scare', waged a notorious campaign against the 'enemies from within' in the US establishment (particularly in the State Department), to the extent that McCarthy and McCarthyite soon became synonymous with witch-hunter and witch-hunting. At the same time in fiction, Mike Hammer, the ultra-hard-boiled hero created by the pulp writer Mickey Spillane, was disposing of forty communists with a machine gun at the climax of *One Lonely Night* (1951) – the number of corpses was double that in the original text but the publishers got cold feet at all the gore. As with 'commie', red did not excite quite such extreme reactions in the UK but it was and remains a useful headline word or a disparaging tag, so that Hewlett

Johnson, a clergyman, acquired the nickname 'The Red Dean of Canterbury' because of his uncompromising support for the Soviet Union in the 1930s and 1940s, while Derek Robinson, a high-profile trade union organiser at British Leyland in the 1970s was soon christened 'Red Robbo' by the tabloids. During Ed Miliband's five-year tenure as leader of the Labour Party he was christened Red Ed, partly because he was slightly further to the left than his predecessors (Gordon Brown and Tony Blair), partly by association with his father, the Marxist academic Ralph Miliband, and partly because it's the kind of rhyming wordplay that tabloids like.

For those who didn't go to the extreme of embracing full-blooded communism the expressions 'pink' and 'pinko' were good enough. Once again the terms originate in the US during the 1920s, as people became aware of a new and threatening social order emerging in the Soviet Union. The associations of the colour pink – unemphatic, soft, feminised – are rather like the 'wet' label attached to those Conservatives who couldn't give their whole-hearted support to Mrs Thatcher and her policies when she was Prime Minister. 'Pinko' remains a useful slur delivered by the right to the left, because it suggests that the person so designated is liberal or socialist (therefore bad) but not very ardent in their beliefs (therefore also bad because feeble, lacking the courage to go all the way, etc.). It's unsurprising that the term has frequent outings in right-leaning publications: 'What made the committed bachelor and pinko-liberal TV presenter opt for a fairy-tale beach wedding in a millionaire's playground?' opined the *Daily Telegraph* of the Channel 4 news anchor Jon Snow in June 2010; 'For example, in the old days I would definitely have reviewed [the TV version of] *Howards End*, even though I can't stand E. M. Forster or the ghastly pinko Schlegel sisters,' wrote the *Spectator*'s James Delingpole, a reflex baiter of 'libtards', in November 2017.

Several other derogatory words and phrases relating to communism have outlived the Soviet period and are still in intermittent and pejorative use. An 'apparatchik' or member of the Soviet bureaucracy now describes an organisation man, someone who toes the party line either out of stupidity or cynical ambition. It works well as a harsher and more knowing alternative to American or British equivalents such as 'suit' or 'jobsworth'. 'Agitprop', a shortening of *Agitpropbyuro*, originally the office tasked with spreading political propaganda, is now applied to any organisation or play, film, etc. that appears to be pushing a left-wing agenda. Film-makers such as Ken Loach or playwrights such as David Hare regularly find themselves tagged with the 'agitprop' label, while the BBC and the subsidised theatre are regarded by the right-wing outlets as nests of agitprop-ery ('the BBC's fresh take on *Lady Chatterley's Lover* hollowed out the original and injected its own up-to-date agitprop', *Daily Telegraph*, 20 September 2015).

The altogether more sinister word 'gulag' derives from the first letters of a lengthy Russian title for the bureaucratic organisation that administered the system of labour camps during the Soviet period. In general the word is used with accuracy, either in application to the Soviet camps or their contemporary equivalents in, say, North Korea, but occasionally it's applied out of context – and applied tastelessly, one might think – to sum up a horrible holiday camp or a grim housing estate. And then there is the word to describe the people who would never have seen the inside of a gulag, unless they came into that substantial category who fell foul of Stalin, the 'nomenklatura' or list of names. In the Soviet Union the word denoted Communist Party appointees to posts in government and industry: the important people, the ones to whom you had to listen. The Soviet Union has gone but the word can still be applied to any influential insider-ish group, almost always with the implication that such a group is privileged, self-perpetuating and self-important: an elite with a Soviet twist. 'For a start, the precise shape of the EU that the Scottish nomenklatura is trying to stay in is in doubt' (*Spectator*, 2 July 2016). 'Ukase', a word rarer than nomenklatura, derives from pre-revolutionary Russia, and has been imported direct into several European languages with the meaning of 'order', 'government directive'. Like those other 'foreign' words, the German diktat and the Latin fiat (= let it be done), the application of 'ukase' hints at an overbearing, unaccountable system, and is a word that has a natural if rarefied place in right-wing discourse: 'No more European superstate, no more dominance from Brussels, no more foreign judges issuing left-wing human-rights ukases' (*Spectator*, 16 May 2015).

It is hardly surprising that the deployment of these old and largely communist expressions should occur mostly on the right and be directed against the left. The intention is to summon up the corrupt, coercive atmosphere of the Soviet system and its apparatus, and such words function as upmarket intellectual equivalents of pinko and commie and lefty. There is, however, one pre-Soviet exception in the 'tsar'. Redolent of extravagance, autocracy and even feudalism, this word is enjoying a curious vogue in the English-speaking West, in parallel to the growing rehabilitation of the old imperial empire and its rulers in Russia itself. Now the title for someone given wide powers by government to solve a problem – drugs tsar, school behaviour tsar, entrepreneurship tsar – it is a nice historical irony that if ever contemporary tsars are complained about it's because they don't have sufficient powers, are not autocratic enough. The current application of the word started in the US where a 'czar', from the late nineteenth century, was a casual way of referring to a boss or other overlord.

Two other Soviet phrases, one appropriated by the West and the other often attributed to Lenin himself, are in common use. 'Fellow traveller' comes from a Russian term (*poputchik*) for someone travelling along the same path as you, i.e. a person who may not share all your aims but who is willing to keep you company. The term rapidly spread outside the Soviet Union to characterise those who were not actual communists but were in sympathy with its ideology. It still pops up occasionally – '[Jeremy Corbyn] is furious at being portrayed, on the basis of what he sees as flimsy evidence, as a Communist fellow traveller' (*Daily Telegraph*, 24 February 2018) – but it has an almost historical quality now and any individual so described will be elderly or, more likely, dead. With a mischievous nod to its liberal reputation, the *Guardian* ran a column for a time in which readers asked and answered each other travel questions and titled it 'Ask a fellow traveller'. There have been attempts to apply the label to those at the opposite end of the ideological spectrum, as in the book by academic Richard Griffiths, *Fellow Travellers of the Right: British Enthusiasts for Nazi Germany 1933–39* (1980), in which he shows how admiration for and active cooperation with the Nazi regime permeated the top echelons of British society in the years leading to the outbreak of war.

There's no evidence that Vladimir Ilyich Ulyanov, aka Lenin, actually employed the phrase 'useful idiots' to describe those foreigners who, while not themselves communists, could be valuable in furthering communism's aims, for example by painting a rosy picture of the Soviet regime. Nevertheless he is often referred to as the creator of the phrase, and no doubt the attribution serves to emphasise the naivety of the 'useful idiots' by showing just how manipulative and cynical was the founding father of the Soviet state. Now the term, first noted in English in 1948, is employed about anybody who becomes, unwittingly, the tool of some other agency or institution. The 'useful idiot' seems to have grown more popular as a deprecatory term in the last few years, in keeping with the increased polarisation of politics, discourse and culture. There may not be much to be said for the fellow traveller but at least he has an inkling of where he's going and there is some volition involved. The useful idiot, by contrast, staggers along, helpless, blindfolded, and led by the nose. A survey of a handful of newspapers in 2017–18 throws up the following instances of the useful idiot: 'Sinn Fein's useful idiot', 'Saddam's . . .', 'Michel Barnier's . . .', 'Putin's . . .', 'Russia's . . .', 'Brussels' . . .', 'Labour's . . .', 'Social Media's . . .' This is far from exhaustive. The useful idiot really is very useful if only as ammunition.

As a coda to communist terminology, it's worth noting the satirical application of the People's Republic formula. This title, originating in the nineteenth century, was adopted by a variety of communist-era states from Albania to Romania. Currently, China and North Korea are both styled People's Republics, with Korea bearing the wholly inaccurate addition of 'Democratic'. Whenever a town council or a region seemed to be turning left, and especially if it adopted a rather sanctimonious liberal identity, then it could find itself entitled to the People's Republic laurel. Such places include(d) the People's Republic of Islington, . . . of South Yorkshire, . . . of California, . . . of Berkeley (in California).

Another pair of expressions are historically distinct from communism and communist, but are often blurred with them. This pinkish taint explains why 'socialist' and 'socialism' have rarely been terms of approval outside the circle of true believers. Tony Blair's avoidance of either word was integral to the entire New Labour project and the attempt, which was initially successful, to persuade the public that he and his party had nothing to do with its previous high-taxing, nationalising self as (old) Labour. As words, socialist and socialism go back two centuries and the beginnings of an era of revolutionary theories as to how society should be organised, theories that stressed collective ownership, redistribution of wealth, state regulation and later encompassed the pursuit of social justice and social reform.

It would be difficult now to find a positive use of the words in the mainstream media. At best, references tend to be neutral: 'Labour has never been a socialist party. That is to say, it has never been committed to the replacement of capitalism as opposed to its reform' (*New Statesman*, 12 March 2018). In America, socialism and its adherents are as bad as – and essentially indistinguishable from – all those commies and pinkos: 'The leader of the US gun lobby called for schools to have the same level of security as banks today and warned that the "socialist" left was bent on stripping Americans of their firearms and freedoms' (*The Times*, 22 February 2018). It is reassuring that Wayne LaPierre, head of the National Rifle Association (NRA), should apparently be taking such pains to distinguish between the 'socialist' left and the rest of the left, which is presumably less socialist. In reality, LaPierre is simply administering a two-fisted punch, a right and a left as it were, by coupling together two bad words, socialist + left, using each to intensify the other. 'Lefty', sometimes 'leftie', is a handy and pejorative noun/adjective found frequently on both sides of the Atlantic. There is something faintly infantile and patronising about 'lefty', useful attributes for a mild insult. By contrast, the counterpart of 'rightie' has never really caught on.

PC Snowflake

I N JANUARY 1991 *New York Magazine* carried an article
titled ARE YOU POLITICALLY CORRECT?, which opened
with the story of a Harvard history professor, Stephan
Thernstrom, who was under attack by a group of students
who considered he had been 'racially insensitive'. The
protest against him was, literally, a whispering campaign.
'Whenever he walked through the campus that spring,
down Harvard's brick paths, under the arched gates, past
the fluttering elms, he found it hard not to imagine the
pointing fingers, the whispers. Racist. There goes the
racist. It was hellish, this persecution. Thernstrom couldn't
sleep. His nerves were frayed, his temper raw.' The magazine used this as a peg on which to hang an attack on what
it saw as the prevailing liberal and yet intolerant culture
on college campuses, a culture with an instinctive adher-
ence to the 'politically correct' and possessing a nose for
sniffing out anything or anybody who didn't conform to
PC standards. Ironically, this liberal outlook was earning

itself descriptions such as 'fascist' and 'McCarthyite', terms traditionally directed by the left at the right.

The extent of the whispering campaign against Professor Thernstrom was open to question (a clue might lie in the quote above, 'he found it hard not to imagine'), although there had been a single article in a Harvard student newspaper attacking his decision to make extensive use of the diaries of slave plantation owners during his lectures. But the *New York Magazine* piece helped to seed a belief that in universities, as well as society more generally, there was a witch-hunt going on against those who held traditional beliefs and espoused conservative values. To be acceptable, to make progress in the workplace, or at the least to avoid trouble, one had to demonstrate 'politically correct' views on race and discrimination, on sex and gender, and even on ideas themselves.

In the quarter century and more since Professor Thernstrom heard the whispers of 'Racist' among the fluttering elms of Harvard, the notion of 'political correctness' has grown from a seed to a great, overarching, all-shadowing tree. The phrase, often shortened to PC,* crops up constantly in the media, in political campaigns, in

---

* As with the shift in the sense of 'gay' it is hard to say when the PC abbreviation no longer summoned up the cosy world of *Dixon of Dock Green*. The personal computer sense still survives in the Currys PC World brand.

daily conversation. 'It may not be very PC to say this but I think . . .' is routinely followed by a comment on equal pay/gender balance/sexist language/gay marriage/immigration/racial differences/Islam/colonialism/imperialism/animal rights/ecology/the disappearance of Christmas . . .

One of the oddities of the phrase is that it's never used by its upholders but only by its opponents. As Moira Weigel, also a Harvard academic, says: 'The term is what Ancient Greek rhetoricians would have called an "exonym": a term for another group, which signals that the speaker does not belong to it. Nobody ever describes themselves as "politically correct". The phrase is only ever an accusation' (*Guardian*, 'The long read: Political Correctness: how the right invented a phantom enemy', 30 November 2016). The derogatory use of 'politically correct' was first applied in universities because they were supposedly nests of privileged, liberal, progressive thinking, but the 'PC brigade' – as they're often described in the British press – are now to be detected everywhere at every level of society, from the government, both national and local, to the workplace, to sport, to law and policing, to large chunks of the media.

To speak out against the PC brigade, to try to thwart their plot to bring about a politically correct nirvana, is the self-appointed mission of other individuals and media outlets and pressure groups, generally the very same ones that rail against the elite, the expert and the establishment.

As the icing on the cake, those leading the charge against the PC brigade frequently cast themselves as mavericks or rebels, claiming to speak on behalf of those ordinary people who are afraid to say what they really think in case they incur the displeasure, or worse, of those powerful liberals. Thus the anti-PC brigade transform themselves into stalwarts for freedom, defiant and heroic resisters against the bland tide of *bien-pensants* and wimpy liberals. They have taken on the mantle of rebellion, as did the Brexiteers during the campaign to get Britain out of the EU, and the rebel is always more glamorous than the conformist.

Altogether it's a winning formula. Those very successful people's tribunes, Nigel Farage and Donald Trump, regularly take swipes at political correctness, as do other more conventional British and US politicians. Nor is the phenomenon confined to the English-speaking world. During the 2017 campaign for the French presidency, Marine Le Pen, the leader of the Front National, talked of how the right-wing establishment was obsessed by its fear of clashing with political correctness (*'obnubilée par sa peur de heurter le politiquement correct'*, quoted in *Le Figaro*, 3 September 2016). Germany too has seen plenty of objections to the *politische Korrekheit* regarded as dominating official culture. Altogether, political correctness has been a very productive linguistic export.

Another oddity of the phrase is that it originated not on the right but on the left, and specifically in the communist world. In 1933, according to a report in a US newspaper, Soviet school pupils could be criticised for showing 'superficial and often politically incorrect information in civics and social sciences'. In 1957 the Chinese leader Mao Tse-tung gave a speech that was translated into English with the title 'On the Correct Handling of Contradictions Among the People'. Correctness here is obviously nothing to do with being right in an ethical or scientific sense but refers simply to conforming to whatever is politically orthodox, i.e. what the Party decides. Though political correctness could only be spoken of with a straight face in the East, the expression took on a more ambivalent sense when it travelled to the West. Moira Weigel, pointing out the popularity of Mao's *Little Red Book* in radical circles in the late 1960s and early 1970s, suggests that 'they didn't use it [correct] in the way Mao did. "Politically correct" became a kind of in-joke among American leftists – something you called a fellow leftist when you thought he or she was being self-righteous.'

There the words and the idea might have rested, a faded in-joke among the rapidly diminishing supporters of Chairman Mao or the Soviet Politburo in the West. But the leftist or communist origins of political correctness turned out to be very useful to the right. After all, they hinted at a Stalinist mentality, extreme intolerance of any opposition, even the kind of thought-control that George Orwell satirised in *Nineteen Eighty-Four*. Accordingly, sometime in the late 1980s the notion was picked up by those who were unhappy at the prevailing culture and used to attack a supposed uniformity and orthodoxy in American higher education. A 28 October 1990 article in the *New York Times* by journalist and author Richard Bernstein observed that the PC movement was shaped by the 'view that Western society has for centuries been dominated by what is often called "the white male power structure" or "patriarchal hegemony"' coupled with the 'related belief is that everybody but white heterosexual males has suffered some form of repression and been denied a cultural voice' (Richard Bernstein, 'The Rising Hegemony of the Politically Correct'). Politically correct programmes that flowed from this interpretation included women's studies, gay and lesbian studies, and African-American studies, as well as affirmative action (the policy of protecting and promoting members of groups that have suffered from discrimination). The tone of Bernstein's article wasn't sneering, as so much later PC commentary is. Nevertheless, his choice of politically correct papers delivered at an academic conference – titles included 'Jane Austen and the Masturbating Girl' and 'A Womb of His Own: Male Renaissance Poets in the Female Body' – was a pointer to that mixture of scepticism, derision and impatience that was to characterise coverage of the PC movement in the coming years.

The Christmas wars

Now we live, apparently, in a world where political correctness has gone mad, to use the tabloid formula. Examples are legion. The *Daily Mail*, the anti-PC cheerleader in chief, provided a few of them in an A to Z published on 17 November 2017 and designed to simultaneously appal and delight its readership. In the list were plenty of instances of cultural appropriation that had been objected to as insensitive, from non-Scots wearing kilts to non-Japanese draped in kimonos to whites donning Native American head-dresses or Mexican sombreros. Pembroke College in Cambridge had to change its menu after ethnic minority students complained about culinary items such as 'Jamaican stew' and 'Tunisian rice', names which were 'cultural misrepresentations' since the dishes do not actually exist in their native countries. Then there are long-standing language issues, some of which have been around since the 1970s: 'forefathers', 'manpower' and 'manfully' should be avoided as they are gender-exclusive, while to call an adult woman a girl is belittling, and mothers-to-be ought to be referred to as 'pregnant people' (this is the advice of the British Medical Association). Sussex University Students' Union cautioned members against using the pronouns 'he' and 'she' so as to avoid assumptions about identity, preferring 'they' and 'them' as correct, gender-neutral terms. Meanwhile 'lame' should be avoided, especially when used to mean 'ineffectual' or 'unappealing', as it could be offensive to some disabled people, while seemingly innocent questions such as 'Where are you from?' or 'Where were you born?' could be construed as racist micro-aggressions (according to guidance from the University of California, Berkeley) because they might suggest the person being questioned doesn't belong there.

To judge by the *Daily Mail* feature, the British people are seething in a cauldron of multicultural, social and sexual confusion. Old definitions have been discarded, new ingredients added, and nobody – certainly nobody normal – knows what's what in this nervous new world. Yet are things as bad as the paper claims? Are all the new usages, preferences and prohibitions really so absurd?

Perhaps the oddest example in the paper's list was that of Suffolk County Council, which has stopped using the notice 'Cat's eyes removed' after fears that people might think real cats had been mutilated; now signs across the county read: 'Caution, road studs removed.' This change doesn't seem related to 'political correctness', however defined, but more to do with clarity. I can't be the only person to have been momentarily struck by the alarming ambiguity of the original roadside warning and to think that the rephrasing is an improvement. And the more one looks at the other 'PC gone mad' examples, the more one sees that there is some sense to at least some of them. It is unquestionably condescending to call a woman a girl, and it must be many years since employers stopped referring to 'manpower' rather than their 'workforce' or 'staff'. Another bugbear is the use of 'they' when the writer isn't sure of the gender of the person they are talking about even though this is standard in English. It is objected to by some purists on the grounds that a plural pronoun shouldn't be used when the subject is singular. I have just used this formula two sentences ago – plural 'they' refers back to singular 'writer' – because it avoids the cumbersome 'he or she' formula preferred by grammar pedants, and the sky hasn't fallen in.

One can go through the rest of the *Daily Mail*'s list, suggesting that rather than PC madness there's actually quite a bit if sense and sensitivity there. Questions such as 'Where are you from?' or 'Where were you born?' could well seem intrusive or even hostile in certain circumstances. And any alert user of the English language will know that there are situations where words such as 'lame' or 'blind' or 'deaf' or 'dumb' might be inappropriate. The Pembroke students had a valid point when they said that dishes named after their countries or cultures didn't actually exist, and far from making an extravagant fuss their comments on Facebook, as reported in other newspapers, were generally good-tempered or humorous along the lines of 'Don't get me started on the Yorkshire puddings!'

This is frequently the case with the anti-PC brigade.

The incidents they cry up are often minor one-offs or sometimes based on a (deliberate) misreading of a situation or, occasionally, completely invented, an irony given that 'You couldn't make this stuff up!' is another standard anti-PC comment. For an example of something that is almost completely made up, look at the so-called 'War on Christmas', a motif of right-wing thinking for many years, particularly in the United States. The replacement of 'Happy Christmas' with 'Happy Holidays' in greetings or store displays, or the very occasional prohibition on the public display of a Christmas tree or a nativity scene, is regarded as part of a conspiracy to secularise America. A 2005 book by a Fox News contributor was titled *The War on Christmas: How the Liberal Plot to Ban the Sacred Christian Holiday Is Worse Than You Thought*. In the previous year another Fox contributor, Bill O'Reilly, asserted that the 'secularists' were out to destroy 'religion in the public arena' because it was the only way they could wear down religious opposition and advance their progressive agenda of 'gay marriage, partial birth abortion, euthanasia, legalized drugs, income redistribution through taxation' (item on the Fox News website, 24 December 2004).

This deliberate stoking up of largely unfounded fears goes back at least to the 1950s and the anti-communist paranoia of far-right organisations such as the John Birch Society, which claimed that the Reds wanted to 'to take Christ out of Christmas' at the same time as 'UN fanatics' were planning to substitute 'UN symbols and emblems as Christmas decorations'. Sometimes forgotten amid all this kerfuffle is the separation between religion and the state, guaranteed by the First Amendment to the US Constitution, and upheld by the Supreme Court in, for example, a 1980 ruling that posting the Ten Commandments in public schools is unconstitutional or a 1989 ruling that it is unconstitutional to erect a nativity scene on public property. In other words, the US Constitution, so religiously adhered to by the right in issues such as gun ownership, is in itself sufficient to keep Christianity out of public spaces. Raising the spectres of liberal conspiracy and political correctness is just a way of rallying the tribe, of firing up the base, as when President Trump declared at a conservative rally in October 2017, 'We're saying "Merry Christmas" again'.

The United Kingdom may be something of a slouch compared to the United States and the 'War on Christmas', even if papers such as the *Daily Mail* and the *Telegraph* are ever vigilant against Xmas offenders. Fortunately there are many other fronts in the PC wars. Back in 2012 when the rise of UKIP seemed to pose a real threat to the Conservatives, then in power in their coalition with the Liberal Democrats, Lord Michael Ashcroft suggested that the Tories were losing votes to UKIP not so much out of a concern with the European Union but because 'ordinary people' were affronted by the 'prevailing culture of political correctness'. Ashcroft, a one-time Deputy Chairman of the Conservative Party, summarised their grievances in a piece on his 'ConservativeHome' blog: 'They say, you can't hold nativity plays or harvest festivals any more; you can't fly a flag of St George any more; you can't call Christmas Christmas any more; you won't be promoted in the police force unless you're from a minority; you can't wear an England shirt on the bus; you won't get social housing unless you're an immigrant; you can't speak up about these things because you'll be called a racist; you can't even smack your children' (quoted in the *Daily Express*, 18 December 2012). Ashcroft pointed out that these examples, mentioned in focus groups, were real and imagined. He might also have pointed out that none of them is true. Harvest festivals, St George's flags, England shirts, all are still regularly celebrated, flown and worn. A report by the House of Commons Home Affairs Committee in 2016 revealed that not a single police force in England and Wales had a BME (Black or Minority Ethnic) representation that matched its local demographic, that four forces had no black officers at all and that eleven had no BME officers above the rank of inspector. And, incidentally, in England it is still legal for a parent or carer to smack a child if it counts as 'reasonable punishment'.

But the truth or falsehood of the beliefs enumerated by Ashcroft is really beside the point. One of the cleverest ploys of the anti-PC brigade is to persuade many people that they are somehow living in a country that is no longer theirs but one which is being gradually taken away from them by conspiratorial forces, unelected elites and faceless bureaucrats. Such groups are not only indifferent to ordinary people's concerns, the story goes, but they routinely inhibit discussion ('you can't speak up about these things') by raising the flag of political correctness. Yet if discussion is inhibited it is because any attempt to introduce facts into the picture, for example by pointing out the net contribution made to the UK economy by migrants, is ignored, shouted down or described as 'fake news'. Why bother to have a discussion, which you might lose, when it is altogether easier to go with slogans or even outright lies about not being allowed to fly the St George's flag or say 'Christmas' any more, all the time invoking the spectre of political correctness. If this was a marketing campaign, which in a way it is, then it would be accounted a stunningly successful one. Political correctness has been transformed into a very bad phrase indeed.

Paradoxically, the power lies less with the supposed PC elite than with their opponents. Apprehension, even downright fear, over being accused of being politically correct is such that supposed offenders rush to fall into line. When officials at the local council in Broxtowe, near Nottingham, left the C-word out of publicity over forthcoming Christmas events they were left in no doubt about the consequences if they did it again: 'There were excuses that there was no room for it [the word 'Christmas'] but I am not accepting that. Appropriate words have been said to appropriate staff,' said the council leader. During a by-election campaign in 2014 the Labour politician Emily Thornberry resigned from her position in the shadow cabinet after tweeting a picture of a terraced house decked with three St George flags, and a white van parked outside, accompanied by the comment 'Image from Rochester'. She was accused of sneering and snobbishness, and the then Labour leader Ed Miliband took her to task for a lack of 'decency and respect'.

This isn't to say, of course, that every single PC accusation is trumped-up or based on nothing at all. But the original impulse behind 'political correctness' is fundamentally a decent and humane one. Yes, it is an attempt to shape public discourse, and to avoid insulting or offending individuals and groups, especially those which are vulnerable or have been marginalised in the past. To that extent, the avoidance of insult, etc., might be construed as an encroachment on absolute free speech. But old-fashioned good manners and civility, the absence of which are frequently decried in outlets that also attack political correctness, are also encroachments on absolute free speech. In fact, most of us, most of the time, select and even curb what we're saying and writing because we're aware that we are on some level being judged on our words.

And political correctness isn't only negative. It suggests that, at least in the public arena and in debate, there are more (and less) civil, respectful and aware ways of referring to people and situations, and that the more respectful ones – the more good-mannered ones, if you prefer – offer a better path, if only because they're the ones likely to get your opponents to listen to you. Unless, of course, the speaker or writer wants to cause offence, another perfectly legitimate impulse. But then all they are doing is appealing to their own side or, in electoral terms, firing up the base.

Political correctness has made a linguistic contribution to culture as well, not so much in the alternative or new formulations that are the subject of mockery by the anti-PC brigade ('undocumented worker' for 'illegal immigrant', 'vertically challenged' for 'short'), but in that it has spawned or given new life to a range of insults and put-downs to describe all those adherents of PC. It's as if the infusion of PC-ness into the body politic produced and continues to produce a range of antibodies or anti-toxins, ready to battle back cell by cell against the unwelcome intruders. Any account of bad words would be incomplete if it didn't reckon with a few of these new anti-toxins.

Down and dirty

Words that take on new meanings can be like fashions. They emerge out of nowhere, kick up a storm, and die away to nothing. The primary sense of a 'snowflake' – something minute that falls from the sky in cold weather – has been around in English since the early eighteenth century; 'flakes of snowe' are found in the English of the Middle Ages though it seems to have taken a few hundred years for the words to be shunted around like railway carriages and turn into 'snowflakes'. The singular 'snow-flake' enjoyed a brief, metaphorical existence in the late twentieth century to characterise the unique personality of an individual, especially a child (from the fact that no two snowflakes are identical). But in the early twenty-first century the word took a different and nastier turn. Now the 'snowflake' is someone – always young, possibly a student, and in either case a millennial – who is ready to take offence at opinions at variance with their own, a person who is excessively sensitive, one who feels entitled to special treatment and will likely demand a 'safe space' where they will not feel threatened or upset.

According to the invaluable *OED*, the earliest appearance in this new sense is from a letter to the *Philadelphia Daily News* in January, 2012: 'These [soldiers in Afghanistan] are just kids who are doing the fighting that the precious little snowflakes of the liberal media are not doing.' Whether it was the happy invention of the US letter-writer or whether it was a term that had been in circulation before is not known. One can see the attractions of 'snowflake' as a derogatory term. In addition to a virginal, unworldly purity, which will melt away rather than allow itself to be smudged, the snowflake is small, fragile and insignificant. In human terms, the ultimate in wimpiness. Rarely has a word been so energetically endorsed, generally in right-of-centre outlets, both in the UK and the US. 'Frankenstein has been dubbed "misunderstood" by snowflake students who see the monster as a victim' (*Sun*, 5 March 2018); 'So-called snowflake students are well known for their principled opposition to sombrero hats, applause, Jacob Rees-Mogg, and indeed the word "snowflake"' (*Sunday Times*, 4 February 2018); 'It turns out that Donald Trump is a tender snowflake who needs a safe space where his feelings can't be hurt' (usnews.com, 14 December 2017,). And the word offers punning possibilities, particularly when it comes to the failure of Britain's trains, roads and schools to cope with the onset of winter: A BUNCH OF SNOWFLAKES! HUNDREDS OF SCHOOLS ACROSS BRITAIN ARE CLOSED — A DAY AFTER FIRST SERIOUS SNOW-FALL HITS ROADS AND RAIL (*Daily Mail* headline, 11 December 2017).

A feature that makes a new term such as 'snowflake' consistent with other expressions directed by some elements on the right at the left is that it suggests softness, pliancy, feebleness. I've already noted the feminised quality of 'pinko' and the infantilising quality of 'lefty' but the same tendencies are implicit in other examples of name-calling from the right. A non-macho tendency to melt under pressure, a deficit in full-on, red-blooded, masculine hardihood, a failure to grow up and be a man, these are standard elements in the rhetoric. Yet when it comes to attacking the elites, the constant verbal stress on the feebleness, the effeteness, the lack of masculinity among the politically correct and liberal sits oddly with the contrary impression given of those elites, that they are ruthless, self-interested, cunning and very powerful. In this regard, such attacks, particularly when allied with sneers at their 'cosmopolitan' or 'global' nature, echo those old and contradictory anti-Semitic slurs that simultaneously depict Jews as less than human and also master manipulators.

The range of right-wing invective is impressive. Take, for example, Mark Steyn, one-time columnist on the *Spectator* and the *Daily Telegraph* and now a regular on Fox News, and a master at vituperation (as well as an adept commentator on films and musicals). For Steyn, those on the liberal left – as well as large numbers on the right, dismissively known as RINOS* – are 'squishes', a self-explanatory word

---

* RINO – Republican In Name Only – is a standard US term on the hard right for those Republicans who are insufficiently doctrinaire or too prepared to compromise with their opponents.

which he sometimes jollies up with 'craven' or 'jelly-spined'. 'Effete' is another favourite term, if a slightly dated one, and useful because although its primary meaning now is 'decadent' the sound of the word inevitably suggests 'effeminate', with which it is sometimes confused. An insult that Steyn seems especially drawn to is 'panty-waist', an Americanism that hasn't gained much of a foothold in British English and denotes a 'sissy', a 'cowardly boy or man'. Evidently liking the sound and feel of the word he uses it often: 'But these days it's just as likely that any human being he [a bear in the wild] comes across is some pantywaist Bambi Boomer enviro-sentimentalist trying to get in touch with his inner self' (*After America*, 2011). Writing of the universal popularity of 'My Way', he comments 'even wimpy social-democrat pantywaists dig it: It was the tune Gerhard Schröder asked the German military band to play as he departed his official office following his election defeat by Angela Merkel' (Steyn Online, June 2017). Sometimes coupled with 'panty-waist' is 'milque-toast' for a timid, submissive man, a distinctive US insult deriving from a 1920s cartoon character Caspar Milquetoast, in turn deriving from the US dish which softens toast in milk and serves up the result with honey or syrup. Steyn is a clever and civilised polemicist and we're at some distance here from the 'fag' and 'pussy' insults regularly directed towards some sectors on the left, but the distance is not unbridgeable.

The most toxic and peculiar of all such far-right insults is surely 'cuck', not for once aimed at the left but at 'fellow' conservatives. It's short for 'cuckservative', a portmanteau linking of 'cuckold' and 'conservative'. Cuckold is a good old – i.e. a bad old – English word, describing the deceived husband of an unfaithful wife. It derives from French and is supposedly onomatopoeic, from the cuckoo and its habit of laying eggs in other birds' nests. The 'cuckservative' raised his ugly head, like so much else, around the time Donald Trump was beginning his campaign for the Republican presidential nomination in 2015. The term served to define and demean establishment opponents of Trump such as Jeb Bush and Marco Rubio, individuals regarded by the hard right as soft – squishy – on a range of issues from immigration to the retention of the Confederate flag on public buildings.

Trump was soon acclaimed as the antithesis of the politically correct and cuckolded. After the presidential candidate had a run-in with the TV interviewer Megyn Kelly, who pressed him on past sexist comments, he couldn't let go of the incident. He commented in a later interview on her supposed aggression: 'You could see there was blood coming out of her eye. Blood coming out of her wherever.' When outrage followed, Trump helpfully clarified exactly where the blood might have been coming from with a tweet: 'Re Megyn Kelly quote: "you could see there was blood coming out of her eyes, blood coming out of her wherever" (NOSE). Just got on w/thought'. He didn't apologise but took a familiar if irrelevant side-swipe at political correctness and adopted the equally familiar defence of it's-all-in-your-dirty-mind by saying that 'only a deviant would think that' (it was a reference to menstruation). His remarks certainly didn't offend his hardcore supporters. If anything they were more excited by his refusal to apologise, by his defiance of the politically correct lobby. 'If Trump were your average, ordinary, cuckolded Republican, he would have apologized by now,' said the blow-hard Rush Limbaugh on his radio show (22 July 2015).

From Limbaugh's perspective and that of others even further to the right, the failure to defend one's own (usually white, mostly male) identity and interests, the reluctance to say it like it is, is perceived not just as weakness but as treachery, the product of years of cultural emasculation. Limbaugh didn't coin 'cuckservative' but he knew which way the semantic wind was blowing. As it happens, insinuations about masculine vigour were an explicit feature in the rancid Republican campaign in which Trump came out on top of the pile. Trump, who has a bully's genius for finding just the right wounding epithet, attacked Jeb Bush as 'low energy' and fixed the label 'little' to Marco Rubio. In return, Rubio unwisely tried to get down and dirty by commenting on the size of the Donald's hands. He told a rally of supporters: 'He is taller than me, he's like 6' 2", which is why I don't understand why his hands are the size of someone who is 5' 2". Have you seen his hands? And you know what they say about men with small hands – you can't trust them.' The way the crowd erupted with laughter and Rubio's comic pause before the punchline showed that trustworthiness wasn't what was on everyone's mind. Trump, whose Achilles' heel does indeed seem to be the size of his hands, was more explicit in his response. During one of the many debates among the Republican presidential hopefuls, he held up those questionable hands and nodded towards Rubio. 'Look at those hands,' he said. 'Are they small hands? And he referred to my hands – if they are small, something else must be small. I guarantee you there is no problem. I guarantee you.'

The message was clear. Trump wasn't merely a long way from 'your average, ordinary, cuckolded Republican', in Rush Limbaugh's description, he was the epitome of steely American masculinity, hand size notwithstanding. No cuckold he, no cuckservative either. For the humiliating demeanour of the cuckold gets a further and significantly racist twist with 'cuckservative' since the portmanteau word hints at the online porn speciality in which husbands, usually white, watch their wives have sex with other men who are frequently black. These willing witnesses are analogous to the mainstream conservatives who look on – thrilled and humiliated by their impotence – while the values they are meant to espouse are modified or over-turned in the attempt to adapt to 'liberal' demands. They are sell-outs, and the implication is that they enjoy the sell-out.

'Cuckservative' is representative of contemporary insults in that it was reputedly coined in a tweet, is inventively rancorous and has a racist and sexual undertow. It joins that roster of right-wing insults that impugn the masculinity not just of those on the left but of those on the right who aren't right enough. Equivalents on the left are harder to find. A rare and recent example is 'gammon', describing a red-faced, raging, middle-aged male, an altogether unattractive specimen, a backwoodsman. The journalist Caitlin Moran was possibly the first to coin the expression when she described David Cameron, then Prime Minister, as resembling 'a slightly camp gammon robot' (*The Times*, 16 April 2010). Another expression on the British left and applied to those on their own side regarded as insufficiently hardline is 'melt', a term reminiscent of 'wets' for those Conservatives who disagreed with Mrs Thatcher.

When it comes to insults, though, it is the opponents of the left who show a greater invention, even exuberance, often with a sexual tinge. Speculation about why the far right is so happy to impugn the virility of their opponents would amount to cheap psychology but that doesn't mean it should be resisted. Behind it is surely years of anxiety and denial about what was formerly taken for granted: white male privilege and priority. Gender and racial equality are far from achieved in the United States and the United Kingdom and other Western democracies but the advances made over the last half century are more than enough to feel threatening to those who are, to judge by their language, already insecure.

Like other expressions such as 'squish' and 'snowflake', 'cuck' sounds abusive. The terms, with their hard consonants or their soft hissing ones, are ready made as little verbal bombs for lobbing at others, whether online or in person. Is it possible that more 'refined' terms such as 'elite' and 'expert' will become swearwords? Can one imagine the day, soon perhaps, when 'You expert!' will be ejected with all the energy and venom of 'You shit!' Some might argue that this has already happened, in spirit if not in fact.

Conclusion: The Daily Mirror

UNDERLYING THIS BOOK is the belief that the words people use, and the ones they avoid, reveal things not just about the users and their audience – us, in short – but more generally about the society and culture that surrounds us. So to the anti-PC brigade the avoidance of certain expressions and the espousal of other, perhaps milder or euphemistic terms reveal a mealy-mouthed community in hock to a minority of do-gooders and liberal campaigners. From the other side such new linguistic habits represent a more enlightened, tolerant and considerate community. The remarkable relaxation concerning the old and taboo four-letter terms, especially the f- and c-words, suggests a much less censorious attitude towards sex, while the sensitivity over LGBT terminology, even its very existence, would amaze someone who'd gone to sleep at any time from the 1950s to the 1990s and just woken up to behold this brave new world. Meantime a Rip Van Winkle from that era would likely be surprised at the sneering and venom now directed at experts and elites. The furore over any instance of the n-word, other than its appearance in rap or as part of the shtick of black performers, is in marked contrast to its wide acceptance, in the UK at any rate, little more than a generation ago. Similarly with expressions such as 'queer' and 'poof'. Or 'spastic' and 'schizo'.

What is unsayable may soon become unthinkable, or somewhere near to unthinkable. This is the principle outlined by George Orwell in the appendix to *Nineteen Eighty-Four* where he explains the purpose behind Newspeak, the diminished version of English which is replacing Oldspeak or Standard English. In Orwell's satire, the new impoverished vocabulary is a method of thought control, with the added advantage that its victims have no idea that their thoughts are being controlled. According to Orwell's commentary: 'It was intended that when Newspeak had been adopted once and for all and Oldspeak forgotten, a heretical thought – that is, a thought diverging from the principles of Ingsoc – should be literally unthinkable, at least so far as thought is dependent on words . . . This was done partly by the invention of new words, but chiefly by eliminating undesirable words and by stripping such words as remained of unorthodox meanings, and so far as possible of all secondary meanings whatever.'

Orwell-style accusations of 'thought control' and 'thought police' are routinely lobbed by the right at what they regard as 'progressive' attempts to modify or control linguistic usage. They're generally wrong, as I suggest in the section on political correctness, but the struggle on both sides – whether to try to change old terms or to stick with them, however sexist, racist, etc. – is a tribute to the sheer power of language. Yet the English language isn't quite as susceptible to control as Orwell's satire or the anti-PC brigade imagine. For one thing, it is expanding not shrinking, so that unlike in Orwell's dystopia there are constantly more words with which to think, not fewer. And if there is the semblance of control in some areas, there is little or none in others, especially across the steppes of the internet. The online Urban Dictionary contains, at the time of writing, well over a million and a half words and phrases. A largely unedited free-for-all, it includes opinions, insults and definitions ranging from quirky to offensive. Thus 'beer' is the 'reason I get up in the morning and the reason I pass out at night' while 'nigger' is 'a secret code word to be used by whites who desire quick, free, total dental extractions at the hands of unliscenced [*sic*], amatuer [*sic*] black dentists'.

Another reason why control doesn't work, or nothing like as effectively as its opponents fear it works, is simple human contrariness. The attempt to police what people say generally meets grudging resistance or backfires altogether, at least when it is imposed from the top down. The attempt by the medieval church and authorities to police and penalise 'vain swearing' was itself in vain. The widespread complaints and laments against such language are proof of its frequency and ineradicability. Hundreds of centuries later, the words in question may have changed but the underlying attitude, the bloody-mindedness, has not.

In the summer of 2017, when Humphrey Smith, the owner of a chain of two hundred pubs in the north of England, tried to enforce a policy of zero tolerance to swearing in his bars, the *Guardian* sent in their correspondent who reported, 'As soon as the subject is raised, one woman at a Smith establishment in Oldham leaps from her chair and declares succinctly: "I'll tell you what I think of the fucking swearing ban, it's a load of bullshit"' (1 July 2017). When local authorities attempt to bring in fines against those using 'foul and abusive' language in public, as Rochdale council did in the same year, they run up against the civil liberties lobby as well as the legal problem of how to measure the degree of offence. In 2011 a High Court judge ruled that, in effect, the police must put up with being sworn at during an arrest. A young man repeatedly used the f-word in public while being searched for drugs, without result. The police must have thought they'd secured a minor victory with a £50 public order fine from magistrates, on the grounds that the bad language took place within earshot of a teenage group. But Mr Justice Bean pronounced that not only were the officers likely to hear such expressions too frequently to be offended but that it was 'quite impossible to infer that the group of young people who were in the vicinity were likely to have experienced alarm or distress at hearing these rather commonplace swear words used'.

In the US police arrests for bad language are not infrequent but they run up against the constitutional right to free speech, a protection confirmed by the Supreme Court in a landmark case during the latter stages of the Vietnam War when a protestor's conviction in California for wearing a jacket emblazoned with the words 'Fuck the Draft' was overturned. Australia is generally in advance of the UK and the US in its reluctance to crack down on public bad language and so it was in 2010 when magistrates in Queensland ruled that it was acceptable for people to tell police officers to 'fuck off', after a young man swore at a female officer outside a nightclub. The defendant refused to pay a fine and contested his brief custody, hiring a barrister who made the valid point that there was quite a difference between saying 'fuck off' rather than 'fuck you' or 'you fuck'. He added: 'Really the word has lost its effect due to its use in books, films, and general speech.' The police ended up having to pay part of the costs of the case. This follows other Australian cases where courts have ruled that expressions such as 'shit' or 'prick' are not offensive.

The key element here is a collective but probably tacit agreement as to what is taboo and what isn't. Some years ago it seems the inhabitants of the British Isles decided that a certain degree of effing and blinding* was acceptable in certain circumstances (of which a private pub conversation would be one). By contrast, they decided – without of course formally 'deciding' anything – that racist terminology wasn't going to get the easy pass it received in the 1950s, 1960s or 1970s. The same thing seems to be happening to sexist language even as I write.

In the end one comes back to the power of language, and a realisation that this is not inherent in the words themselves – though the sound of a word and even its shape sometimes may contribute to the effect – but something that is culturally determined. Think of the appalled laughter that resounded through His Majesty's Theatre in April 1914 when Eliza Doolittle declared 'Not bloody likely', or the furore that greeted Ken Tynan's utterance of 'fuck' half a century later on television, or the outrage that follows any use of the n-word now. The shock and outrage may occasionally be played up but the reflexive shrinking away – 'You can't say that!' – is genuine.

Yet, as I've shown through this book, taboos change and may even go into reverse. Jumble the order of events

---

* The 'effing' part is obvious while the 'blinding' bit derives from the old imprecation '(God) blind me!' or 'blimey!' You don't hear 'blimey' much any more but my memory is that around fifty years ago it was regarded as quite 'strong'.

above so that the n-word appears in a play in the earlier part of the twentieth century, with 'bloody' being used on television in the mid-1960s and 'fuck' deployed across the media now. This isn't speculative, of course, but exactly what happened. In his 1932 play *On the Rocks*, George Bernard Shaw has a character say: 'Pandranath: you are only a silly nigger pretending to be an English gentleman.' 'Bloody' was one of the favourite words of Alf Garnett in the long-running sitcom *Till Death Us Do Part*; that and other minor taboo terms such as 'shit' were quite widely used on television in the 1960s and the ensuing decades. And 'fuck' is ubiquitous now on late-night British television. There is or was little or no protest, no shock, no surprise even, about the use of these terms – *at the time*. Just as the n-word must have seemed appropriate to Shaw writing in the early 1930s, so too did 'bloody' become normal in the middle of the last century, while the f-word and occasionally the c-word seem to suit adult audiences in the early twenty-first century.

When it comes to taboo expressions, it's as if history is a mirror showing us everything in reverse. What was over there on the unacceptable side now appears on the acceptable wing, and vice versa. But the mirror also shows us ourselves, with our prejudices and preferences, our fears and embarrassments, and the changing language we use to clothe them.

Index

INDEX